P9-DBV-680
06/20

MILK STREET

The New Rules

Recipes That Will Change the Way You Cook

MILK STREET

The New Rules

Recipes That Will Change the Way You Cook

Christopher Kimball

With writing and editing by
J. M. Hirsch and Michelle Locke

Recipes by
Matthew Card, Diane Unger and the Cooks at Milk Street

Art direction by
Jennifer Baldino Cox and Brianna Coleman

Photography by
Connie Miller of CB Creatives

VORACIOUS

LITTLE, BROWN AND COMPANY
NEW YORK   BOSTON   LONDON

Copyright © 2019 by CPK Media, LLC.

Hachette Book Group supports the right to free expression and the
value of copyright. The purpose of copyright is to encourage writers
and artists to produce the creative works that enrich our culture.

The scanning, uploading, and distribution of this book without permission
is a theft of the author's intellectual property. If you would like
permission to use material from the book (other than
for review purposes), please contact permissions@hbgusa.com.
Thank you for your support of the author's rights.

Little, Brown and Company
Hachette Book Group
1290 Avenue of the Americas, New York, NY 10104
littlebrown.com

First Edition: October 2019

Voracious is an imprint of Little, Brown and Company, a division of
Hachette Book Group, Inc.
The Voracious name and logo are trademarks of
Hachette Book Group, Inc.

The publisher is not responsible for websites (or their content)
that are not owned by the publisher.

The Hachette Speakers Bureau provides a wide range of authors for
speaking events. To find out more, go to hachettespeakersbureau.com
or call (866) 376-6591.

Photography credits: Connie Miller of CB Creatives. Other photography
by page: Brian Samuels, pages XV, 28, 62-63, 76-77, 100, 120-121,
132-133, 206-209 (single spices), 220-221, 246, 256, 271, 280-281;
Channing Johnson, page IX, Benjamin Schaefer, page 303 (upper and
bottom right images).

Styling credits: Christine Tobin except as noted; Catherine Smart, front
cover and pages XIV, 6, 9 (upper image), 12 (upper image), 26, 33, 40,
47, 56, 58, 60, 68, 70, 74, 84, 86, 89, 90, 94 (top), 118, 136, 142, 145, 146
(upper image), 149, 150, 152, 172, 176, 180, 182, 185, 186, 237, 242,
244 (upper image), 255, 268, 288; Brianna Coleman, 54, 55, 62, 63,
178-79, 196 (lower images), 206-209, 220-221, 280.

Prop styling by Brianna Coleman

ISBN 978-0-316-42305-2 (hardcover) / 978-0-316-53814-5 (signed) /
978-0-316-53813-8 (B & N signed) /
978-0-316-42709-8 (B & N signed Black Friday)
LCCN 2019937736

10 9 8 7 6 5 4 3 2 1

IM

Print book interior design by Gary Tooth / Empire Design Studio
Printed in China

INTRODUCTION

Rules are a mixed blessing. They are useful in building a foundation of knowledge, whether in music or cooking. But they also create boundaries that can dampen improvisation.

The New Rules is our attempt to do both, to create a communal starting point for a new way to cook (well, new to the classic American table) while also inspiring home cooks to abandon rigid culinary notions drawn from America's European roots and ersatz adaptations of Chinese, Italian and Mexican cuisines.

A few examples. Water for stock. Putting the sweet back into savory. Blooming spices. Bitter and charred as flavors. Herbs as greens. Ginger as a vegetable. Don't stir polenta. Season early. And late. Cook pasta in its sauce, not water.

This is not a license to discard culinary history. It's an opportunity to learn from others and rethink what we do at the stove. These rules may be new to us but they are conventional wisdom for millions of home cooks around the world.

New Rules. Old Rules. It all comes down to the same thing. Fresh, bold dishes made with an enthusiasm for the joy of cooking.

CHANGE THE WAY YOU COOK

No. 1
Banish One-Note Flavors and Textures

Simplistic flavors and textures lack interest. A balance of contrasting flavors and textures allows each to shine without dominating.

No. 2
Tenderize Tough Greens with Salt

Raw greens can be off-puttingly tough; massaging the leaves with kosher salt tenderizes them.

No. 3
For Sweeter Root Vegetables, Grab Your Grater

When root vegetables are cut, their cells are ruptured, releasing sugars and volatile hydrocarbons, the source of their sweetness and aromas. Grating ruptures the most cells, producing sweeter vegetables.

No. 4
For Dressing That Sticks, Salt Your Vegetables

Slick and watery vegetables can be hard to flavor; dressings and seasonings slide right off. Salting them first draws out moisture, leaving behind firmer, drier vegetables to which seasonings can stick.

No. 5
Treat Herbs as Greens, Not Garnish

For full-flavored but still simple salads, add herbs by the cupful rather than as a delicate sprinkle.

No. 6
Stagger Your Cooking

Dumping everything in the pot at once creates a uniformity of texture and can overcook more tender ingredients. Stagger them based on how long they should cook.

No. 7
Bloom Seasonings in Fat for Bigger Flavor

Heating spices and seasonings in fat intensifies their flavors, drawing them into the liquid and allowing them to better permeate the dish.

No. 8
Jumpstart Your Potatoes

For potatoes that are tender on the inside and crispy on the outside, we start them in the microwave.

No. 9
Beat Bitterness by Charring

Roasting cabbage and other sulfurous vegetables at high heat reduces their bitterness and gives them a subtle sweetness.

No. 10
Braise Low and Slow to Tenderize Tough Greens

Sturdy greens like kale can be leathery and tough if not cooked long enough. But a gentle simmer gives them time to become tender, sweet and to meld with other ingredients.

No. 11
Sear and Steam for Perfectly Crisp-Tender Vegetables

For perfectly crisp and tender vegetables, we combine cooking techniques. Start by searing them in a hot pan to develop browning and flavor. Then add water and a tight-fitting lid to steam them until tender.

No. 12
For Bolder Sauces, Lose the Liquid

Reducing the amount of liquid used in sauces allows the flavors to concentrate and better coat the other ingredients.

No. 13
Stop Stirring Your Polenta

For the creamiest, easiest polenta, all you need is an oven, a couple vigorous stirs and no endless whisking.

No. 14
Seize the Starch for Better Beans and Grains

Use the natural starches in beans, lentils and grains to improve the texture of the finished dish.

No. 15
Move Rice from the Side to the Center

Rethink chicken soup by making starchy rice the star while relegating chicken to the role of flavorful garnish.

No. 16
Hold the Herbs Until the End

Delicate herbs make the most impact when they're kept fresh. This often means adding them last, as heat can dull their flavor.

No. 17
Put a Chill on Rice for Frying

Chill cooked rice, then toss it with oil before using it for stir-frying. Freshly cooked rice will otherwise turn soft or gluey in the pan.

No. 18
Don't Let Neutral Ingredients Stand Alone

Pair neutral ingredients—such as lentils or grains—with brighter, sharper flavors for balance and impact.

No. 19
Season Your Water

Adding hearty seasonings to the cooking liquid for grains and beans infuses them with bolder flavor.

No. 20
Warm Beans for Bolder Seasoning

Improve the flavor of canned beans by heating them before seasoning. The heat makes the beans swell; as they cool and contract they better absorb other flavors.

No. 21
Create Creaminess Without Cream

A creamy sauce doesn't have to be made with cream. Grating corn kernels releases their milky pulp and starches to create the base of a rich sauce.

No. 22
Put Pasta Water to Work

Don't throw pasta water down the drain. The starchy water is a great way to create sauces that coat and cling to the cooked noodles.

No. 23
Get Bigger Flavor from Supermarket Tomatoes

Use a slow simmer to transform supermarket tomatoes from bland to bold.

No. 24
Boil Your Noodles Without Water

Cooking noodles in a seasoned liquid, rather than boiling them separately in water and finishing them with a sauce, is an easy way to build flavor.

No. 25
Caramelize Pasta for Deeper, Richer Flavor

Toasting dry pasta caramelizes some of the starches, producing nutty flavors similar to caramelized sugar.

No. 26
Parcook Pasta for Better Flavor

Boiling pasta until just shy of al dente, then finishing it directly in the sauce (fortified with some of the starchy cooking water), allows the pasta to better absorb other flavors.

No. 27
Stop Pureeing Your Pesto

Processing the ingredients in a particular order—and only until grainy, not pureed—produces a dramatically better pesto with layers of texture and flavor.

No. 28
Punch Up Pasta and Noodles with Savory Flavors

Savory flavors are key to combatting the bland nature of noodles and pasta. It's why tomatoes, olives, anchovies, garlic and cheese are essential to Italian recipes, and mushrooms, fish sauce and soy sauce show up so often in Asian noodles.

No. 29
Super-Starch Your Pasta

Create silkier, thicker sauces by cooking pasta and noodles in less water than typically called for, concentrating the starches that leach out of the noodles and into the cooking water.

No. 30
Use Cornstarch to Smooth Out Lumpy Sauces

Some cheese-based sauces are notoriously difficult to make without clumping. Adding cornstarch to the mixture stabilizes the cheese as it melts, creating a silky-smooth sauce.

No. 31
Add Air to Your Carbonara

Classic carbonara can be heavy and dense. Whisking the egg-and-cheese sauce as it cooks slowly over gentle heat lightens it by pumping air into it.

No. 32
Beat Back Soggy Noodle Salads

Use Asian somen noodles for pasta salads that won't turn starchy and mealy when cooled.

No. 33
Some Pasta Needs Nuts

Pasta can suffer from a singular, soft texture. So we borrow a trick from Sicily, where cooks add textural contrast—plus sweet and savory notes—with nuts, such as crushed pistachios and almonds.

No. 34
Add Yogurt to Make Dough Flavorful and Flexible

Adding tangy yogurt to dough is an easy way to boost flavor. It also makes the dough more tender and easier to work with.

No. 35
Add Moisture Without Adding Liquid

Adding mashed potatoes to dough yields a lighter, more tender crumb. Using sweet potatoes multiplies the impact, adding color and flavor as well as tenderness.

No. 36
Change the Flour to Change the Chew

Different flours—such as starchy, sweet rice flour—can change the texture of breads for the better.

No. 37
Go Low for the Perfect Poached Egg

For the easiest poached eggs, use a low-sided skillet, not a tall saucepan. And once the eggs are in, turn off the burner. The residual heat will gently and perfectly poach the eggs.

No. 38
Add Crunch to Your Eggs

Eggs don't have to be soft. Crisp-edged whites can offer a pleasant contrast to tender yolks and vegetables.

No. 39
Steam, Don't Boil, Your Eggs

Safeguard soft- or hard-cooked eggs against rubbery whites and overdone yolks by steaming instead of boiling. Steam transfers less energy to the eggs, cooking them more gently.

No. 40
End the Cooking Early

Omelets are easily overcooked. To prevent this, we pull the pan off the heat when the curds are still slightly wet. The eggs finish cooking using just the residual heat in the pan.

No. 41
Start on the Stovetop, Finish in the Oven

To ensure thicker flat omelets are perfectly done edge to edge, we start the cooking on the stovetop, then slide the pan into the oven, where the eggs finish cooking gently and evenly.

No. 42
For Lighter Eggs, Borrow a Baking Ingredient

Baking powder can help lighten baked frittatas. Just as it does in traditional baking, the baking powder reacts with the heat of the oven to form carbon dioxide gas—or bubbles—that adds air to the frittata's structure.

No. 43
Cook Gentle, Season Strong

A gentle, even heat is best for keeping the delicate flesh of fish tender. Steaming is ideal because the heat surrounds the fish, cooking it from all sides without movement.

No. 44
Stick with Single-Sided Searing

Fish and shellfish can quickly overcook. This makes it a challenge to develop a crisp, flavorful crust. So we sear seafood on just one side, then finish cooking off the burner with just residual heat.

No. 45
Tame Garlic with an Acid Touch

Briefly soaking garlic in an acid, such as lime juice, tames its bite and mellows its pungency without sacrificing flavor.

No. 46
For Tender Fish Stews, Think Big

Small chunks of fish are easy to overcook, turning them dry and tasteless. So when making fish stew, we use thick fillets and leave them whole so we can better control their rate of cooking.

No. 47
Use Marinades to Help Brown Shrimp

Shrimp tend to overcook on the inside before the outside has time to develop flavorful browning and caramelization, especially when grilling. To help with this, we briefly marinate shrimp in ingredients that speed browning, such as sugar and fat.

No. 48
Keep Seafood Tender by Saving Acids for the End

Acids can toughen the texture of raw seafood. So when we want to add tangy flavor, we add them after cooking as a sauce.

No. 49
Flat Birds Cook Faster, Crisp Better

Spatchcocking puts the breasts and thighs on an even plane so they cook at the same time. Flattening the bird also exposes all of the skin to heat, resulting in crisper skin.

No. 50
Roast on Baking Sheets, Not Roasting Pans

Roasting on a low-rimmed baking sheet rather than in a deep pan allows for better air circulation around the food, accelerating cooking and boosting browning.

No. 51
Build Better Skewers with Strips, Not Chunks

Think thin strips rather than thick chunks when making meat skewers. They cook faster and provide plenty of surface area for applying flavorful rubs and sauces.

No. 52
Shred Your Chicken for Bolder Flavor

Shredding cooked chicken not only makes the meat more tender, it also can result in better flavor. Shredded chicken has more surface area to better absorb seasonings and sauces.

No. 53
Hit Repeat for Better, Bigger Flavor

Repeating flavors is a signal-boosting tactic that creates bold layers of flavor. We often use the same spice mixture twice—first to coat chicken before cooking, then again to dust the finished dish.

No. 54
Spice Under the Skin

When seasoning chicken with spices, we often apply them under the skin where they can directly flavor the meat and stay in place better.

No. 55
Season Crumbs for Better Crust

Breading often is bland. But seasoning the breadcrumb coating itself—rather than just the meat—is an easy opportunity to build flavor into a dish.

No. 56
Tangy Sides Lighten and Brighten Heavy Mains

Fried and other oily foods often taste heavy. But serving them with sides spiked with acidic ingredients like slaws and quick-pickles balances the richness.

No. 57
Cook First, Flavor Last

Marinades rarely deliver much flavor. They don't penetrate deeply enough and the heat of cooking can dull their flavors. So we instead turn them into sauces we apply at the end.

No. 58
Use a Low, Slow Simmer to Keep Meat Moist

Cooking meat in liquid that's kept at a gentle simmer makes for moister meat. The liquid itself doesn't add moisture, but the milder heat cooks the meat more gently, keeping it tender and moist.

No. 59
Stop Tossing Your Stems

Don't trash your cilantro stems; they are full of flavor. We frequently puree them into sauces, salsas and moles, and use them to flavor rice dishes and soups.

No. 60
Put a Lid on It for Richer Low-Liquid Cooking

Cooking chicken in a covered pot with a small amount of liquid cooks the meat mainly in its own juices, keeping flavors rich and concentrated.

No. 61
Cut Meat Cold for Thin, Tender Slices

Tough cuts of meat can be made more tender by thinly slicing them, shortening the otherwise chewy muscle fibers. Sometimes we freeze the meat to make the slicing easier.

No. 62
Use Steam Power for More Tender Meat

Adding water to the pan doesn't directly add moisture to the meat, but it does create a moist environment that transfers heat to the meat more efficiently than dry air, cooking it fast and keeping it tender.

No. 63
Don't Marinate Without Also Saucing

Marinades are slow to penetrate meat, so they add limited flavor. To get around this, use them twice—first to season the meat before cooking, then later as a sauce for the finished dish.

No. 64
Give Meats an Acidic Finish

Adding acidic ingredients at the end of cooking lightens and brightens otherwise rich and heavy meats.

No. 65
Sear on the Stovetop, Cook in the Oven

Searing a spice-crusted pork tenderloin on the stovetop not only browns the meat, it also toasts the seasonings, heightening their flavors. But it's easy to overcook, so we finish it in the gentler and more even heat of the oven.

No. 66
Lose the Lid to Concentrate Flavors

We often start long-cooked stews covered so the ingredients' natural moisture is trapped in the pot and cooking begins gently and slowly. But we like to remove the cover toward the end to allow the liquid to reduce and the flavors it contains to concentrate.

No. 67
Use Less Liquid for More Flavor

Braising meats with minimal liquid in a covered pot allows the meat to cook gently in its own juices. The method concentrates juices that can later make richly flavored sauces.

No. 68
Finish the Dish the Way You Start

Finishing a dish with a repeat hit of seasoning used during cooking creates layers of interest and helps reinforce flavor.

No. 69
Sauce Meat as It Rests

As meat rests, the muscle fibers relax, allowing flavors to be better absorbed.

No. 70
Treat Meat as a Flavoring

Meat doesn't have to be the main event. Much of the world treats it more as a garnish, adding deep savory flavor without weighing down the dish.

No. 71
Treat Fresh Ginger as a Vegetable

Don't consign ginger to a mere flavoring. Up the volume and treat it like a vegetable. And don't worry about the spiciness. Ginger's bite mellows with cooking.

No. 72
Stop Searing Your Meat

Skip the searing. It's easier to build flavor into a stew by adding handfuls of herbs and plenty of robust spices. You'll save the time and hassle.

No. 73
Chill Your Meatballs

Chilling meatballs firms them up so they hold their shape better and won't fall apart as they cook.

No. 74
Tenderize Beef with Baking Soda

Lowering the acidity of beef makes it more tender. Balkan and Chinese cooks do this by adding an alkali, such as baking soda. This forces the muscle proteins apart, which makes them easier to bite through and better able to retain moisture.

No. 75
Salt Your Drinks, Not Your Glassware

Unlike salting the rim of a glass—which overwhelms the flavors inside—a tiny amount of salt added to the drink itself enhances and brightens the other ingredients.

THE MILK STREET WAY

Give Your Meals a **Foundation**, a **Counterpoint** and an **Embellishment**

At Milk Street, every recipe needs to offer a diversity of tastes, textures and sensations. While balance and harmony are important, so is contrast between those elements, which changes how we experience a dish. Think about a classic chicken soup of soft carrots and noodles with broth vs. a bowl filled with broth and chicken, dolloped with bright, hot and tangy condiments and topped with crunchy raw radish and cabbage and handfuls of fresh herbs. We're partial to the bold, fresh and bright flavors of the latter.

Getting the balance of a dish right is easier to do when you think about recipes in three parts. The dominant taste, texture and sensation of a recipe make up its **foundation.** Any taste, texture or sensation that contrasts the foundation makes up the recipe's **counterpoint.** And finishing items— the flourishes and additions that punctuate the dish—are the **embellishment,** sometimes a garnish, sometimes not.

For example, in classic Italian-American spaghetti marinara, the foundation is the wheaty, chewy and warming pasta. The acidic, bright and smooth/ slippery marinara serves as the counterpoint. A final sprinkle of grated Parmesan and chopped basil are the embellishments, adding salty, savory and fresh flavors that accent both the foundation and its counterpoint.

In traditional American and Western European cooking, the foundation takes center stage, with counterpoints typically playing an often subtle role in the dish. At Milk Street, we do things differently. Our counterpoints and embellishments play as vital a role in a recipe as the foundation.

Take classic bean salad, typically a mix of canned beans coated in a slightly sweet dressing, a dish that is one-note soft. Now imagine Georgian-style salad (p. 75) where instead of three beans and a sprinkling of herbs we take a one-bean (kidney), three-herb approach, adding fresh dill, parsley and cilantro by the fistful. The beans (foundation) are dressed with a tangy shallot-vinegar dressing and herbs (counterpoint), all finished with toasted walnuts (embellishment). We don't give up the ease of canned beans, but we do heat them in the microwave before dressing; it boosts their ability to absorb flavor. The classic salad is mostly textureless and can easily veer into bland and mealy territory. The second bursts with layers of sweet, earthy, crunchy, spicy flavor and will always be our preference.

This approach can be applied to any dish. When we make a red-sauced pasta, as in our bucatini with cherry tomato sauce and fresh sage (p. 87), the pasta is the foundation and the sauce of slow-simmered cherry tomatoes is the counterpoint. They're good on their own. But they get even better with the embellishment of fresh sage, shaved pecorino cheese and peppery olive oil.

A FEW NOTES ON OUR METHOD

Though we prefer dishes that feature multiple flavors and sensations, we don't always want them to be extreme. Bitterness can be subtle, as in the olive oil in a salad dressing. Crunchy can cover a wide spectrum, from gently crisp raw scallions to brittle tortilla chips. And preparation makes a difference. Roasted and charred sweet potatoes are crisped and bitter on the outside, soft and sweet on the inside. Steamed, the whole vegetable is soft and sweet only. Both are fine, in the correct context. Not every dish will contain every element, but the majority should be present.

AND A NOTE ON INGREDIENTS

At Milk Street, we don't call for unusual equipment or hard-to-find ingredients. But we do travel the world searching for recipes and ideas, and some ingredients we find become indispensable additions to our pantry—one-stroke solutions that add big, bold flavor that isn't easily replicated. We highlight these finds—Aleppo pepper, fish sauce, pomegranate molasses and more—in special sections throughout the book with information on where to find, how to use and how to store.

LEARNING THE ELEMENTS
Every element of a dish adds flavor, texture and sensation

TEXTURE	FLAVOR		SENSATION
Crunchy	Bitter	Pungent	Warming
Chewy/Toothsome	Sweet	Rich	Cooling
Slippery/Smooth	Sour	Fresh	
	Salty	Peppery	
	Spicy		

FOUNDATION

COUNTERPOINT

EMBELLISHMENT

VEGETABLES

RECIPES & RULES

VEGETABLES

At Milk Street, we create **flavorful salads** with handfuls of herbs. We **grate root vegetables** to enhance their natural sweetness. We **turn up the heat** to char brassicas like broccoli and cabbage to bring out their nutty, earthy sweetness. And we **stir-fry vegetables with high-impact ingredients** to deliver rich flavor in every bite.

Too often we leave vegetables on the sidelines, blandly boiling or roasting them without much thought to building flavor. Or over and again we construct the same basic green salads from all the usual suspects. But there is a world of alternatives.

Salads can be so much more than limp and leafy. They can be as decadent as the creamy, avocado-based dishes of Latin cooking. Or as bold as a vibrantly orange Moroccan carrot salad. And with the right mix of flavors and textures, just about any vegetable can move from the side of the plate to the center.

Vegetables—just like any protein—are best when served with a **balance of flavors and contrasting textures.** In our bitter greens and orange salad, walnuts and goat cheese provide meaty richness while oranges add sweetness to balance the pleasant bitterness of mixed greens such as endive and frisée. Likewise, smoked almonds give nutty contrast to an avocado and arugula salad.

Sometimes vegetables are tough, and we need to tenderize and sweeten them. When we plan to eat kale raw, we massage the leaves with salt, a technique also used on cabbage when making sauerkraut. This breaks down tough cell walls and softens the leaves. For our Moroccan carrot salad, **we grate the carrots, which releases more sugars than simply slicing or dicing**. For our smashed cucumber salad, we again use salt, but this time simply sprinkled on. It keeps the cucumbers crisp and removes moisture that would dilute the other flavors.

Fresh herbs often are considered a garnish—a dainty sprinkle to finish a dish. We turn that concept on its head with salads that **treat herbs like the main ingredient,** piling them on. We pair summer squash with basil and mint and balance the sweetness of cherry tomatoes with plenty of parsley and dill. For our take on a Chinese-style cucumber salad, we add texture and flavor with chopped nuts, sliced scallions and tender cilantro.

We **pay attention to texture** in our cooked vegetables, too. For dishes such as caponata, each vegetable is cooked separately so they don't turn into mush. And we aren't afraid to **season vegetables as boldly as we would meat.** In our sautéed spinach, we follow the Indian technique of making a tarka, blooming spices in butter to enhance their flavors and aromas.

Brassicas such as cabbage and Brussels sprouts can be bitter and sulfurous. But not if you **cook them at high heat, which neutralizes the bitterness and brings out the vegetables' sweetness.** Our cabbage is quartered, buttered and roasted to a char. Broccoli, meanwhile, is cooked to a deep brown in a cast-iron skillet. In our Portuguese rice with kale and tomatoes, lacinato kale is stewed until the leaves are supple and tender.

And we blend techniques—such as steaming and stir-frying—to ensure we get vegetables perfectly seared outside and wonderfully tender inside. Our stir-fried green beans, for example, start in a hot pan—undisturbed to boost browning. We then add water and clap on a tight-fitting lid so the vegetables steam to doneness. A bit of stir-fried ground pork with garlic, ginger and scallions adds savory flavor. Our stir-fried cauliflower benefits from the same fry-then-steam approach.

No. 1

Banish One-Note Flavors and Textures

Simplistic flavors and textures lack interest. A balance of contrasting flavors and textures allows each to shine without dominating.

Bitter Greens and Orange Salad
with Walnuts and Goat Cheese

3 medium oranges (see note)

¼ cup red wine vinegar

2 tablespoons fresh oregano, finely chopped

Kosher salt and ground black pepper

1 medium shallot, halved and thinly sliced

½ cup pitted Kalamata olives, finely chopped

⅓ cup walnuts, toasted and finely chopped

¼ cup extra-virgin olive oil

4 ounces fresh goat cheese (chèvre), crumbled

12 cups lightly packed mixed bitter greens (see note), in bite-size pieces

This salad is full of bold flavors, a mixture of bitter, sweet, briny and creamy. Meanwhile, crunchy walnuts and creamy goat cheese add layers of texture. Navel oranges do well, but colorful Cara Cara or blood oranges are great if they are in season. As for greens, use a combination of sturdy varieties so the leaves can stand up to the other ingredients. Our favorite was a mixture of endive, radicchio and frisée; you'll need one head of each to get 12 cups.

Don't leave the walnuts and olives in large pieces. *Make sure to chop finely enough so that they mix into the dressing.*

Cut ½ inch off the top and bottom of each orange. One at a time, stand each on a cut end and, slicing from top to bottom, cut away the peel and pith following the contour of the fruit. Cut the oranges vertically into quarters, then trim away the seedy core from each. Cut each quarter crosswise into ½-inch-thick slices.

In a large bowl, combine the vinegar, oregano, ¾ teaspoon salt and ½ teaspoon pepper. Add the shallot and oranges, along with their juice, and toss. Let stand for 10 minutes.

To the oranges, add the olives, walnuts, oil and all but 3 tablespoons of the goat cheese, then stir gently until combined and the cheese begins to break down and become creamy. Add the greens and toss. Taste and season with salt and pepper, then transfer to a serving platter. Sprinkle with the remaining goat cheese.

Avocado and Arugula Salad
with Smoked Almonds

2 tablespoons extra-virgin olive oil, plus more to serve

¾ teaspoon smoked paprika, divided

¾ teaspoon sweet paprika, divided

3 tablespoons sherry vinegar

Kosher salt and ground black pepper

5-ounce container baby arugula

2 ripe avocados

¼ cup roughly chopped smoked almonds, divided

We use a handful of Spanish flavors—including two varieties of paprika—to make a salad with woodsy, smoky notes and deep richness. Smoked almonds add nuttiness and texture that contrasts the silkiness of the avocados. Once assembled, serve the salad right away, as the delicate arugula wilts easily after it is dressed and the avocados will discolor.

Don't use underripe avocados. *The smooth, creamy texture of fully ripe avocados balances the earthiness of the paprika and bitterness of the arugula.*

In a small skillet over medium, heat the oil until shimmering. Add ½ teaspoon each smoked paprika and sweet paprika, then cook, stirring, until fragrant and the oil is red, about 2 minutes. Immediately pour into a small heatproof bowl, then whisk in the vinegar, ½ teaspoon salt and ¼ teaspoon pepper. Set aside to cool.

Meanwhile, in a small bowl, stir together ½ teaspoon salt and the remaining ¼ teaspoon each smoked paprika and sweet paprika; set aside. Halve, pit and peel the avocados, then cut each half in half again.

Place the arugula in a large bowl along with half the almonds. Add the cooled dressing and toss to combine. Transfer the arugula to a platter, then place the avocado wedges on the arugula. Sprinkle the salt-paprika mixture onto the avocados, drizzle with additional oil and scatter the remaining almonds on top.

Chopped Kale Salad
with Cilantro and Walnuts

⅓ cup red wine vinegar

3 medium garlic cloves, finely grated

1½ cups walnuts, chopped

2 teaspoons ground coriander

1 teaspoon dry mustard

1 teaspoon fennel seeds, finely ground

¼ teaspoon cayenne pepper

1 bunch curly kale, stemmed

2 tablespoons grapeseed or other neutral oil

Kosher salt

1 bunch cilantro, leaves and tender stems, chopped

This hearty chopped salad is inspired by the Georgian dish ispanakhis pkhali, which is made with spinach. It sometimes is so finely chopped that it is almost a dip or condiment, but we prefer the versions that maintain the different textures and crunch of the ingredients. Instead of spinach, we opted for heartier kale. Along with garlic, oil and vinegar, the greens and walnuts often are dressed with blue fenugreek, which usually requires a trip to a specialty market. While it cannot be copied, we find that a combination of coriander, mustard and fennel approximate its unique flavor.

Don't skip toasting the nuts and spices. *It brings out their nutty, vibrant aromas, adding wonderful depth to the dish.*

In a liquid measuring cup or small bowl, combine the vinegar and garlic; set aside. In a small skillet over medium-low, toast the walnuts, stirring often, until fragrant and golden brown, 7 to 10 minutes. Transfer to a large plate. To the same skillet, add the coriander, mustard, ground fennel and cayenne. Return to medium-low and toast, stirring, until fragrant and slightly darker, about 1 minute. Push the

walnuts to the side of the plate, then transfer the spices to the clearing.

In a large bowl, toss the kale with the oil and 2 teaspoons salt until evenly coated. Using your hands, firmly massage the kale until darkened in color and the volume has reduced by about half.

Working in 2 batches, pulse the kale in a food processor until finely chopped, about 10 pulses. Return the kale to the

large bowl. Add the vinegar mixture, all but ¼ cup of the walnuts, the spices and the cilantro. Toss, then taste and season with salt. Transfer to a serving bowl and sprinkle with the remaining walnuts.

No. 2

Tenderize Tough Greens with Salt

Raw greens can be off-puttingly tough; massaging the leaves with kosher salt tenderizes them.

HOW TO TENDERIZE KALE

1. Drizzle 2 tablespoons neutral oil onto the kale.

2. Sprinkle 2 teaspoons kosher salt onto the leaves.

3. Using your hands, toss to evenly distribute the oil and salt.

4. Rub the leaves until darkened in color and reduced in volume.

CHANGE THE WAY YOU COOK

No. 3

For Sweeter Root Vegetables, Grab Your Grater

When root vegetables are cut, their cells are ruptured, releasing sugars and volatile hydrocarbons, the source of their sweetness and aromas. Grating ruptures the most cells, producing sweeter vegetables.

Moroccan Carrot Salad

2 tablespoons lemon juice

1 tablespoon pomegranate molasses

½ teaspoon ground turmeric

Kosher salt and ground black pepper

¼ cup extra-virgin olive oil

⅓ cup dried apricots, thinly sliced

1½ teaspoons cumin seeds, toasted

1 pound carrots, peeled and shredded

½ cup shelled roasted pistachios, toasted and chopped

¾ cup pitted green olives, chopped

½ cup roughly chopped fresh mint, plus more to serve

Our take on the classic Moroccan carrot salad transforms average grocery-store carrots into a delicious side dish. Shredding both minimizes the fibrousness of the carrots and increases their sweetness. We then dress the carrots with a fruity, tangy-sweet dressing infused with spices. Dried apricots, toasted pistachios and fresh mint are perfect accents. Pomegranate molasses, often used in Middle Eastern cooking, is a dark, thick syrup with a sweet-sour flavor; look for it in the international aisle of the grocery store or in Middle Eastern markets.

Don't shred the carrots too finely or too coarsely. *Fine shreds quickly turn limp and lack texture, but very coarse shreds are tough and unpleasant to eat. The large holes on a box grater work well, as does a food processor fitted with the medium shredding disk.*

In a large bowl, whisk together the lemon juice, molasses, turmeric and ½ teaspoon salt. While whisking, slowly pour in the oil. Add the apricots and cumin, then let stand for 5 minutes to allow the apricots to soften.

Add the carrots and stir until evenly coated. Stir in the pistachios, olives and mint. Taste and season with salt and pepper, then transfer to a serving bowl. Sprinkle with additional mint.

No. 4

For Dressing That Sticks, Salt Your Vegetables

Slick and watery vegetables can be hard to flavor; dressings and seasonings slide right off. Salting them first draws out moisture, leaving behind firmer, drier vegetables to which seasonings can stick.

HOW TO SMASH CUCUMBERS

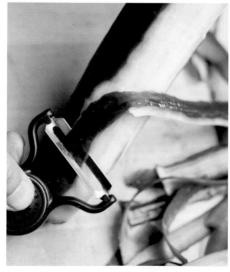

1. Trim the end of the cucumbers, then peel them.

2. Using a rolling pin or the flat side of a chef's knife, smack the cucumbers.

3. The cucumbers will split and crack, and will release some of the seeds.

Smashed Cucumber Salad
with Peanuts, Scallions and Cilantro

2 medium garlic cloves,
finely grated

2 teaspoons finely grated
fresh ginger

¼ cup lime juice

1½ teaspoons Sriracha

½ teaspoon white sugar

Kosher salt and ground black pepper

3 English cucumbers, trimmed
and peeled

½ cup roasted unsalted peanuts,
finely chopped

4 scallions, thinly sliced

1 serrano chili, stemmed, halved,
seeded and thinly sliced

½ cup lightly packed fresh cilantro,
finely chopped

This refreshing, boldly textured and flavored salad is from the Yunnan province in southern China. Smashing cucumbers helps release the seeds, which are the source of much of the vegetables' wateriness. It also creates craggy surfaces that are better at absorbing flavors. Salting the cucumbers draws out excess moisture, preventing it from diluting the other flavors. Serve with grilled meats or seafood along with jasmine rice.

Don't use regular cucumbers; *they contain a large amount of seeds that will quickly water down the salad, even if first salted to remove excess moisture. And don't forget to peel the cucumbers. The skins, if left on, will block the salt from drawing out the maximum amount liquid.*

In a small bowl, stir together the garlic, ginger, lime juice, Sriracha, sugar and ½ teaspoon salt. Set aside. Place the cucumbers on a cutting board. With the flat side of a chef's knife or a rolling pin, hit the cucumbers until they split and crack.

Slice the cucumbers ½-inch thick on the diagonal and transfer to a large colander set over a large bowl. Add 2 teaspoons salt and toss. Top with a plate smaller than the diameter of the colander; weigh down the plate with 2 or 3 cans. Let stand until liquid has pooled in the bowl, about 15 minutes. Discard the liquid, then rinse and dry the bowl.

In the same large bowl, combine the cucumbers, peanuts, scallions, chili and cilantro. Add the dressing and toss to coat. Taste and season with salt and pepper.

No. 5

Treat Herbs as Greens, Not Garnish

For full-flavored but still simple salads, add herbs by the cupful rather than as a delicate sprinkle.

Summer Squash and Herb Salad
with Almonds and Parmesan

1½ teaspoons grated lemon zest,
plus 3 tablespoons lemon juice

3 tablespoons extra-virgin olive oil

Kosher salt and ground black pepper

One 8-ounce zucchini, trimmed,
quartered lengthwise, cored and
thinly sliced on the diagonal

One 8-ounce summer squash,
trimmed, quartered lengthwise, cored
and thinly sliced on the diagonal

¾ cup lightly packed fresh basil,
torn if large

½ cup lightly packed fresh mint,
torn if large

⅓ cup sliced almonds, toasted

1½ ounces Parmesan cheese,
shredded on the large holes of
a box grater (about ½ cup)

This quick, yet elegant salad is the perfect accompaniment to grilled meats or a simple pasta dish. Crisp yet tender summer squash and crunchy toasted almonds create a salad full of contrasts, while plenty of fresh herbs take the place of traditional salad greens. Any salty, aged cheese, such as manchego or aged Gouda, could be substituted for the Parmesan.

Don't dress the salad *until you are ready to serve. The herbs are delicate and wilt quickly. Also, don't forget to cut out the core from each squash and zucchini quarter. The soft, porous center will soak up dressing and become mushy.*

In a small bowl, whisk together the lemon zest and juice, oil, 1 teaspoon salt and ½ teaspoon pepper. Set aside.

In a large bowl, toss together the zucchini, summer squash, basil, mint, almonds and all but 2 tablespoons of Parmesan. Add the dressing and toss. Taste and season with salt and pepper. Transfer to a serving dish and sprinkle with the remaining Parmesan.

Grape Tomato Salad
with Parsley and Dill

2 pints grape or cherry
tomatoes, halved

Kosher salt and ground black pepper

¼ cup lemon juice

3 medium garlic cloves, minced

1 medium shallot, halved
and thinly sliced

¾ cup lightly packed fresh
flat-leaf parsley

2 tablespoons extra-virgin olive oil

½ cup lightly packed fresh dill,
roughly chopped

In this simple salad with vibrant, contrasting colors, grape tomatoes are halved and salted to soften them slightly and season them through. Steeping the garlic and shallot in lemon juice for 10 minutes mellows their bite. To be efficient, use this time to prep the parsley and dill. The salad is especially good with grilled meats or seafood or spooned into pita bread.

Don't add the dill *until just before transferring the salad to a serving vessel; the delicate leaves wilt quickly. The parsley is added sooner because it is sturdier.*

In a large bowl, toss the tomatoes with ½ teaspoon salt. Set aside. In a small bowl, stir together the lemon juice, garlic, shallot and ½ teaspoon each salt and pepper. Set aside for about 10 minutes.

Add the shallot mixture, parsley and oil to the tomatoes and toss well. Taste and season with salt and pepper. Add the dill and toss. Using a slotted spoon, transfer to a serving dish.

Cilantro, Scallion and
Cucumber Salad (Lao Hu Cai)

2 tablespoons unseasoned rice vinegar

1 tablespoon soy sauce

½ teaspoon white sugar

Kosher salt

2 medium garlic cloves, finely grated

1 bunch scallions, sliced ½ inch thick, whites and greens reserved separately

½ English cucumber, halved lengthwise and thinly sliced on the diagonal

3 jalapeño chilies, stemmed, halved lengthwise, seeded and thinly sliced on the diagonal

½ cup roasted salted peanuts, roughly chopped

Leaves and tender stems from 1 bunch cilantro (about 4 cups lightly packed), cut into 2-inch lengths

Chili oil, to serve (optional)

This punchy salad with plenty of texture is our take on Chinese tiger salad (lao hu cai), a popular dish from the northern part of the country. Instead of the customary raw onion, we use scallions and grated garlic, and we soften their harsh flavors by steeping them in the dressing before tossing with the remaining ingredients. The bold flavors make the salad a good side for rich grilled meats and oily fish. For a heat-free version, replace the jalapeños with a small green bell pepper, stemmed, seeded and sliced into thin strips.

Don't use only the cilantro leaves; *use the tender stems, too, as they pack plenty of flavor. Pluck small sprigs off the thick main stem—this makes the salad more voluminous and visually interesting.*

In a large bowl, whisk together the vinegar, soy sauce, sugar and ½ teaspoon salt. Stir in the garlic, scallion whites and cucumber, then let stand for about 10 minutes.

Add the jalapeños, peanuts and scallion greens, then toss. Taste and season with salt. Add the cilantro and toss, then transfer to a serving dish. Serve with chili oil (if using).

Parsley and Arugula Salad
with Lemon and Sesame

1½ teaspoons grated lemon zest, plus 3 tablespoons lemon juice

2 tablespoons extra-virgin olive oil

Kosher salt

Leaves and tender stems from 1 bunch flat-leaf parsley (about 3 cups lightly packed)

2 cups lightly packed baby arugula

4 scallions, thinly sliced

1 tablespoon sesame seeds, toasted

Parsley is the primary leafy green in this salad; a handful of baby arugula adds a pepperiness that rounds out the herbal, grassy notes, while scallions offer pungency. Serve the salad right away, as the acidity of the lemon juice will quickly wilt the leaves. It's perfect tucked into a sandwich wrap, as an accompaniment to fish or as a flourish for hearty stews and braises.

Don't use curly parsley; *the flat-leaf variety has more flavor and is more pleasant to eat. And don't pick off every individual leaf of parsley. It's fine to use the tender stems, so simply pluck off the small sprigs attached to the thick main stems. Small sprigs give the salad volume as well as visual appeal.*

In a large bowl, whisk together the lemon zest and juice, the oil and ¼ teaspoon salt. Add the parsley, arugula and scallions, then toss. Sprinkle on the sesame seeds and toss again. Taste and season with salt.

No. 6

Stagger Your Cooking

Dumping everything in the pot at once creates a uniformity of texture and can overcook more tender ingredients. Stagger them based on how long they should cook.

Sicilian Caponata

6 tablespoons extra-virgin
olive oil, divided

1 medium eggplant (about 1 pound),
trimmed and cut into 1-inch chunks

Kosher salt and ground black pepper

1 medium zucchini, trimmed, halved
lengthwise and cut into 1-inch pieces

1 large yellow onion, cut into
1-inch pieces

1 red bell pepper, stemmed,
seeded and cut into 1-inch pieces

½ cup red wine vinegar

2 tablespoons white sugar,
plus more to serve

1 tablespoon tomato paste

¼ cup lightly packed fresh basil, torn

Caponata, a sweet-and-sour eggplant dish from Sicily, gets its distinctive flavor from a blending of the island's Mediterranean and North African influences. We stagger the cooking of the vegetables to better preserve the character of each. This keeps the caponata bright and full of texture rather than stewy and one-dimensional. Vinegar, sugar and tomato paste, added at the end of cooking, bring the elements together. If you prefer a sweeter caponata, stir in additional sugar when seasoning with salt and pepper. Serve warm or at room temperature with crusty bread as an appetizer or as a side to grilled or roasted meats and seafood.

Don't forget to stir the vegetables while they cook. Occasionally moving them around the pan ensures they cook and brown evenly. To preserve the basil's bright color, don't tear and add the leaves until you are ready to serve.

In a nonstick 12-inch skillet over medium, heat 4 tablespoons of oil until shimmering. Add the eggplant and 1 teaspoon salt, stir, then distribute in an even layer. Cover and cook, stirring occasionally, until the eggplant is browned and a skewer inserted in the largest piece meets no resistance, 10 to 15 minutes. Using a slotted spoon, transfer to a large bowl.

In the same skillet over medium, heat 1 tablespoon of the remaining oil until shimmering. Add the zucchini and ¼

teaspoon salt, stir, then distribute in an even layer. Cover and cook, stirring occasionally, until the zucchini is browned and a skewer inserted in the largest piece meets no resistance, 5 to 8 minutes. Transfer to the bowl with the eggplant.

In the same skillet over medium, heat the remaining 1 tablespoon oil until shimmering. Add the onion, bell pepper and ¼ teaspoon salt, stir, then distribute in an even layer. Cover and cook, stirring occasionally, until the vegetables are

lightly browned and softened, 7 to 10 minutes. Add the vinegar, sugar and tomato paste, then stir until the sugar has dissolved and the mixture is well combined. Continue to cook, stirring, until the liquid begins to turn syrupy, 1 to 2 minutes. Add to the bowl with the eggplant and zucchini and stir. Taste and season with salt, pepper and sugar. Serve warm or at room temperature, stirring in the basil just before serving.

No. 7

Bloom Seasonings in Fat for Bigger Flavor

Heating spices and seasonings in fat intensifies their flavors, drawing them into the liquid and allowing them to better permeate the dish.

South Indian Sautéed Spinach

4 tablespoons (½ stick) salted butter, cut into 4 pieces

1 teaspoon cumin seeds

1 teaspoon yellow mustard seeds

4 medium garlic cloves, chopped

1 jalapeño chili, stemmed and minced

1 tablespoon finely grated fresh ginger

1 medium yellow onion, finely chopped

1½ teaspoons curry powder

Kosher salt and ground black pepper

1½ pounds bunch spinach, trimmed of bottom 1½ inches, roughly chopped

This simple spinach sauté, inspired by a dish called palakura vepudu, is quick to make and has a wonderfully rich aroma and flavor. The secret is infusing the dish with a tarka—spices toasted in butter to bloom their flavors and fragrances. We use cumin seeds and mustard seeds as the flavor foundation for the dish; alliums and other aromatics are cooked briefly in the tarka to soften their bite.

Don't use baby spinach for this dish, as the leaves quickly turn soggy and limp. Mature spinach is sturdier and more flavorful. Look for bunches with large, dark green leaves and snappy stems.

In a large Dutch oven over medium, melt the butter. Add the cumin and mustard seeds, then toast, stirring often, until fragrant and sizzling, 45 to 90 seconds. Add the garlic, jalapeño, ginger, onion, curry powder, 1 teaspoon salt and ½ teaspoon pepper, then cook, stirring occasionally, until the onion is softened, 3 to 5 minutes.

Add the spinach, turning to coat with the butter. Cover and cook until the stems are tender, about 4 minutes, stirring once about halfway through. Remove from the heat, then taste and season with salt and pepper.

Hot-and-Sour Curried Chickpeas

Start to finish: **25 minutes**

Servings: **4**

2 medium red onions, halved

1 jalapeño chili, stemmed and finely chopped

¼ cup lemon juice

2 teaspoons finely grated fresh ginger, divided

3 large plum tomatoes, halved lengthwise and cored

3 tablespoons salted butter, divided

2 teaspoons garam masala

1½ teaspoons curry powder

Kosher salt

Two 15½-ounce cans chickpeas, rinsed and drained

¼ cup chopped fresh cilantro, plus more to serve

Khatte chole, a popular Indian street food, was our starting point for this quick-and-easy vegetarian curry. Amchoor, or dried green mango powder, usually supplies the dish's characteristic tartness, but instead we steep chopped onion and jalapeño in lemon juice to make a quick pickle that adds crunch as well as acidity. For less heat, remove the seeds from the jalapeño before chopping. A box grater makes quick work of reducing the onions and tomatoes to a pulp—no food processor or blender needed. Serve the chickpeas with naan or basmati rice.

Don't stir all of the onion-jalapeño pickle into the chickpea mixture in the saucepan. Reserve about ⅓ cup for scattering on top as a garnish.

Finely chop 1 onion half, then in a small bowl, combine it with the jalapeño, lemon juice and 1 teaspoon of ginger. Set aside. On the large holes of a box grater set over a large bowl, grate the remaining 3 onion halves. Next, grate the tomato halves starting on the cut sides and grating down to the skin; discard the skins.

In a large saucepan over medium, heat 2 tablespoons of butter, the garam masala and curry powder, stirring, until fragrant,

about 30 seconds. Add the onion-tomato pulp, the remaining 1 teaspoon ginger and 1 teaspoon salt. Increase to medium-high and cook, stirring occasionally, until a spoon leaves about a 5-second trail when drawn through the mixture, 8 to 10 minutes.

Add the chickpeas and cook, stirring, until the chickpeas are warmed through, 1 to 2 minutes. Remove the pan from the heat. Measure out and reserve about ⅓ cup of the onion-jalapeño pickle, then

add the remainder to the pan along with the cilantro, the remaining 1 tablespoon butter and ½ teaspoon salt. Stir to combine, then taste and adjust the seasoning with salt. Transfer to a serving dish and sprinkle with the reserved onion-jalapeño pickle and additional cilantro.

BLANCHING AND ROASTING VEGETABLES

Skip the Foil, Monitor the Boil and Know When to Leave Them Alone

Done right, blanching and roasting are fast, no-fuss ways to highlight the natural flavor of vegetables. Done wrong, they can be a disaster, from withered green beans to sulfurous broccoli. We took more than a dozen vegetables and cooked them by blanching or roasting, taking notes along the way so we could assemble a go-to reference for both methods. A lot of the results were straightforward, but there were some surprises. For instance, most of the vegetables blanched faster than suggested by many of the sources we consulted. Here's a rundown of what we did and the guidelines we came up with.

BLANCHING

Blanching is the technique we turn to when we want crisp-tender vegetables. The technique is simple—briefly plunge vegetables into boiling water, then cool them in ice water to stop the cooking. But the timing has to be just right. Boil too long and the vegetables turn mushy. Chill too long and they get soggy.

We blanched 11 vegetables and determined different timing depending on whether they were to be refrigerated for later use or used immediately. (Vegetables intended for storage and later cooking or reheating should be blanched for slightly less time than those for immediate use.) Overall, we found it was best to use ample water—we prefer **4 quarts seasoned with 2 tablespoons Diamond Crystal kosher salt.** For best flavor, we also salt the chilling water—**3 quarts cold water mixed with 2 tablespoons kosher salt and 1 quart ice.** A slotted spoon or long-handled tongs are best for transferring vegetables to and from the ice bath.

We recommend cutting large, firm vegetables such as broccoli into pieces. More tender produce, such as green beans, can be blanched whole. Hearty greens such as kale and chard should be stemmed. After chilling, always drain blanched vegetables in a colander

BLANCHING TIMES

VEGETABLE:	SIZE PIECES:	TIME TO BLANCH FOR STORAGE:	TIME TO BLANCH TO CRISP-TENDER:	TIME IN ICE BATH:
Asparagus- small to medium	Whole, trimmed	30 secs	1 min	1 min
Asparagus-large	Whole, trimmed	1 min	2 mins	1 min
Broccoli	1-inch florets	1 min	1½ mins	1 min
Broccoli rabe	2-inch pieces	30 secs	40 secs	30 secs
Cauliflower	1-inch florets	1½ mins	2 mins	1 min
Corn	Whole ear, shucked	5 mins	7 mins	1 min
Curly kale	Stemmed	30 secs	40 secs	30 secs
Green beans	Whole, trimmed	2 mins	3 mins	1 min
Haricots verts	Whole	1½ mins	2 mins	1 min
Lacinato kale	Stemmed	30 secs	40 secs	30 secs
Snap peas	Whole, trimmed and stringed	1 min	1½ mins	1 min
Swiss chard	Stemmed	20 secs	30 secs	30 secs

and pat dry with kitchen towels to remove excess water.

Uses: Blanched vegetables are great in salads, pastas and sandwiches. They also store well up to three days—wrapped in a kitchen towel and sealed in a plastic bag—for later use (quickly sauté or stir-fry to rewarm).

ROASTING

Roasting uses dry heat to release natural sugars, creating new aromatic compounds and sweet, toasted flavors. Often, all that's needed is a toss with oil and salt before sliding the pan into the oven. But there are plentiful variables. From cauliflower to carrots, each has a different form, water content and density—meaning each can require different prep, roasting time and temperature.

We took nine vegetables and tossed them with varying amounts of olive oil and salt before roasting them on low-rimmed baking sheets. We started with common weights—a medium butternut squash, for instance, weighs about 2 pounds—and basic cuts, using 1-inch pieces in most cases. Thinner items like asparagus and green beans needed only trimming. For pan prep, we skipped any kitchen parchment or foil. The former can burn at high temperatures, and the latter tends to cause sticking. We used a metal spatula to loosen, lift and stir vegetables, and found that holding it upside-down provided the best leverage for scraping. While stirring prevented scorching on the bottom of the pan, not all of the vegetables benefitted from it. Leaving some undisturbed actually was better for browning, as with the sprouts and green beans.

We gauged tenderness and browning to come up with recommended times and temperatures. Generally, sturdier items such as squash and broccoli develop better color at higher temperatures; they also are more forgiving, requiring less attention under the high heat. More delicate vegetables, such as asparagus and green beans, fare better at slightly lower heat—which produces browning while still preserving their texture—but require closer monitoring. To determine doneness, we inserted a paring knife into large pieces to check for tenderness, but also made sure the vegetables were browned as well. Some items, like potatoes, soften early but aren't truly done until they're brown and crispy.

Uses: Roasted vegetables are great as a snack, as a side to proteins like grilled fish or chicken, or as a topping for pizzas. They also can be tucked into pita or flatbread for a quick sandwich or used as fillings for omelets and frittatas.

ROASTING TIMES

T: Tablespoon / C: Cup / t: Teaspoon

VEGETABLE	WEIGHT	PREPARATION	ROASTING TEMP	EXTRA VIRGIN OLIVE OIL	KOSHER SALT	COOK TIME (IN MINUTES)	STIR HALFWAY THROUGH?
Asparagus	1 lb	Tough bottoms trimmed, about 1-inch removed	475°F	1 T	¼ t	7–12	No
Broccoli	1½ lbs	1-inch wide florets, stems peeled and cut into ¼-inch coins	500°F	3 T	1 t	15–20	Yes
Brussels Sprouts	1½ lbs	Trimmed, halved	475°F	2 T	1 t	15–20	No
Butternut Squash	2 lbs (~1 med.)	Peeled, seeded, 1-inch pieces	500°F	1½ T	1 t	35–40	Yes
Carrots	2 lbs	Peeled, 1-inch pieces	500°F	2 T	1½ t	20–25	Yes
Cauliflower	2 lbs (~1 med.)	Cored, 1-inch florets	500°F	¼ C	1½ t	10–15	No
Green Beans	1 lb	Whole, trimmed	475°F	2 T	½ t	12–17	No
Sweet Potatoes	2 lbs	Peeled, 1-inch pieces	500°F	2 T	2 t	30–35	Yes
Yukon Gold Potatoes	3 lbs	Peeled, 1-inch pieces	500°F	¼ C	2 t	45–50	Yes

Jumpstart Your Potatoes

For potatoes that are tender on the inside and crispy on the outside, we start them in the microwave.

Spicy Potatoes
with Peanuts and Scallions

Start to finish: **40 minutes**

Servings: **4 to 6**

2½ pounds Yukon Gold potatoes, peeled and cut into ¾-inch cubes

7 tablespoons peanut oil, divided

Kosher salt and ground black pepper

½ cup roasted salted peanuts, roughly chopped

1 bunch scallions, white parts minced, green parts thinly sliced, reserved separately

3 medium garlic cloves, minced

½ teaspoon smoked paprika

1 teaspoon Sichuan peppercorns, finely ground

3 to 4 tablespoons Asian chili-garlic sauce

3 tablespoons unseasoned rice vinegar

2 teaspoons toasted sesame oil

This dish was inspired by stir-fried potatoes from the Yunnan province in southern China. For a touch of spice, we season them with Sichuan peppercorns. To grind the peppercorns, process them in an electric spice grinder, shaking it as needed if the blades aren't catching the bits, until the peppercorns are reduced to a powder. The recipe calls for 3 to 4 tablespoons of chili-garlic sauce, but you can use as little or as much as you like.

Don't microwave the potatoes *without first rinsing them to wash away excess surface starch. Otherwise, the exteriors will be sticky and gummy after microwaving. Also, make sure to drain the potatoes in a colander after microwaving. Removing as much moisture as possible helps ensure the potatoes brown well in the skillet.*

Place the potatoes in a large microwave-safe bowl and add water to cover. Stir to release some of the starch, then drain in a colander. Return the potatoes to the bowl and add 1 tablespoon of oil and 1 teaspoon salt, then toss. Cover and microwave on high for 4 minutes. Stir, re-cover and microwave until a skewer inserted into the largest piece of potato meets no resistance, 3 to 4 minutes. Drain again in the colander; set aside.

In a nonstick 12-inch skillet over medium, heat 2 tablespoons of the remaining oil until shimmering. Add the peanuts and cook, stirring, until beginning to brown, about 1 minute. Add the scallion whites, garlic, paprika and Sichuan pepper, then cook, stirring, until fragrant, about 30 seconds. Transfer to a small bowl and stir in the chili-garlic sauce, vinegar and sesame oil; set aside. Wipe out the skillet.

In the same skillet, heat the remaining 4 tablespoons oil over medium-high until barely smoking. Add the potatoes and distribute in an even layer. Cook without stirring until golden brown on the bottoms, about 4 minutes. Stir and continue to cook, stirring occasionally, until golden brown all over, 4 to 6 minutes.

Reduce to low and add the peanut mixture. Using a silicone spatula, gently incorporate the peanut mixture, scraping the bottom of the pan and turning to coat the potatoes. Off heat, stir in the scallion greens, then taste and season with salt and pepper.

Indian-Spiced Potatoes and Peas
with Chilies and Ginger

Start to finish: **40 minutes**

Servings: **4**

2 pounds russet potatoes, peeled and cut into ½-inch chunks

Kosher salt and ground black pepper

2 tablespoons coconut oil

2 teaspoons yellow or brown mustard seeds

1 medium yellow onion, chopped

2 serrano chilies, stemmed, seeded and minced

3 medium garlic cloves, minced

2 teaspoons finely grated fresh ginger

½ teaspoon ground turmeric

1 medium plum tomato, cored and chopped

1 cup frozen peas

1 cup lightly packed fresh cilantro leaves

This boldly flavored dish is a hybrid of two Indian classics: aloo matar (a tomatoey potato and pea curry) and the potato filling used in samosas. Microwaving the potato chunks simplifies and speeds up the cooking, while finishing them in a skillet ensures they are browned and crisp. For a good kick of chili heat, leave the seeds in the serranos before mincing. These potatoes are a great side dish, but served with basmati rice and yogurt they're hearty enough to be a vegetarian meal.

Don't use waxy potatoes such as red or white varieties. *Starchy russets better absorb the seasonings and become tender with cooking. And don't bother thawing the peas; they'll defrost and cook directly in the skillet.*

In a large microwave-safe bowl, combine the potatoes with 1 teaspoon salt. Cover and microwave for 4 minutes. Stir, re-cover and continue to microwave until a skewer inserted into the potatoes meets no resistance, another 3 to 4 minutes. Drain in a colander and set aside.

In a nonstick 12-inch skillet over medium-high, melt the coconut oil, then add the mustard seeds and cook, swirling the pan, until sizzling, 45 to 90 seconds. Add the potatoes in an even layer and cook without stirring until golden brown on the bottom, 3 to 5 minutes.

Stir in the onion, chilies, garlic, ginger, turmeric, 1 teaspoon salt and ½ teaspoon pepper. Cover and cook, stirring occasionally, until the onions are softened, 6 to 8 minutes. Stir in the tomato and peas and cook, uncovered and stirring occasionally, until warmed through, about 2 minutes. Taste and season with salt and pepper. Off heat, stir in the cilantro.

No. 9

Beat Bitterness by Charring

Roasting cabbage and other sulfurous vegetables at high heat reduces their bitterness and gives them a subtle sweetness.

Roasted Cabbage
with Cilantro and Sesame

2-pound head savoy cabbage, tough outer leaves removed, cut into 4 even wedges

4 tablespoons (½ stick) salted butter, cut into 4 pieces and softened

Kosher salt and ground black pepper

¼ cup unseasoned rice vinegar

2 tablespoons soy sauce

1 tablespoon grapeseed or other neutral oil

2 teaspoons honey

2 teaspoons sweet paprika

½ teaspoon cayenne pepper

2 tablespoons sesame seeds, toasted

1 cup lightly packed fresh cilantro, roughly chopped

Inspired by a wood fire-roasted cabbage dish at Firedoor in Sydney, this dish turns a simple green cabbage into a tender, richly charred side with tons of flavor. Our dish adapts the idea to a standard oven, cutting the cabbage into quarters and roasting it covered for 15 minutes to tenderize the leaves, followed by another 15 minutes uncovered to render them deeply browned and superbly tasty. An Asian-leaning vinaigrette pairs perfectly with the cabbage's natural sweetness and nutty roasted notes.

Don't use regular green cabbage; *we much preferred the texture and appearance of frilly-leaved savoy cabbage. Don't forget to soften the butter. Cold butter is too firm to spread onto the cabbage. And don't be afraid to really work the butter between the layers of leaves.*

Heat the oven to 475°F with a rack in the middle position. Line a rimmed baking sheet with foil. Using your hands and 1 tablespoon of the butter per cabbage wedge, rub the butter on all sides and into the layers of the cabbage. Sprinkle each wedge with ¼ teaspoon each salt and black pepper. Place the cabbage wedges cut-side down on the prepared baking sheet. Cover tightly with foil and roast until a skewer inserted at the thickest part of the cabbage meets a little resistance, about 15 minutes.

Uncover the baking sheet and continue to roast until deeply browned on all sides, another 15 minutes, flipping the wedges with wide metal spatula about halfway through.

Meanwhile, in a small bowl, whisk together the vinegar, soy sauce, oil, honey, paprika, cayenne, 1 teaspoon salt and ½ teaspoon black pepper. Set aside.

Transfer the cabbage to a cutting board, then trim off and discard the core from each wedge. Place the cabbage on a platter and drizzle each wedge with 1 tablespoon of the sauce. Sprinkle with the sesame seeds and cilantro, then serve with the remaining sauce on the side.

Charred Broccoli
with Japanese-Style Toasted Sesame Sauce

1¼ pounds broccoli, florets
cut into 1-inch pieces, stems peeled,
halved and sliced ½-inch thick

2 tablespoons grapeseed
or other neutral oil

Kosher salt

Japanese-style
sesame sauce (recipe below)

In Japanese cooking, gomae refers to foods dressed with a salty-sweet toasted sesame sauce. Here we use broccoli. To maximize flavorful browning, distribute the broccoli evenly in the skillet and pat down the pieces so they make contact with the pan's hot surface. You will need a 12-inch cast-iron skillet for this recipe.

Don't cut the broccoli *larger than specified or the pieces may not cook through in the time indicated in the recipe.*

In a large bowl, toss the broccoli with the oil and ½ teaspoon salt. Heat a cast-iron 12-inch skillet over high for 3 minutes, or until a drop of water evaporates in 1 to 2 seconds. Add the broccoli and use a wooden spoon to pat it in a snug, even layer; reserve the bowl.

Cook without stirring until deeply browned in spots, about 4 minutes. Stir, turning the broccoli, and continue to cook until charred and crisp-tender, another 4 to 5 minutes. Return the broccoli to the bowl and spoon the sesame sauce on top. Stir until evenly coated. Taste and season with salt.

JAPANESE-STYLE SESAME SAUCE

Start to finish: **15 minutes**

Makes **⅓ cup**

⅓ cup sesame seeds

4 teaspoons mirin

4 teaspoons soy sauce

4 teaspoons sake

1 tablespoon white sugar

⅛ to ¼ teaspoon cayenne pepper
(optional)

In a small skillet over medium, toast the sesame seeds until fragrant and golden brown, about 4 minutes. Transfer to a plate and cool to room temperature.

In a spice grinder, pulse the seeds until coarsely ground, about 3 pulses. Transfer to a small bowl and stir in the mirin, soy sauce, sake, sugar and cayenne (if using).

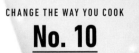

No. 10

Braise Low and Slow to Tenderize Tough Greens

Sturdy greens like kale can be leathery and tough if not cooked long enough. But a gentle simmer gives them time to become tender, sweet and to meld with other ingredients.

Portuguese Rice
with Kale and Plum Tomatoes

⅓ cup extra-virgin olive oil

1 medium yellow onion, chopped

4 medium garlic cloves,
finely chopped

3 medium plum tomatoes,
cored and chopped

Kosher salt

1 bunch lacinato kale (about 1 pound),
stemmed, leaves torn into 1½-inch
pieces

½ cup long-grain white rice,
rinsed and drained

1 tablespoon lemon juice

A staple on the Portuguese table, arroz de grelos customarily is made with spicy turnip greens (grelos), but in our version we opted for easier-to-find lacinato kale. Bunches of kale vary in size, so to make sure you purchase enough for this recipe, weigh it on the produce scale at the grocery store; you need 1 pound. Serve this simple yet remarkably flavorful one-pot dish as the center of a vegan or vegetarian meal, or offer it alongside almost any simply prepared meat, poultry or seafood.

Don't uncover the pot *while the rice is cooking; it will release too much steam and the end result will be too dry.*

In a large pot over medium-high, heat the oil until shimmering. Add the onion, garlic, a third of the chopped tomatoes and 1 tablespoon salt. Cook, stirring occasionally, until the tomatoes have broken down and the bits stuck to the bottom of the pot are dark golden brown, 7 to 10 minutes.

Add the kale, stirring and scraping up any browned bits, until wilted, about 1 minute. Stir in 2½ cups water and bring to a simmer, then cover and reduce to medium-low. Cook for 10 minutes, then stir in the rice and remaining chopped tomatoes.

Return to a simmer, cover and reduce to low. Cook, without stirring or lifting the cover, until the rice is tender and only a little liquid pools at the bottom of the pot, 15 to 20 minutes. Stir in the lemon juice and 1 teaspoon salt. Taste and adjust the seasoning with salt.

No. 11

Sear and Steam for Perfectly Crisp-Tender Vegetables

For perfectly crisp and tender vegetables, we combine cooking techniques. Start by searing them in a hot pan to develop browning and flavor. Then add water and a tight-fitting lid to steam them until tender.

Stir-Fried Green Beans
with Pork and Oyster Sauce

Start to finish: **20 minutes**
Servings: **4**

¼ cup dry sherry

¼ cup oyster sauce

2 teaspoons lightly packed brown sugar

2 teaspoons Asian chili-garlic sauce

3 tablespoons peanut oil, divided

1 pound green beans, trimmed, thoroughly dried

4 ounces ground pork

4 medium garlic cloves, finely grated

1 tablespoon finely grated fresh ginger

1 bunch scallions, white parts minced, green parts cut into 1-inch pieces, reserved separately

1 tablespoon sesame seeds, toasted (optional)

A combination of steaming and stir-frying yields crisp-tender green beans. You'll need a nonstick skillet with a tight-fitting lid for this recipe; the lid traps the steam that cooks the beans. Serve as a side dish or light main course with steamed jasmine rice.

Don't forget to thoroughly dry the green beans before cooking to wick away any excess moisture. *Also, don't stir the beans for the first 3 minutes after adding them to the skillet. This allows them to brown, which develops flavor.*

In a small bowl, stir together the sherry, oyster sauce, sugar, chili-garlic sauce and 2 tablespoons water; set aside. In a nonstick 12-inch skillet over medium-high, heat 2 tablespoons of oil until barely smoking. Add the green beans in an even layer and cook without stirring until they begin to brown, about 3 minutes. Stir, then add ¼ cup water and immediately cover the pan. Cook until the beans are bright green and crisp-tender, 2 to 3 minutes. Transfer to a medium bowl, along with any water remaining in the pan.

In the same skillet over medium-high, heat the remaining 1 tablespoon oil until barely smoking. Add the pork and cook, stirring to break it up, until no longer pink, 3 to 5 minutes. Add the garlic, ginger and scallion whites, then cook, stirring, until fragrant, about 30 seconds. Pour in the sherry mixture and cook, stirring, until the mixture is thick enough that a spatula drawn through it leaves a trail, 2 to 3 minutes.

Return the beans to the pan and cook, stirring to coat, until heated through, about 1 minute. Stir in the scallion greens. Transfer to a serving dish and sprinkle with the sesame seeds, if using.

Stir-Fried Cauliflower
with Chilies and Scallions

2 tablespoons grapeseed or other neutral oil, plus more if needed

1¼ pounds cauliflower (about ½ large head), trimmed and cut into 1-inch florets (about 5 cups)

Kosher salt

3 to 4 ounces pancetta, chopped

1¼ teaspoons cumin seeds

1 serrano chili, stemmed and sliced into thin rounds

3 dried árbol chilies, broken in half

4 scallions, white parts chopped, green parts thinly sliced on the diagonal, reserved separately

3 medium garlic cloves, thinly sliced

2 tablespoons dry sherry

1½ teaspoons soy sauce

1 teaspoon unseasoned rice vinegar

Served in the Hunan and Sichuan regions of China, this dish traditionally makes use of a long-stemmed variety of cauliflower with loosely packed florets that can be stir-fried in a flash. Dense Western-style cauliflower needs longer cooking, so we first brown the florets in a hot skillet, then add a little water to create steam to finish cooking them through. Be sure to cut the cauliflower into 1-inch pieces to keep the cooking time brief. Traditionally, thinly sliced pork belly flavors the stir-fry, but we opt for easier-to-find pancetta.

Don't use cooking sherry, *which contains salt and sometimes preservatives. Instead, look for an inexpensive bottle of dry sherry from the wine store or the spirits section of your supermarket.*

In a 12-inch skillet over medium-high, heat the oil until barely smoking. Add the cauliflower and stir to coat, then arrange in an even layer. Cook without stirring until beginning to brown, about 3 minutes. Stir, add ¼ cup water and ½ teaspoon salt, then immediately cover. Cook until just tender and the liquid has evaporated, about 5 minutes, stirring once halfway through. Transfer to a large plate, then wipe the skillet with paper towels.

In the same skillet over medium-low, cook the pancetta, stirring, until the fat has rendered and pieces are just shy of crisp, 4 to 5 minutes. There should be a thin layer of fat in the pan; if needed, add 1 to 2 teaspoons of oil. Add the cumin, both chilies, scallion whites and garlic, then cook, stirring, until fragrant, 1 minute.

Increase to medium-high, then return the cauliflower to the pan and add the sherry and soy sauce. Cook, stirring occasionally, until the liquid evaporates, 1 to 2 minutes. Off heat, stir in the vinegar and scallion greens.

No. 12

For Bolder Sauces, Lose the Liquid

Reducing the amount of liquid used in sauces allows the flavors to concentrate and better coat the other ingredients.

Spiced Stir-Fried Asparagus
with Coconut

3 tablespoons coconut oil
(preferably unrefined), divided

1½ pounds thick asparagus (see note),
trimmed and cut ½ inch thick on the
diagonal

⅓ cup unsweetened shredded coconut

1 large shallot, halved and thinly sliced

1 jalapeño chili, stemmed and sliced
into thin half rings

1 teaspoon yellow or brown
mustard seeds

1 teaspoon cumin seeds

½ teaspoon ground turmeric

Kosher salt

In the southern Indian state of Kerala, vegetables often are stir-fried with spices and coconut. These dishes, known as thoran, generally have just enough liquid to help the vegetables cook, but not so much as to create a sauce. Hence, they are called dry curries. For our version, we stir-fry asparagus, not a typical vegetable on the Indian table, but its sweet, grassy flavor pairs well with the spices and coconut. For less chili heat, seed the jalapeño before slicing.

Don't use pencil-thin asparagus; *it will quickly overcook and turn soft and soggy. Opt for thicker stalks.*

In a 12-inch skillet over medium-high, heat 1 tablespoon of oil until shimmering. Add the asparagus in an even layer and cook without stirring until deeply browned in spots, about 3 minutes. Transfer to a medium bowl and set aside.

Return the skillet to medium and heat the remaining 2 tablespoons oil until shimmering. Stir in the coconut, shallot, jalapeño, mustard seeds, cumin seeds, turmeric and 1 teaspoon salt. Cook, stirring often, until the shallot is softened and lightly browned, about 4 minutes.

Return the asparagus to the pan, increase to medium-high and stir in 1 tablespoon water. Cook, stirring often, until the asparagus is just tender, 1 to 2 minutes. Taste and season with salt.

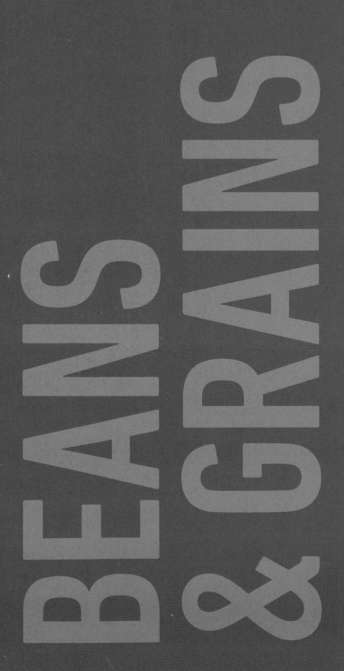

BEANS
& GRAINS

At Milk Street, **we let the sweet flavor of grains shine** by lightening up on fat. We **add herbs at the end of cooking to preserve their delicate flavor.** We layer earthy lentils with bold seasonings and we **keep grains light and fluffy** by chilling, toasting and coating them so they cook separately and evenly.

Basic beans and grains rarely inspire, but they should. **Married to the right herbs and spices**—or cooked any number of inventive, low-labor ways beyond bland boiling—**beans and grains can boldly transform a meal.**

Throwing heaps of ingredients into the pot or using labor-intensive techniques just adds extra work and results in muddled flavors. Better to **focus on just a few powerhouse ingredients and techniques** for dishes that deliver simpler and better results.

Take polenta, which we'd considered a tedious dish requiring endless standing and stirring at the stove, not to mention a fair amount of cheese and fat to give it flavor. But in a hilltop village in Italy, we learned that simpler is better. **No fat, no cheese and just a couple strong stirs.** The simplicity lets the natural sweetness of the corn come through. Good as is, our polenta also pairs well with robust sauces.

We like to **get more out of beans by changing their texture.** In our light and crispy black-eyed pea fritters, we **work with the beans' natural starchiness to create a batter that fries up crisp and light.** Rice, too, can benefit from a textural rethink. In the U.S., we typically see steamed rice that's light, fluffy and neutral. But cooks

elsewhere know that's just a start. In our Vietnamese-inspired take on rice soup—a popular dish often eaten for breakfast—we **use short-grain rice for its creaminess, cooking it to a thick and velvety texture** in a garlic- and ginger-seasoned broth.

Texture is a key component in making the most of grains, which is why we **toss cold, cooked rice with a couple tablespoons of oil before frying,** as in our fried rice with edamame and ham. The chilling firms the rice's starches so the grains are separate and won't fry up soft and soggy; the oil is added insurance against sogginess.

And to get maximum benefit, **we pay attention to when we season.** In our arroz verde, we add the fresh herbs last to preserve their delicate flavors. But to infuse sturdy legumes like lentils and black beans with flavor, we start early and add spices and other seasonings to the cooking liquid.

While there's no denying the convenience of canned beans, we sometimes find they need a little help. In our kidney bean salad, we **warm the beans before adding the dressing.** It's an easy step that improves flavor absorption.

No. 13

Stop Stirring Your Polenta

For the creamiest, easiest polenta, all you need is an oven, a couple vigorous stirs and no endless whisking.

Creamy Polenta
with Savory Sauces

2 cups coarse stone-ground yellow cornmeal (see note)

Kosher salt and ground black pepper

Polenta, a savory cornmeal porridge, can be a disappointment in the U.S., tasting mostly of the cheese and fat that weighs it down. Not to mention it requires near-constant whisking to get a lump-free consistency. But in Cossano Belbo, Italy, we found a better way with no cheese, no butter and not much stirring. The finished polenta is light and fresh, and the flavor of the corn really shines. We use more water than called for in conventional recipes. And we found that combining the cornmeal with cold, not boiling, water, then bringing the entire pot to a simmer, prevents clumping. We finished the polenta in the more gentle and even heat of the oven. For the best flavor and texture, use coarse stone-ground cornmeal; fine cornmeal produced pasty, gluey polenta, while steel-ground cornmeal had less flavor. We liked Bob's Red Mill coarse-ground cornmeal and its polenta corn grits, but found that different brands cook up with slightly different consistencies. The finished polenta should be pourable; if it's too thick, thin it with water as needed. This polenta is a perfect side to braises. It also can be paired with a flavorful sauce (see following recipes). And if you'd like to have leftovers to serve fried the next day, see our recipe (p. 53) for instructions on scaling up and storage.

Don't use white cornmeal. *Its flavor is milder than yellow cornmeal. In Italy, it is used mostly for sweet dishes. And don't skip the whisk for stirring the polenta; its wires are more effective than a wooden spoon for breaking up lumps.*

Heat the oven to 375°F with a rack in the lower-middle position. In a large Dutch oven, whisk together the cornmeal, 1 tablespoon salt and 11 cups water. Bring to a gentle simmer over medium-high, stirring to prevent clumping. Transfer the pot, uncovered, to the oven and bake for 1 hour.

Remove the pot from the oven. Carefully whisk the cornmeal mixture until smooth, then use a wooden spoon to scrape along the bottom and into the corners of the pot to loosen any stuck bits. Return the pot, uncovered, to the oven and cook until the cornmeal is thick and creamy and the granules are tender, another 10 to 30 minutes, depending on the cornmeal used.

Remove the pot from the oven. Vigorously whisk the polenta until smooth and use the wooden spoon to scrape the bottom, sides and corners. Let stand for 5 minutes. The polenta should thicken just enough for a spoon to leave a brief trail when drawn through; whisk in additional water, if needed, to adjust the consistency. Taste and season with salt and pepper. Serve immediately.

SPINACH, PANCETTA AND CREAM SAUCE

Start to finish: **25 minutes**
Makes **2½ cups**

Spinach with pancetta and cream is a luxurious topping for polenta, as well as a delicious way to work a vegetable into your meal. We let the microwave do half the work—it wilts the leaves in just a few minutes and with little effort. If you like, use bacon instead of pancetta.

Put 1 pound baby spinach in a large microwave-safe bowl, cover and microwave on high until almost fully wilted, 2 to 4 minutes, stirring once. Uncover and set aside until cool enough to handle. Using your hands, squeeze the spinach dry, then roughly chop; set aside. In a large saucepan over medium, cook **3 ounces pancetta** (chopped), stirring occasionally, until golden brown and crisp, about 8 minutes. Using a slotted spoon, transfer to a paper towel–lined plate. Add **1 medium shallot** (halved and thinly sliced), 1 teaspoon kosher salt and ½ teaspoon ground black pepper to the fat in the pan, then cook over medium, stirring occasionally, until the shallot is light golden brown, about 2 minutes. Stir in **1 cup heavy cream** and **⅛ teaspoon grated nutmeg.** Bring to a simmer and cook, stirring often, until thickened enough that a spatula drawn through it leaves a brief trail, 4 to 6 minutes. Off heat, stir in **1 ounce finely grated Parmesan cheese** (½ cup), **1 tablespoon finely grated lemon zest,** the spinach and pancetta. Taste, then season with salt and pepper.

BUTTER, GARLIC AND ANCHOVY SAUCE

Start to finish: **25 minutes**
Makes **1 cup**

This sauce is a heady blend of butter, olive oil, lightly toasted garlic and umami-rich anchovies. Bay and rosemary offer herbal notes, while lemon juice adds brightness to balance the deep, rich flavors.

In a small saucepan over low, combine **8 tablespoons (1 stick) salted butter, ¼ cup extra-virgin olive oil, 12 medium garlic cloves** (minced), **3 tablespoons minced drained oil-packed anchovies, 2 bay leaves, 2 small rosemary sprigs** and **¾ teaspoon red pepper flakes.** Cook, stirring occasionally, until the garlic is lightly toasted and the anchovies have disintegrated, 15 to 20 minutes. Off heat, remove and discard the bay and rosemary, then stir in **2 tablespoons lemon juice.**

SPICY TOMATO SAUCE WITH GARLIC AND ANCHOVIES (BAGNA DELL'INFERNO)

Start to finish: **20 minutes**
Makes **2 cups**

We developed this bold sauce—named for the devil's bath—as a topping for polenta, but it also would be delicious over pasta.

In a nonstick 12-inch skillet over medium, combine **2 tablespoons extra-virgin olive oil, 5 oil-packed anchovies** and **5 medium garlic cloves** (minced). Cook, stirring occasionally and breaking up the anchovies, until the garlic is light golden brown, 2 to 3 minutes. Stir in **½ teaspoon red pepper flakes** and **2 pints grape tomatoes** (1 pint halved, 1 pint left whole), then cover and cook, stirring occasionally, until most of the whole tomatoes have burst, 5 to 7 minutes. Using a fork or potato masher, gently mash the tomatoes. Off heat, stir in **3 tablespoons red wine vinegar** and **2 tablespoons extra-virgin olive oil.** Taste and season with salt and ground black pepper, then stir in **¼ cup chopped fresh basil.**

FRIED POLENTA

Start to finish: **25 minutes**

Servings: **4**

Soft polenta loses its creamy, pourable consistency with chilling. But Italians transform those firm leftovers by cutting the polenta into squares and frying until crisp outside and creamy inside. If you plan to serve soft polenta one night and fried polenta in the next few days, scale up the recipe for soft polenta so you have enough for both occasions: Increase the cornmeal to 2½ cups, the water to 13¾ cups and the salt to 5 teaspoons. While the polenta cooks, coat an 8-inch square baking dish with 1 tablespoon extra-virgin olive oil. When the soft polenta has finished cooking, ladle 4 cups into the prepared baking dish and smooth it to an even layer. Cool to room temperature, cover with plastic wrap and refrigerate until firm, or up to two days. Fried polenta is a great accompaniment to stews, or it can be topped with cheese or sauce and served as an appetizer or light main course. In Italy, it often is eaten as a starter topped with chunks of Gorgonzola cheese and a drizzle of honey.

Don't use polenta that has not been chilled until very firm. It's best to give the polenta at least a full day in the refrigerator before cutting and frying.

8-inch square firm, chilled soft polenta
⅓ cup all-purpose flour
Kosher salt and ground black pepper
6 tablespoons extra-virgin olive oil, divided

Remove the polenta from the baking dish by inverting it onto a cutting board. Cut into 9 squares. In a shallow dish, whisk the flour and ½ teaspoon each salt and pepper. Add the polenta squares to the seasoned flour and turn to coat on all sides, then shake off the excess.

In a 12-inch nonstick skillet over medium-high, heat 3 tablespoons of oil until barely smoking. Add 4 or 5 of the squares and cook until lightly browned, about 4 minutes. Carefully flip each square and cook until lightly browned on the second sides, another 3 to 4 minutes. Transfer to a large plate and wipe out the skillet. Repeat with the remaining oil and polenta.

SPICE UP YOUR SPICES

Bloom Them, Toast Them and Keep Them Coarse

The key to getting the most flavor and aroma from your spices is knowing how to unlock their volatile oils. The two most common techniques for doing this are applying heat and grinding. Depending on the recipe, sometimes both are employed. Applying heat (by either blooming in fat or toasting in a dry pan) tends to deepen and soften a spice's sharp, raw flavor notes. But there are occasions when we prefer raw spices over bloomed or toasted. For grinding whole spices, a spice mill or an electric coffee grinder dedicated to the purpose work well (cinnamon sticks are the exception, as they aren't easily pulverized at home). Spices can be ground in their raw state or after toasting and cooling. The degree to which they are ground impacts flavor and texture as well as the appearance of a dish.

Here are some of the ways we get the most out of all our spices.

BLOOMING

Blooming spices—or heating them in hot fat, such as butter, ghee or oil—changes their flavor in two ways. First, many of the flavor compounds in spices are fat soluble, which means when you bloom them in hot oil, aromas and flavors are extracted. Second, spices bloomed in hot fat are transformed by heat and oxidation, creating new and more complex flavor and aroma compounds.

Bloom spices—rather than toast them in a dry pan—when you not only want deeper flavor, but also want the fat to help

carry the flavor more evenly throughout a dish. We do this in our South Indian sautéed spinach (p. 25), toasting cumin and mustard seeds in butter for a burst of fragrant flavor.

How to bloom: To bloom spices perfectly, there are just two rules to remember. First, **size determines time.** Larger spices, such as whole seeds (cumin, coriander) and cinnamon sticks require more time for the heat to draw the oil-soluble compounds to the surface of the spice. Ground spices require less time because the surface area of the ground spice is much larger. Second, **start spices in cool or warm oil and heat slowly** over low to medium heat. Gradual cooking gives you a wider window to determine when the spices are done so there's less chance of overheating or scorching, which results in bitter, acrid flavors.

TOASTING

Toasting spices in a dry skillet—that is, without any fat—is another way to intensify their flavors and aromas. Spices that are made into seasoning blends or rubs often are toasted before mixing, as are spices in a recipe that wouldn't otherwise have a chance to see dry heat.

How to toast: Start spices, whole or ground, in a cool pan and toast them over low to medium heat, stirring frequently for even cooking. Most spices are done after just a couple minutes, when their aroma becomes more pronounced and they darken by just a shade or two—don't expect a dramatic change in color. Some spices, such as mustard seeds, may pop as they toast. To prevent scorching, immediately transfer the toasted spices to a plate or bowl to cool. Whole spices that will be ground should be allowed to cool completely before grinding to prevent clumping. Toast only as much as needed for your recipe or that you can use quickly because the flavorful oils released by heating will dissipate more rapidly than with raw spices.

When not to toast: Leave spices raw when they'll encounter intense heat during cooking. For instance, when you're making a spice rub to coat steak with a flavorful crust, the spices will toast while the meat cooks. We also don't toast when we want the brighter flavor of untoasted spices. In our shrimp with Kerkennaise sauce (p. 175), the caraway seeds are coarsely ground and left raw to retain their unique flavor.

WHOLE VS. COARSELY GROUND VS. FINELY GROUND

Use whole spices when you want the discrete flavor of a spice to pop in a dish and when you want a brighter flavor. **Use coarsely ground spices when you want a final dish with layers of flavor** that are semi-integrated. Some bites will taste more intensely spiced than others. **Use finely ground spices when you want the flavors to blend into the foundation** of a dish.

USE SPICE FOR TEXTURE

To experiment with the impact spice size has on taste, make dukkah, the Egyptian nut-and-seed mix. (For more information on dukkah and its uses, see p. 220), Start with the basic recipe; in a large skillet over medium, toast **½ cup raw cashews** for 3 to 4 minutes. Add **2 tablespoons sesame seeds** and toast for 1 to 2 minutes. Add **2 tablespoons each coriander seeds** and **cumin seeds** and **1 tablespoon caraway seeds,** then toast for 1 minute. Remove from the heat and let cool, then pulse in a food processor with **1 teaspoon dried oregano** and ½ teaspoon each kosher salt and ground black pepper until coarsely ground. Transfer half of the mix to a bowl, then process the remaining dukkah until finely ground. The coarsely ground dukkah should still taste like its component parts; the finely ground batch will be an entirely new ingredient with its own cohesive flavor.

Use coarsely ground dukkah **on toast with cream cheese, ricotta or fresh goat cheese; sprinkled onto roasted root vegetables** such as carrots and beets; or stirred into olive oil as a dip for pita bread.

Use finely ground dukkah mixed with flour to coat chicken cutlets, add it to salad dressings for nutty-spicy flavor or use it as a seasoning for all sorts of egg dishes.

KEEP IT FRESH

BUYING
When possible and practical, buy whole spices in small quantities from the bulk section of a grocery store or from a reputable online vendor.

STORING
Store spices in airtight containers away from heat and light. It is best to store them whole, then toast and grind them in small batches to use over a short period of time.

SHELF-LIFE
Spices lose their potency over time and eventually lose all of the volatile oils that made them flavorful. However, before you throw away any spice, toast it in a dry skillet. If it becomes aromatic, go ahead and use it.

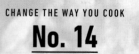

No. 14

Seize the Starch for Better Beans and Grains

Use the natural starches in beans, lentils and grains to improve the texture of the finished dish.

Black-Eyed Pea Fritters

1 cup dried black-eyed peas

Kosher salt

1 teaspoon baking powder

1 bunch scallions, finely chopped

2 Fresno chilies, stemmed, seeded and finely chopped

1½ cups peanut oil

Tomato-curry dipping sauce, recipe below, to serve

In West Africa, cooks turn black-eyed peas into crisp fritters reminiscent of falafel, often serving them with an assertively spiced dipping sauce that contrasts nicely with the earthy legumes. It's essential to use dried peas here, not canned, and they must be soaked for at least 12 hours, so plan accordingly. But after soaking and draining, the beans don't need to be cooked—they go directly into the food processor to make a doughy batter. We process most of the peas to a fine puree, but leave some coarse to give the fritters more texture. To monitor the temperature of the frying oil, a digital thermometer works best. Serve the fritters as an appetizer or snack with the dipping sauce (see following recipe) or treat them like falafel and tuck a few into folded flatbread along with lettuce, tomato and onion.

Don't skip the step of rubbing the soaked peas with your hands to remove some of their skins. This gives the fritters a lighter, finer texture. And don't shortcut the 30-minute refrigeration time for the batter; chilling helps the fritters hold together during frying.

In a large bowl, combine the peas with 8 cups water and 1 tablespoon salt. Soak at room temperature for at least 12 hours or up to 24 hours.

With the peas still in the soaking water, rub them together with your hands to release as many skins as possible. Pour off the water and loosened skins, then drain the peas in a colander and rinse well; you should have about 3 cups drained peas.

In a food processor, process 2 cups of the peas and 2 tablespoons water until nearly smooth, about 2 minutes, scraping the bowl as needed. Add the remaining peas and process until coarsely ground, about 30 seconds. Transfer to a bowl and stir in the baking powder, scallions, chilies and 2 teaspoons salt. Cover and refrigerate for about 30 minutes.

Set a wire rack in a rimmed baking sheet and line half of the rack with a triple layer of paper towels. In a 12-inch nonstick skillet over medium-high, heat the oil to 350°F. Working quickly, drop 8 heaping tablespoons of the bean mixture into the hot oil, then use a wide slotted spoon to flatten each mound into a round about ½ inch thick. Cook until the bottoms are deep golden brown, 1 to 2 minutes, adjusting the heat as needed to keep the oil at 350°F. Using 2 forks, flip each fritter and cook until the second sides are deep golden brown, another 1 to 2 minutes. Using the slotted spoon, transfer the fritters to the paper towels and let drain for 20 to 30 seconds, then transfer to the other side of the wire rack. Return the oil to 350°F and repeat with the remaining bean mixture. Sprinkle the fritters with salt and serve with the dipping sauce.

TOMATO-CURRY DIPPING SAUCE

Start to finish: **10 minutes**

Makes about **¾ cup**

2 tablespoons curry powder

½ cup ketchup

2 tablespoons packed dark brown sugar

2 tablespoons lime juice

1 tablespoon hot sauce

Kosher salt and ground black pepper

In a small skillet over medium, toast the curry powder, stirring constantly, until fragrant, about 30 seconds. Transfer to a small bowl and add the ketchup, sugar, lime juice, hot sauce and 3 tablespoons water. Whisk until the sugar dissolves, then taste and season with salt and pepper.

No. 15

Move Rice from the Side to the Center

Rethink chicken soup by making starchy rice the star while relegating chicken to the role of flavorful garnish.

Vietnamese Rice Soup
with Chicken (Cháo Gà)

2 quarts low-sodium chicken broth

1 cup Japanese-style short-grain rice

3 medium garlic cloves, finely grated

2 teaspoons finely grated fresh ginger

1 bunch scallions, thinly sliced, white and green parts reserved separately

Kosher salt and ground black pepper

Two 8- to 10-ounce boneless, skinless chicken breasts

1 tablespoon fish sauce

½ cup lightly packed fresh cilantro, finely chopped

Lime wedges, to serve

This is a hearty but not heavy bowl of soupy rice. It often is served with garnishes that offer textural and flavor contrasts. In Vietnam, it's known as cháo and frequently is eaten for breakfast. Seasoned with modest amounts of garlic, ginger and fish sauce, our version is built from simple, clean yet wholly satisfying flavors. Cilantro and scallions add bright color and fresh notes, and ground black pepper lends a touch of heat and pungency. The soup will continue to thicken as it stands; to adjust the consistency, stir in water or chicken broth a few tablespoons at a time.

Don't use long- or medium-grain rice. The high starch content of short-grain rice gives the soup its thick, creamy consistency. And don't rinse the rice before cooking; you want the grains to retain as much starch as possible.

In a large pot over medium-high, combine the broth, rice, garlic, ginger, scallion whites and ½ teaspoon pepper. Bring to a boil, then add the chicken breasts, fully submerging them. Cover, reduce to low and cook, adjusting the heat to maintain a gentle simmer, until the thickest part of the chicken reaches 160°F, 18 to 24 minutes.

Using tongs, transfer the chicken to a medium bowl and set aside. Bring the rice mixture to a rapid simmer over medium, then stir in the fish sauce. Cover and continue to cook, stirring occasionally and adjusting the heat as needed to maintain a simmer, until the broth is thickened and the grains of rice no longer settle beneath the surface, about 20 minutes.

While the rice continues to cook, shred the chicken and set aside. When the rice and broth are ready, taste and season with salt and pepper, then ladle into individual bowls. Top with shredded chicken, scallion greens, cilantro and additional pepper. Serve with lime wedges.

No. 16

Hold the Herbs
Until the End

Delicate herbs make the most
impact when they're kept fresh.
This often means adding them last,
as heat can dull their flavor.

Arroz Verde
(Green Rice)

1 tablespoon grapeseed or other neutral oil

1½ cups long-grain white rice (see note), rinsed and drained

½ teaspoon ground cumin

3 scallions, thinly sliced

4 jalapeño chilies, stemmed, seeded, 2 finely chopped, 2 roughly chopped

4 medium garlic cloves, finely chopped

Kosher salt

2 cups lightly packed fresh cilantro stems and leaves, roughly chopped

This flavorful, vibrant Mexican side dish pairs well with almost any type of main, from Indian curries to simple roasted chicken. It often is made by adding pureed cilantro and chilies to the liquid at the start of cooking, but this produces rice that's army green and dull in taste. To keep the color and flavor fresh, we cook our rice with just the hardier flavorings—garlic, scallions and half the chilies—then stir in the puree after cooking. Seeding all the jalapeños keeps this dish mild; if you want some heat, leave the seeds in one or more of the chilies.

Don't use basmati rice *in place of the regular long-grain rice the recipe calls for. Though basmati is a long-grain variety, it cooks a little differently. (Jasmine rice, on the other hand, does work here.) Don't worry about carefully chopping the cilantro. A few quick cuts are sufficient for preventing the stems from wrapping around the blender blade during pureeing.*

In a large saucepan over medium, heat the oil until shimmering. Add the rice and cumin, then cook, stirring, until the grains are translucent and the cumin is fragrant, about 2 minutes. Stir in the scallions, the finely chopped jalapeños, three-fourths of the garlic, 2 cups water and 2 teaspoons salt. Bring to a simmer over high, then cover, reduce to low and cook until the rice absorbs the liquid, 10 to 15 minutes.

While the rice cooks, in a blender, combine ¼ cup water, the cilantro, the roughly chopped jalapeños, the remaining garlic and 1 teaspoon salt. Blend until smooth, about 1 minute, scraping the blender as needed.

When the rice is done, remove the pan from the heat. Uncover, then drape a kitchen towel across the top of the pan. Replace the lid and let stand for 5 minutes.

Using a fork, gently fluff the rice. Transfer to a large bowl, then add the cilantro puree and fold with a rubber spatula until fully incorporated.

RETHINK RICE

Go Green With Herbal Add-Ins, Switch Up Cooking Liquids and Chill the Leftovers

There are an amazing 40,000 varieties of rice. And yet all too often we limit ourselves to just one kind, cooked one way; white rice, steamed. At Milk Street, we sometimes **use long-grain brown rice for fried rice** instead of the traditional white; its nutty, earthy taste adds contrast. (And we save ourselves trouble by **freezing rice for future use**; it's ready when we want it.) We don't waste time with merely decorative sprinkles of herbs, instead **adding a robust herb puree at the end of cooking** for maximum flavor and color. And we **don't limit ourselves to plain water,** using swaps such as coconut milk to build flavor into the cooking process.

Milk Street Method

Before we cook any rice, we rinse and thoroughly drain it. We use a large saucepan over medium high heat. These are our master cooking directions for 3½ to 4 cups cooked rice.

LONG-GRAIN WHITE RICE:

Bring 2¼ cups water, **1½ cups long-grain white rice** (rinsed and drained) and ½ teaspoon kosher salt to a simmer, then reduce to low, cover and cook until tender and the water is absorbed, about 15 minutes. Fluff with a fork.

Uses: As is, this is a classic, starchy side that is good with robustly flavored dishes like curries. But with the addition of an aromatic oil puree it's transformed into a noteworthy dish that is excellent with just about anything, including simple roasted chicken, grilled fish or as part of a Mexican-inspired meal.

Cilantro Rice

To make cilantro rice, in a medium saucepan over high, stir together **1½ cups long-grain white rice** (rinsed and drained), 2 cups water and 1 teaspoon kosher salt. Bring to a simmer, then cover, reduce to low and cook until the liquid is absorbed, 15 to 20 minutes. Meanwhile, in a blender combine ¼ cup water, 1 teaspoon kosher salt, **2 cups lightly packed fresh cilantro** (roughly chopped), **1 jalapeño chili** (stemmed, seeded and roughly chopped), **3 scallions** (roughly chopped), **3 medium garlic cloves** (peeled) and **2 tablespoons extra-virgin olive oil.** Puree until smooth, about 1 minute. If necessary, add additional water 1 teaspoon at a time to reach a smooth consistency. When the rice is done, remove the pan from the heat, lift the cover, then drape a kitchen towel over the pan. Replace the cover and let stand for 5 minutes. Using a fork, gently fluff the rice. Add the cilantro puree and **1 teaspoon lime juice,** then gently fold in. Serve with **lime wedges.**

LONG-GRAIN BROWN RICE:

Bring 1¾ cups water, **1 cup long-grain brown rice** (rinsed and drained) and ¾ teaspoon kosher salt to a simmer, then reduce to low, cover and cook until tender and the water is absorbed, about 25 minutes. Remove from the heat and let stand, covered, for 10 minutes. Fluff with a fork.

Uses: Swap out long-grain brown rice anywhere you might use long-grain white. We like its chewy texture and full flavor when used in fried rice with black beans and topped with diced avocado, pico de gallo and shredded pepper jack cheese. Since long-grain brown rice isn't as sticky as white rice, the grains tend to stay separate. We also don't have to chill it before frying, as with white rice.

Brown Rice with Crispy Prosciutto and Rosemary

For brown rice with crispy prosciutto and rosemary, in a medium saucepan, bring 1¾ cups water, **1 cup long-grain brown rice** (rinsed and drained) and ¾ teaspoon kosher salt to a simmer, then reduce to low, cover and cook until tender and the water is absorbed, about 25 minutes. Remove from the heat and let stand, covered, for 10 minutes. Meanwhile, in a small skillet over medium, heat **2 teaspoons extra-virgin olive oil** until shimmering. Add **2 ounces thinly sliced prosciutto** (chopped) and cook, stirring often, until the pieces are crisp, about 7 minutes. Transfer to a small bowl and set aside. Fluff the rice, then fold in the prosciutto, 2 tablespoons extra-virgin olive oil and **1½ teaspoons finely chopped fresh rosemary.** Serve drizzled with additional olive oil and sprinkled with **flaky sea salt.**

Cool Tip: Freeze Rice for Future Use

There are countless quick-and-easy recipes predicated on leftover rice, but who has the time to cook rice and chill it for hours before a weeknight meal? So we freeze it ahead of time. When you have a moment, cook an extra batch or two of rice, cool, and stick it in a zip-close bag in the freezer. Or simply save leftover rice from your dinner and collect it. With a quick defrost on the countertop or in the microwave, it'll be ready to make fried rice, a quick rice soup with broth, greens, and a bit of meat, or to bulk up a quick quesadilla. (Toss the cold rice with a bit of oil before frying for added protection against sticky, clumpy rice.)

JASMINE RICE

Bring 2 cups water, **1½ cups jasmine rice** (rinsed and drained) and ½ teaspoon kosher salt, if desired, to a simmer, then reduce to low, cover and cook until tender and fluffy and the water is absorbed, 15 to 18 minutes. Fluff with a fork.

Uses: Slightly stickier and sweeter than regular long-grain white, plain jasmine rice also is good as a side. But we like to up the flavor with a double dose of coconut. We use coconut oil to fry shallots, ginger and lemon grass, and add coconut milk to the cooking water for a fragrant and delicate rice that's especially good with Southeast Asian grilled meats and satay, as well as spicy curries.

Coconut-Ginger Rice

To make coconut-ginger rice, in a large saucepan over medium-high, heat **1 tablespoon coconut oil** (preferably unrefined) until barely smoking. Add **2 medium shallots** (halved and thinly sliced) and cook, stirring frequently, until lightly browned, 3 to 5 minutes. Stir in a **1-inch piece fresh ginger** (peeled, sliced into thirds and lightly bruised) and **1 lemon grass stalk** (trimmed to the lower 6 inches, outer leaves discarded, lightly bruised), and cook until fragrant, about 30 seconds. Stir in **1½ cups jasmine rice** (rinsed and drained), 1½ cups water, **½ cup coconut milk** and 1 teaspoon kosher salt; bring to a simmer. Cover, reduce to low and cook until the rice absorbs the liquid, 15 to 20 minutes. Remove and discard the ginger and lemon grass, then fluff the rice with a fork. Taste and season with salt.

Fried Rice
with Edamame and Ham

4 cups cooked rice, chilled

4 tablespoons grapeseed
or other neutral oil, divided

3 large eggs

2 ounces sliced deli ham,
cut into ½-inch pieces

1 bunch scallions, thinly sliced,
white and green parts reserved
separately

1 cup frozen shelled edamame

1 tablespoon soy sauce,
plus more to serve

1 tablespoon unseasoned rice vinegar

1 tablespoon mirin

The best fried rice has grains that are separate, not stuck together in clumps. Some cooks have turned to mayonnaise, as recommended by the website of the popular Kewpie Japanese mayonnaise, stirring a squirt of it into the cooked rice before frying. We find that a light toss in oil works well. The rice must be cooked, then chilled—using freshly cooked rice will result in sogginess—so you'll need to plan ahead. This recipe works with long-, medium- or short-grain rice—no adjustments needed. The savory-sweet Japanese seasoning blend called furikake adds a tasty flourish when sprinkled on each portion.

Don't bother thawing the edamame. *The beans will thaw and cook directly in the skillet.*

In a medium bowl, toss the rice with 2 tablespoons of oil until evenly coated, breaking up any clumps. In a small bowl, beat the eggs until well combined. In a nonstick 12-inch skillet over medium-high, heat 1 tablespoon of the remaining oil until shimmering. Add the ham and scallion whites, then cook, stirring constantly, until the ham begins to brown and the pieces no longer stick together, about 2 minutes. Add the edamame and cook, stirring, until warmed through, about 2 minutes. Transfer to a bowl and set aside.

In the same skillet over medium-high, heat the remaining 1 tablespoon oil until shimmering. Add the rice and cook, stirring to break up any lumps, until warmed through, about 2 minutes. Push the rice to one side of the pan and add the eggs to the clearing. Cook, stirring and pulling the eggs away from the rice, until mostly set but still glossy, 30 to 60 seconds.

Reduce to medium-low and stir in the ham mixture, breaking the eggs into small pieces. Remove from the heat and stir in the soy sauce, vinegar, mirin and scallion greens. Serve with additional soy sauce on the side.

No. 17

Put a Chill on Rice for Frying

Chill cooked rice, then toss it with oil before using it for stir-frying. Freshly cooked rice will otherwise turn soft or gluey in the pan.

No. 18

Don't Let Neutral Ingredients Stand Alone

Pair neutral ingredients—such as lentils or grains—with brighter, sharper flavors for balance and impact.

Lentils with Swiss Chard
and Pomegranate Molasses

½ bunch Swiss chard, stems thinly
sliced, leaves chopped into rough
¾-inch pieces (about 5 cups),
reserved separately

3½ tablespoons lemon juice, divided

1 cup brown lentils, rinsed
and drained

4 medium garlic cloves,
finely chopped, divided

Kosher salt and ground black pepper

5 tablespoons extra-virgin olive oil,
divided, plus more to serve

1 large yellow onion, halved
and thinly sliced

2 tablespoons pomegranate molasses

1 bunch fresh cilantro, finely chopped

This hearty vegetarian dish combines quick-cooking brown lentils and silky, sweet caramelized onion. The earthy, deep flavors are brightened with lemon juice and tangy-sweet pomegranate molasses, while Swiss chard lends mineral notes and cilantro brings freshness. We quick-pickle the chard stems in lemon juice and add them at the end; they offer a pleasant textural contrast to the lentils. Use rainbow chard if available—the bright stems add pops of color. The lentils are especially good with seared salmon fillets, runny-yolked eggs or hunks of warm, crusty bread.

Don't bother picking off just the leaves *from the bunch of cilantro. The tender parts of the stems are fine to use, too. Simply lop off the stems from the entire bunch, removing just the thicker, more fibrous sections.*

In a small bowl, combine the chard stems and 2 tablespoons of lemon juice; set aside. In a large saucepan over high, combine 5 cups water, the lentils, half the garlic and 2 teaspoons salt. Bring to a boil, then stir, **reduce to medium-high** and cook, adjusting the heat as needed to maintain a rapid simmer, until the lentils are tender, 20 to 25 minutes.

Meanwhile, in a nonstick 12-inch skillet over medium-high, heat 2 tablespoons of oil until shimmering. Add the onion and ½ teaspoon salt, then cook, stirring often, until softened, 3 to 5 minutes. Reduce to medium and cook, stirring occasionally, until the onion is deeply browned, another 3 to 5 minutes. Stir in the remaining garlic and the chard leaves. Continue to cook, stirring often, until the chard is wilted and tender, 3 to 5 minutes. Transfer to a large bowl.

When the lentils are tender, drain them in a colander, then transfer to the bowl with the onion mixture. Drain off and discard the liquid from the chard stems, then add the stems to the lentils and onion. Add the remaining 3 tablespoons oil, the remaining 1½ tablespoons lemon juice, the pomegranate molasses and 1 teaspoon each salt and pepper. Stir, then fold in the cilantro. Taste and season with salt and pepper. Serve warm or at room temperature, drizzled with additional oil.

Spanish Chorizo, Ham
and White Bean Stew

1 tablespoon extra-virgin olive oil

1 medium yellow onion, chopped

6 medium garlic cloves, chopped

1 teaspoon saffron threads

Kosher salt and ground black pepper

8 ounces Spanish chorizo, casings removed, halved and thinly sliced

8 ounces ham steak, cut into ½-inch cubes

1½ quarts low-sodium chicken broth

Three 15½-ounce cans white beans, rinsed and drained

3 bay leaves

4 scallions, thinly sliced

Warmed crusty bread, to serve

This is a quick-and-easy version of the Spanish dish known as fabada asturi- ana, a hearty stew of dried beans, sausage and other smoky, porky ingredients. We pared back on the meats, using only chorizo and ham, both of which lend deep flavor to the broth. The dish gets its name from the large beans that traditionally are used in its preparation, but we found that canned white beans worked well. We especially liked the relatively large size and creamy texture of cannellinis, but great northern and navy beans are fine, too. A pinch of saffron adds a Spanish flavor and fragrance, while giving the stew an alluring golden hue.

Don't overcook the chorizo and ham *after adding it to the sautéed onion mixture. If the pieces begin to sear or brown, they'll be chewy and rubbery in the finished dish. Cook only until the chorizo begins to release some of its fat.*

In a large pot over medium, heat the oil until shimmering. Add the onion, garlic, saffron and ½ teaspoon each salt and pepper. Cook, stirring occasionally, until the onion is slightly softened, 5 to 8 minutes.

Add the chorizo and ham, then cook, stirring, just until the chorizo begins to release its fat, about 1 minute. Stir in the broth, beans and bay. Bring to a simmer over medium-high, then reduce to medium and cook, stirring occasion- ally and adjusting heat as needed to maintain a simmer, for 10 to 15 minutes.

Remove and discard the bay, then stir in the scallions. Taste and season with salt and pepper. Serve with bread.

Lebanese Lentils and Rice
with Crisped Onions (Mujaddara)

Start to finish: **50 minutes**
Servings: **4**

4 medium garlic cloves,
smashed and peeled

4 bay leaves

2½ teaspoons ground cumin

½ teaspoon ground allspice

Kosher salt and ground black pepper

1 cup brown lentils, rinsed and drained

1 cup basmati rice, rinsed and drained

⅓ cup extra-virgin olive oil

2 medium yellow onions, halved
and thinly sliced

1 bunch scallions, thinly sliced

Plain whole-milk yogurt, to serve

Rice and lentils with caramelized onions is a much-loved food in the Middle East. This is our take on the version we had in Lebanon, where the dish is called mujaddara. The rice and lentils are simmered together in the same pot, with the longer-cooking lentils getting a 10-minute head start so both finish at the same time. Meanwhile, the onions are fried until crisp and deeply caramelized—almost burnt, really—to coax out a savory bittersweet flavor. Serve hot, warm or at room temperature with a dollop of plain yogurt. It's a delicious accompaniment to grilled or roasted meats, but it's hearty enough to be the center of a vegetarian meal.

Don't use French green lentils (*lentils du Puy*) *in place of the brown lentils called for. Even when fully cooked, green lentils retain a firm, almost al dente texture, while brown lentils take on a softness that combines well with the rice. Don't worry if the onions turn quite dark at the edge of the skillet; deep browning is desirable. But do stir the browned bits into the mix to ensure the onions color evenly. If the onions brown deeply before they soften, lower the heat a notch or two and keep stirring until the pan cools slightly.*

In a large Dutch oven over medium-high, combine 5 cups water, the garlic, bay, cumin, allspice, 1 tablespoon salt and 1 teaspoon pepper. Bring to a boil, then stir in the lentils and reduce to medium. Cover and cook, stirring occasionally and adjusting the heat to maintain a simmer, until the lentils are softened but still quite firm at the center, about 10 minutes.

Stir in the rice and return to a simmer. Cover, reduce to medium-low and cook until the liquid is absorbed and the lentils and rice are tender, about 25 minutes.

Meanwhile, in a 12-inch skillet over medium-high, heat the oil until shimmering. Add the onions and cook, stirring only occasionally at the start then more frequently once browning begins at the edges of the pan, until the onions are deeply caramelized and crisped, 10 to 15 minutes; adjust the heat if the onions brown too quickly. Using a slotted spoon, transfer the onions to a paper towel–lined plate and spread evenly. Sprinkle with ¼ teaspoon salt and set aside; the onions will crisp as they cool.

When the lentils and rice are tender, remove the pot from the heat. Uncover and lay a kitchen towel across the pan, then replace the lid and let stand for 10 minutes.

Using a fork, fluff the lentils and rice, removing and discarding the bay. Taste and season with salt and pepper. Stir in half the scallions, then transfer to a serving bowl. Top with the fried onions and remaining scallions. Serve hot, warm or at room temperature with yogurt on the side.

Oaxacan Refried Black Beans

4 tablespoons lard or refined coconut oil, divided

1 large white onion, chopped

1 pint grape or cherry tomatoes

5 guajillo chilies, stemmed and seeded

1 pound dried black beans, rinsed and drained

10 medium garlic cloves, peeled and kept whole, plus 5 medium garlic cloves, minced

3 bay leaves

1 teaspoon aniseed

Kosher salt and ground black pepper

4 teaspoons ground cumin

4 teaspoons ground coriander

1 tablespoon ancho chili powder

1 teaspoon dried oregano

In Oaxaca, black beans are part of almost every meal. Though they sometimes are served whole, we especially liked the balanced, complex flavor and smooth, velvety consistency of refried black beans. Traditionally, the beans are flavored with avocado leaves. We mimicked that flavor with a combination of bay leaves, aniseed and dried oregano. And we bloomed cumin, coriander, dried oregano, ancho chili powder and minced garlic in the fat before adding the pureed beans for deeper flavor. Lard gives these beans a rich meatiness, but coconut oil is a good vegetarian substitute. The beans can be stored in an airtight container in the refrigerator for up to a week. We liked this topped with crumbled cotija cheese and fresh cilantro.

Don't soak the beans before cooking. Unlike other types of dried beans, black beans soften readily without soaking. And don't forget to reserve the bean cooking liquid; you'll need 2 cups when pureeing the beans in the food processor. The liquid also is useful for thinning the beans when reheating (they thicken as they stand).

In a large pot over medium-high, heat 1 tablespoon of lard until barely smoking. Add the onion, tomatoes and guajillo chilies, then cook, stirring occasionally, until the onion is well browned, 5 to 7 minutes. Add the beans, whole garlic cloves, bay and aniseed, then stir in 10 cups water. Bring to a boil, cover partially and reduce to low. Cook, stirring occasionally, until the beans are completely tender, 1½ hours to 2 hours.

Stir in 2 teaspoons salt. Set a colander in a large bowl and drain the beans, reserving the cooking liquid. Remove and discard the bay leaves. Transfer the drained beans to a food processor and pulse a few times to break up the beans. With the machine running, add 1½ cups of the reserved cooking liquid and process until smooth, 2 to 3 minutes, scraping the bowl as needed. Taste and season with salt, then set aside.

In a 12-inch nonstick skillet over medium, heat 2 tablespoons of the remaining lard until shimmering. Add the minced garlic, cumin, coriander, ancho chili powder and oregano, then cook, stirring, until fragrant, about 30 seconds.

Stir in the pureed beans and cook, stirring frequently, until beginning to brown on the bottom, 8 to 10 minutes. Continue to cook and stir, adding reserved cooking water as needed, until the mixture has the consistency of mashed potatoes, 5 to 7 minutes. Off heat, stir in the remaining 1 tablespoon lard, then taste and season with salt and pepper.

No. 20

Warm Beans for Bolder Seasoning

Improve the flavor of canned beans by heating them before seasoning. The heat makes the beans swell; as they cool and contract they better absorb other flavors.

Kidney Bean Salad
with Spiced Vinaigrette and Herbs

Start to finish: **35 minutes**

Servings: **6**

2 medium shallots, halved
and thinly sliced

⅓ cup cider vinegar

2 teaspoons ground coriander

1 teaspoon ground fennel seeds

1 teaspoon dry mustard

½ cup walnuts

Four 15½-ounce cans kidney beans,
rinsed and drained

Kosher salt and ground black pepper

3 tablespoons extra-virgin olive oil,
plus more to serve

2 medium garlic cloves, finely grated

½ cup roughly chopped fresh dill

½ cup roughly chopped fresh
flat-leaf parsley

½ cup roughly chopped fresh cilantro,
plus more to serve

Georgian kidney bean salad is spiced and herbal, not sugary like American three-bean salad. Toasted walnuts add crunch that contrasts with the starchy creaminess of the beans. For convenience, we use canned kidney beans, but to ensure they're seasoned throughout, we heat them in the microwave before tossing them with the dressing. As the beans cool, they absorb the seasonings so every bite is flavorful. If you can't find ground fennel, grind your own by processing 1 teaspoon whole fennel seeds in a spice grinder until fine and powdery.

Don't forget to cover the beans *before microwaving so they don't dry out. And don't forget to stir them halfway through so they heat evenly.*

In a small bowl, stir together the shallots and vinegar; set aside. In a 10-inch skillet over medium, combine the coriander, fennel and dry mustard, then toast, stirring frequently, until fragrant, about 2 minutes. Transfer to a small bowl. Add the walnuts to the same skillet and toast over medium, stirring frequently, until golden brown and fragrant, 3 to 5 minutes. Transfer to cutting board and let cool.

While the nuts cool, in a large microwave-safe bowl, toss the beans with 1 teaspoon salt. Cover and microwave on high just until hot, 3 to 3½ minutes, stirring once halfway through.

To the hot beans, add the shallot-vinegar mixture, the toasted spices, the oil, garlic, 2 teaspoons salt and ¾ teaspoon pepper. Toss, then let stand for 5 minutes, stirring once about halfway through.

Roughly chop the walnuts, then reserve about half for sprinkling. Add the remaining walnuts to the bean mixture along with the dill, parsley and cilantro. Toss to combine, then taste and season with salt and pepper. Transfer to a platter, sprinkle with the reserved walnuts and additional cilantro. Serve warm or at room temperature.

RAMP UP THE SWEET AND SAVORY

For Everything from Vinaigrette to Vodka, You Need Pomegranate Molasses and Fish Sauce

When a dish needs a quick flavor boost there are two ingredients we often reach for. The first, pomegranate molasses, comes from the Middle Eastern pantry. The second, fish sauce, is popular across Southeast Asian cooking. We love the way both boldly and easily transform whatever we add them to.

POMEGRANATE MOLASSES

What it is: Pomegranate molasses is made by boiling down the juice of sweet-and-sour pomegranates until thick. The resulting syrup—which is not related to nor can it be substituted for the cane sugar-based molasses most Americans know—is tangy, sweet and brightly acidic. We like Mymouné brand best.

How to Use

AS A GLAZE

Slather pomegranate molasses on **roast lamb, pork or chicken** while the meat rests after cooking, then whisk a tablespoon of butter into the pan juices and drippings for an instant sauce. For grilling, brush the molasses directly on the meat during the final moments over the heat. (Don't add too soon; it will burn).

IN A DRESSING

In a small bowl, whisk together **3 tablespoons pomegranate molasses, 1 tablespoon red wine vinegar, 2 teaspoons Dijon or whole-grain mustard, ½ teaspoon minced fresh thyme,** ½ teaspoon kosher salt and ¼ teaspoon ground black pepper. While whisking, gradually pour in **¼ cup extra-virgin olive oil.** Taste and season with salt and pepper. Toss with **leafy greens,** especially robust options such as radicchio, arugula, spinach and escarole, or drizzle over blanched, steamed or roasted vegetables. To change the flavor, omit the thyme and add **1 to 2 tablespoons chopped fresh mint** and/or **parsley.** For a **quick chickpea salad** using the dressing, drain and dry a **15½-ounce can chickpeas** and toss with a handful of **parsley leaves, finely chopped radishes** or **cucumbers,** and **toasted, crumbled pita bread.** Dress liberally, as both the chickpeas and pita will soak it up.

AS A SEASONING

Drizzle over **roasted vegetables,** then sprinkle with **za'atar** and **smoked paprika.** It pairs particularly well with the earthy flavors of roasted or pureed **sweet potatoes** or **winter squash,** especially with a handful of **toasted walnuts** to counter the sweetness. Add a spoonful to a bowl of **braised lentils** with a garnish of **feta cheese** and **fresh herbs**—the fruitiness of the molasses offsets the starchiness of the legumes. Use it to accentuate the sweet-tart flavor of sliced **tomatoes;** just add torn **mint** or **basil,** a little **extra-virgin olive oil** and coarse salt.

AT BREAKFAST

Try brightening your **oatmeal**—or any **hot cereal**—with a spoonful of **pomegranate molasses** and **dried cherries** and **pistachios, almonds** or **tahini.** Swirl into **plain yogurt** before adding your favorite **granola** and **banana slices.**

WITH DESSERT

Spoon a thin stream on top of **ice cream, sorbet** or **fruit salad.** It can boost **apple pie filling** or intensify the flavor of **plums** or **peaches** in any dessert.

AS A BEVERAGE BRIGHTENER

Think of pomegranate molasses as a lighter, brighter **grenadine.** Mix with **vodka** and **seltzer water.** Or skip the booze and add to **ginger beer, lemonade** or **iced tea** with a squeeze of **lime.**

FISH SAUCE

What it is: Fish sauce is made from salted and fermented fish. It's been used in cooking for thousands of years in many parts of the world but is especially associated with Thai, Vietnamese and other Southeast Asian cuisines. We learned from Andrea Nguyen, author of "The Pho Cookbook," that the best fish sauce is made by fermenting anchovies in large barrels with nothing but salt for about a year. Lesser brands ferment for less time, use different fish or just the viscera, or add herbs and spices, hydrolyzed proteins and preservatives. The longer the fermentation, the less fishy and the nuttier—and more umami-rich—the flavor. There's no "extra-virgin" fish sauce, but there is a first pressing, which means the first draining of liquid from the bottom of the barrel. In Vietnam, the highest quality (the first pressing) is used as a table condiment; the second for making dipping sauces; and the third for cooking.

How to Use

AS A DIPPING SAUCE

To make the classic Vietnamese dipping sauce, nuoc cham, in a small bowl, combine ⅓ cup water, **¼ cup lime juice, 2 tablespoons fish sauce, 2 tablespoons white sugar, 1 small garlic clove** (minced) and **1 red Thai chili** (stemmed and thinly sliced). Stir until the sugar dissolves. Serve with grilled beef, pork, chicken or seafood, or offer as a dipping sauce for potstickers, spring rolls or Asian dumplings.

IN A DRESSING

Mix equal parts **fish sauce, lime juice** and **sugar,** add a little **grated garlic** and **minced chili.** Use as a salad dressing for Southeast Asian-style salads.

IN SOUPS AND STEWS

Stir a small spoonful into soups, braises, stir-fries and sauces for instant umami without any noticeable fishiness.

RECIPES & RULES

NOODLES & BREADS

NOODLES & BREADS

At Milk Street, we look for quick and simple sauces that rely on a **few, bold ingredients for standout flavor.** We find easy ways to **use multidimensional ingredients,** such as **tangy yogurt rather than one-note cream. We finish cooking noodles in the sauce to let them absorb more flavor.** We don't toss out our pasta water; we use it to add body and richness to sauces. And **we toast noodles to bring out nutty flavors.**

Noodles plus liquid plus heat equals dinner. The trick is getting the formula right. Try too hard to infuse bland noodles with flavor and you end up with a muddle. Don't try at all and dinner becomes a dull routine—red sauce, green sauce, butter, full stop.

Like noodles, breads start with flour and water. But their precise measurements, times and temperatures can make them daunting for the home cook. And even when a baked good is technically successful it can be disappointingly bland.

Fortunately, we don't have to look too far to find fixes for both issues.

We **add flavor and tenderness to doughs with ingredients such as yogurt and sweet potatoes.** And we shake up our pasta routine—noodles can be chilled and spicy or turned into flavorful stir-fries, as Asian cooks make them. They can be sauced with nut-based pestos the Sicilian way. They can be dressed with a cream sauce made with no cream at all—just reach for tangy yogurt as Middle Eastern cooks do. And even tried-and-true favorites can be improved; in Rome, we learned how to lighten and brighten carbonara.

One of the best ways to improve a pasta dish also is one of the easiest: **Don't toss the pasta cooking water down the drain.** Following the Italian tradition, we routinely use the starchy cooking liquid to add body that creates silky, clingy sauces.

The cooking water also can add flavor. In our pasta with sweet corn, tomatoes and basil, **we boil leftover corn cobs and use that water to cook the pasta.** Some of the corn- and pasta-enriched cooking water also goes into the sauce for multiple layers of sweet, earthy flavor. In Asia, **noodles often are cooked directly in the seasoning mixture,** a technique we use in our mee goreng, an Indonesian stir-fry. Noodles cooked this way absorb flavor, rather than just water.

For creamy sauces without the heft of heavy cream, we often use yogurt, as in our spaghetti with yogurt and cilantro. Thinned with pasta cooking water, the yogurt creates a creamy sauce that coats the noodles without weighing them down. Tangy yogurt also offers more nuanced flavor than one-note cream.

For deep, nutty flavor, we toast noodles much as we do with nuts, seeds and spices. Toasting not only adds color and flavor, it also helps prevent the pasta from getting soggy, as in our pearl couscous pilaf. In our toasted noodles with shrimp, we double down on the technique, toasting the noodles before cooking them in the sauce, then sliding the skillet under the broiler to crisp the tips for a finishing crunch.

We also revisit the classics. In Genoa, Italy, we learned that real pesto alla Genovese is all about the basil, and lots of it. **The order in which the ingredients are mashed also matters.** We found that **a pantry staple is the key to Rome's flawlessly creamy and smooth cacio e pepe.** And in Sicily, we discovered that **nuts can add both flavor and texture** to pasta dishes.

For simple, yet bold sauces, we focus on one or two powerhouse ingredients, such as chilies or olives. We do this with two Italian-style dishes, such as spaghetti with garlic, olive oil and chilies and fettuccini with olives and arugula. And we turn to Malaysia's hakka mee for a quick noodle dish with the deep flavor of umami-rich mushrooms balanced by the sharpness of quick-pickled jalapeños.

We make sure **we pick the right noodle for the right sauce.** The shape of pasta changes how well it holds a sauce. And for pasta salads, we're not fans of cold Italian noodles; they turn extra-starchy and mealy with refrigeration. Instead, **when we want a refreshing cold noodle dish, we look to Asia.** Korean bibim guksu is made with skinny, delicate somen noodles that are well-suited to be served at room temperature or chilled. We rev their flavor with spicy gochujang and kimchi.

Flatbreads are a good way to get fresh-baked flavor without hours of effort. We **make ours better by adding yogurt to produce a more flexible dough.** We give four pizza recipes here and list several more quick and easy toppings on pp. 132-133.

CHANGE THE WAY YOU COOK

No. 21

Create Creaminess Without Cream

A creamy sauce doesn't have to be made with cream. Grating corn kernels releases their milky pulp and starches to create the base of a rich sauce.

Campanelle Pasta
with Sweet Corn, Tomatoes and Basil

Start to finish: **30 minutes**

Servings: **4**

1 pint grape or cherry
tomatoes, halved

Kosher salt and ground black pepper

4 ears corn, husked

4 tablespoons (½ stick) salted butter,
cut into 1-tablespoon pieces, divided

2 medium shallots, minced

1 habanero chili, stemmed,
seeded and minced

12 ounces campanelle or
other short pasta

1 cup lightly packed fresh
basil, sliced

This recipe was inspired by a pasta dish served at Al Forno, a landmark restaurant in Providence, Rhode Island. There, ears of corn are blanched, then the kernels are sliced off and mixed with chopped tomatoes, minced habanero peppers and fresh herbs, then tossed with olive oil and hot pappardelle. We instead grate the corn off the cobs, which yields a coarse puree of kernels and starchy corn "milk." To reinforce the corn flavor, we boil the bare cobs in the water later used to cook the pasta. Using a minimal amount of water—just 2½ quarts—means the flavors and starches are concentrated in the liquid. We put some of this liquid to good use in the sauce. The ingredients in this summery pasta dish are few, so fresh corn and ripe tomatoes are key. Yellow corn gave the dish a golden hue, but white corn worked, too. Whichever you use, make sure to remove as much of the corn silk as possible before grating. Short, sauce-catching pasta shapes are best here—if you can't find campanelle (a frilly, trumpet-like shape), look for penne rigate, fusilli or farfalle.

Don't fear the habanero chili in this dish. It does add a little heat (seeding the chili removes much of its burn), but it's here mostly because its fruity notes are a nice complement to the corn, tomatoes and basil.

In a small bowl, stir together the tomatoes and ½ teaspoon salt; set aside. Set a box grater in a large bowl or pie plate. Using the large holes, grate the corn down to the cobs; reserve the cobs.

In a large pot, bring 2½ quarts water to a boil. Add the corn cobs and 1 tablespoon salt, reduce to medium and cook, covered, for 10 minutes. Using tongs, remove and discard the cobs, then remove the pot from the heat.

In a 12-inch nonstick skillet over medium, melt 2 tablespoons of the butter. Add the grated corn, shallots, habanero and 1 teaspoon salt. Cook, stirring, until the shallots soften, about 5 minutes. Stir in 1½ cups of the cooking liquid. Cook over medium-low, uncovered and stirring occasionally, until slightly thickened (a spatula should leave a brief trail when drawn through), 10 to 15 minutes.

Meanwhile, return the remaining corn-infused water to a boil. Add the pasta and cook, stirring occasionally, until al dente. Reserve 1 cup of the cooking water, then drain the pasta. Add the pasta to the skillet and cook over medium, stirring constantly, until the pasta is coated and the sauce is creamy, about 2 minutes; if needed, add the reserved cooking water 2 tablespoons at a time to reach the proper consistency.

Off heat, add the remaining 2 tablespoons butter, basil and tomatoes with their juice, then toss until the butter has melted. Taste and season with salt and pepper.

No. 22

Put Pasta Water to Work

Don't throw pasta water down the drain. The starchy water is a great way to create sauces that coat and cling to the cooked noodles.

Spaghetti with Cilantro Yogurt

4 cups lightly packed fresh cilantro

½ cup pine nuts or slivered almonds, toasted

4 tablespoons (½ stick) salted butter, softened

3 tablespoons extra-virgin olive oil, divided

1 cup plain whole-milk Greek yogurt

3 teaspoons Aleppo pepper (see note)

Kosher salt and ground black pepper

12 ounces spaghetti, 10 ounces whole, 2 ounces broken into 1-inch pieces

1 teaspoon grated lemon zest

Mediterranean cooks from Greece to Lebanon save time and add flavor by using yogurt as the base for no-cook sauces. We use a generous amount of cilantro for freshness and color, toasted nuts for depth of flavor and softened butter for richness. Toasting a portion of the pasta adds another layer of earthy, wheaty flavor. We especially liked the subtle heat and fruity notes of Aleppo pepper in this dish, but if it isn't available, substitute 1½ teaspoons sweet paprika plus ⅛ teaspoon cayenne pepper or red pepper flakes in the yogurt mixture, then sprinkle the finished dish with ½ teaspoon sweet paprika just before serving.

Don't process the cilantro if it's damp. Make sure it's completely dry, otherwise the processor blade will leave it soggy and bruised. Don't use regular yogurt, which will separate when combined with the hot pasta. And don't use low-fat or nonfat Greek yogurt, as they lack the richness needed for a full-flavored dish. Plain whole-milk Greek yogurt is the best choice.

In a food processor, roughly chop the cilantro, about 30 seconds, scraping the bowl as needed. Add the nuts, butter and 2 tablespoons of oil, then process until smooth. Scrape down the bowl, then add the yogurt, 2 teaspoons Aleppo pepper and 1½ teaspoons salt, then process until well combined, about 30 seconds; set aside.

Set a colander in a large bowl. In a large pot, bring 2 quarts water to a boil. Add the whole pasta and 1 tablespoon salt, then cook, stirring frequently, for 5 minutes. Drain in the colander, then set the pasta and cooking water aside.

In the same pot over medium, heat the remaining 1 tablespoon oil until shimmering. Add the broken pasta and cook, stirring frequently, until golden brown, 1 to 2 minutes. Carefully stir in 2 cups of the reserved cooking water and bring to a boil. Add the whole pasta, bring to a boil and cook, stirring frequently, until the liquid has thickened slightly and the pasta is al dente, 2 to 3 minutes. Remove from the heat and let stand for 3 minutes to cool slightly.

Add the yogurt mixture and toss to coat, adding additional cooking water 2 tablespoons at a time as needed to make a creamy sauce. Stir in the lemon zest, then taste and season with salt and black pepper. Transfer to a serving bowl and sprinkle with the remaining 1 teaspoon Aleppo pepper.

No. 23

Get Bigger Flavor from Supermarket Tomatoes

Use a slow simmer to transform supermarket tomatoes from bland to bold.

Bucatini Pasta
with Cherry Tomato Sauce and Fresh Sage

Start to finish: **1¼ hours**
(30 minutes active)

Servings: **4**

⅓ cup extra-virgin olive oil,
plus more to serve

4 medium garlic cloves, thinly sliced

¼ teaspoon red pepper flakes

2 bay leaves

1 pound cherry or grape tomatoes,
halved

½ teaspoon white sugar

Kosher salt

2 tablespoons chopped fresh sage,
divided

12 ounces bucatini or spaghetti pasta

¾ teaspoon smoked paprika

Shaved pecorino Romano, to serve

This is our adaptation of a recipe from Yotam Ottolenghi's "Simple." With gentle simmering and a bit of water to draw out the cooking time, supermarket cherry or grape tomatoes are transformed into a bold pasta sauce. To boost flavor, we've added herbs, red pepper flakes and pecorino Romano. Spaghetti or bucatini (a tubular pasta resembling thick spaghetti) pairs well with the sauce, but short shapes such as penne and ziti are great, too. We like this on pasta, but it's also terrific spooned over polenta, folded into braised lentils or white beans, or smeared on a pizza crust and topped with a creamy cheese.

Don't simmer the tomatoes *until there is no liquid remaining. Some moisture is needed for the sauce to cling to the pasta.*

In a 12-inch skillet over medium-high, heat the oil until shimmering. Add the garlic, pepper flakes and bay, then cook, stirring, until fragrant, about 30 seconds. Add the tomatoes, sugar, 1 teaspoon salt and 1 cup water. Bring to a simmer and cook, stirring occasionally, until the tomatoes begin to break down, about 4 minutes.

Reduce to medium-low and cook, uncovered and stirring occasionally and adjusting the heat as needed to maintain a steady simmer, until the tomatoes have fully broken down and the sauce is thick enough that a spatula drawn through it leaves a trail, 45 to 55 minutes. Remove from the heat and remove and discard the bay. Stir in 1 tablespoon of sage and the smoked paprika, then cover to keep warm.

When the sauce is almost ready, in a large pot, bring 4 quarts water to a boil. Add 2 tablespoons salt and the pasta, then cook, stirring occasionally, until al dente. Drain the pasta, then return to the pot. Add the sauce and toss until well combined. Transfer to a serving bowl. Sprinkle with the remaining 1 tablespoon sage and shaved pecorino, then drizzle with additional oil.

TRANSFORM SUPERMARKET TOMATOES

Bring Bold Flavor to Bland Tomatoes

Supermarket tomatoes almost always are a disappointment, particularly when raw. But we've found four simple ways to transform them from bland and mealy to bright and bursting with flavor.

SLOW-ROAST

Slowly roasting low-moisture tomatoes—such as plum and Roma—concentrates their flavor and caramelizes their natural sugars for a mellow sweetness with just a touch of tang. We add them to sandwiches, soups or stews, or toss with pasta. Serve over polenta or grilled or fried fish. Chop a few and toss with fresh herbs, such as basil, parsley and thyme, for a quick relish. For a quick version of fagioli all'uccelletto (beans braised in tomato sauce), toss a handful of chopped slow-roasted tomatoes with a drained can of white beans, chopped fresh sage, a pinch of red pepper flakes and a few tablespoons olive oil. Heat until bubbling and creamy, then serve with crusty bread.

To make, heat the oven to 325°F with a rack in the middle position. Line a rimmed baking sheet with kitchen parchment. In a large bowl, whisk **¼ cup white balsamic vinegar, ¼ cup tomato paste,** 2 teaspoons kosher salt and 1 teaspoon ground black pepper. Add **4 pounds plum tomatoes,** cored and halved lengthwise, and toss to coat. Arrange, cut side up, on the baking sheet. Drizzle with **¼ cup extra-virgin olive oil.** Roast until the tomatoes are shriveled, caramelized and lightly charred, 3 to 3½ hours, rotating the pan halfway through. Use immediately or cool, transfer to an airtight container and refrigerate up to 1 week.

MAKE CONSERVA

Tomato conserva—fresh tomatoes cooked down into an intense, concentrated paste—is an old Italian recipe devised as a way to preserve summer produce. At Milk Street, we've found that slowly cooking down cherry or grape tomatoes in olive oil transforms them into a sauce that is thick, sweet and rich. Adding water slows the cooking, allowing the tomatoes to fully break down and soften. We like to spread tomato conserva on grilled bread for bruschetta or serve as part of a cheese platter. Also use it as a base for pasta sauce, or mix into cooked rice or other grains, such as bulgur and farro. And try it in paninis or grilled cheese sandwiches, or spooned onto polenta or grits.

To make, in a large pot over medium, combine **1 cup extra-virgin olive oil** with **4 medium garlic cloves** (smashed and peeled). Cook, stirring often, until the garlic begins to brown, 1 to 2 minutes. Stir in **4 pints grape or cherry tomatoes, 1 teaspoon white sugar, 2 large bay leaves,** 1 teaspoon kosher salt and 2 cups water. Bring to a boil over high, then reduce to medium-high and cook, stirring occasionally and adjusting the heat to maintain a steady but not too vigorous boil, until the tomatoes burst and begin sticking to the bottom of the pot, 30 to 35 minutes. Reduce to medium and cook, stirring frequently and breaking up the tomatoes, until the oil separates to the surface, 20 to 25 minutes; be sure to scrape the bottom. Remove from the heat and cool for about 5 minutes. Use immediately or transfer to a pint-size jar, cool completely, cover and refrigerate for up to 1 week.

QUICK-PICKLE

We often steep raw alliums such as garlic and onion in an acid to tame their harshness and bite. We find that a similar technique can wake up the flavors of supermarket tomatoes, too. A quick pickle in seasoned vinegar highlights and brightens the tomatoes natural sugars and acidity. We spoon quick-pickled tomatoes on top of cooked beans, stir them into grain salads and tuck them into sandwiches or wraps. Dollop on top of creamy or chunky soups or use as a garnish for scrambled or fried eggs.

To make, in a medium bowl, stir together **12 ounces plum tomatoes** (cored, seeded and diced), **3 tablespoons cider vinegar, 1 tablespoon chopped fresh dill, 1 teaspoon red pepper flakes, 1 teaspoon white sugar** and ½ teaspoon kosher salt. Cover and refrigerate for at least 1 hour or up to 3 hours.

SLOW-SIMMER

One of our favorite, and simplest, ways to take store-bought tomatoes from mealy to silky is by way of a slow simmer. We use this technique to create versatile sauces, such as this one spiked with garlic, red pepper flakes and sage. Toss it with cooked pasta or use as pizza sauce. We also like it topped with fried eggs, a dollop of ricotta and some sautéed kale or Swiss chard.

To make, in a 12-inch skillet over medium-high, heat ⅓ **cup extra-virgin olive oil** until shimmering. Add **4 medium garlic cloves** (thinly sliced), **¼ teaspoon red pepper flakes** and **2 bay leaves,** then cook, stirring, until fragrant, about 30 seconds. Add **1 pound cherry or grape tomatoes,** halved, **½ teaspoon white sugar,** 1 teaspoon kosher salt and 1 cup water. Bring to a simmer and cook, stirring, until the tomatoes begin to break down, about 4 minutes. Reduce to medium-low and cook, uncovered, stirring occasionally and adjusting the heat to maintain a steady simmer, until the tomatoes have fully broken down and the sauce is thick enough that a spatula drawn through it leaves a trail, 45 to 55 minutes. Remove from the heat, then discard the bay. Stir in **1 tablespoon chopped fresh sage** and **¾ teaspoon smoked paprika.**

No. 24

Boil Your Noodles Without Water

Cooking noodles in a seasoned liquid, rather than boiling them separately in water and finishing them with a sauce, is an easy way to build flavor.

Thai Stir-Fried Glass Noodles
with Carrots and Roasted Peanuts (Pad Woon Sen)

4 ounces cellophane noodles

2 tablespoons soy sauce

2 tablespoons oyster sauce

2 tablespoons fish sauce

2 tablespoons lime juice, plus lime wedges to serve

2 teaspoons packed light or dark brown sugar

Kosher salt and ground white pepper

4 large eggs

6 teaspoons peanut oil, divided

1 medium yellow onion, halved and thinly sliced

¼ small head green cabbage, cored and chopped (about 3 cups)

2 medium carrots, peeled and shredded on the large holes of a box grater

3 medium garlic cloves, minced

½ cup roughly chopped fresh cilantro

¼ cup chopped roasted salted peanuts

Glass noodles—also called cellophane noodles, bean threads or sai fun (in Thai they're known as woon sen)—are made from the starch of mung beans. Dried, the noodles are thin, wiry and white, but they plump and turn translucent after cooking. They're fast to prepare, but essentially bland; finishing them off in a sauce spiked with savory soy, oyster and fish sauces is a good way to add flavor. To prepare cellophane noodles for stir-frying, they need only to be soaked in room-temperature water for about 20 minutes; use this time to prep the other ingredients. As with all stir-fries, once cooking starts, the process goes quickly, so have your ingredients and equipment ready before you start cooking.

Don't forget to cut the soaked noodles *into shorter lengths using kitchen shears, or you'll end up with a tangled nest in the pan.*

In a medium bowl, cover the noodles with room-temperature water. Let stand until pliable but not fully softened, about 20 minutes. Drain, then use kitchen shears to snip into shorter lengths; set aside.

Meanwhile, in a small bowl, whisk together the soy sauce, oyster sauce, fish sauce, lime juice, sugar and ½ teaspoon white pepper; set aside. In another small bowl, beat the eggs with ½ teaspoon each salt and white pepper.

When the noodles are ready, in a 12-inch nonstick skillet over medium-high, heat 1½ teaspoons of oil until

barely smoking. Pour in the eggs and cook, stirring constantly with a silicone spatula, until just set, about 30 seconds. Transfer to a plate, then carefully wipe out the skillet with paper towels. Using the spatula, break the eggs into small pieces; set aside.

Return the skillet to medium-high, add the remaining 4½ teaspoons oil and heat until shimmering. Add the onion and cook, stirring occasionally, until beginning to brown, about 3 minutes. Add the cabbage, carrots and garlic, then cook, stirring occasionally, until wilted, 2 to 3 minutes. Distribute the noodles in the

pan and, using tongs, toss to combine with the vegetables. Add the soy sauce mixture and cook, tossing frequently, until most of the liquid has been absorbed, about 1 minute. Add the eggs and toss. Transfer to a platter and sprinkle with the cilantro and peanuts. Serve with lime wedges.

Indonesian Stir-Fried Noodles
with Red Pepper (Mee Goreng)

¼ cup soy sauce

1 tablespoon oyster sauce

4 teaspoons packed light or dark brown sugar

¼ teaspoon ground cumin

Kosher salt and ground black pepper

1 pound fresh yellow Asian wheat noodles

4 tablespoons peanut oil, divided

¼ medium head green cabbage, cored and sliced (3 to 4 cups)

3 large shallots, halved and sliced lengthwise

1 small red bell pepper, stemmed, seeded and thinly sliced

5 medium garlic cloves, minced

1 bunch scallions, cut into 1-inch lengths

Lime wedges, to serve

Sambal oelek or chili-garlic sauce, to serve

Mee goreng (literally, "fried noodles") is a savory, slightly sweet Indonesian dish in which the noodles retain a satisfying chew that contrasts with the crunch of stir-fried vegetables. The noodles absorb the flavorings and remain pleasantly dry. Use fresh yellow-hued Asian noodles with the shape and thickness of spaghetti. They may be labeled "pancit," a Filipino term; "oil noodles" work well, too. For a more robust meal, add 12 ounces seasoned and seared shrimp at the end.

Don't forget to rinse the noodles *before cooking. It also allows you to loosen the strands so they are easier to distribute in the skillet.*

In a small bowl, stir together the soy sauce, oyster sauce, sugar, cumin, ¼ teaspoon pepper and ⅓ cup water. Place the noodles in a colander and rinse under cool water, gently loosening the strands. Using kitchen shears, snip the noodles into shorter lengths. Drizzle 1 tablespoon of oil over the noodles and toss; set aside.

In a 12-inch nonstick skillet over medium-high, heat 1 tablespoon of the remaining oil until barely smoking. Add the cabbage in an even layer and cook until charred in spots, about 2 minutes, stirring only once halfway through.

Transfer to a medium bowl. Add 1 tablespoon of the remaining oil and heat until barely smoking. Stir in the shallots and bell pepper, distribute in an even layer, then cook until browned in spots, about 2 minutes, stirring only once halfway through. Add the garlic and cook, stirring occasionally, until no longer raw, about 1 minute. Transfer to the bowl with the cabbage.

Return the skillet to medium-high, add the remaining 1 tablespoon oil and heat until barely smoking. Distribute the noodles in an even layer and cook without stirring until spotty brown, 2 to

3 minutes. Toss, then redistribute in an even layer and cook without stirring for about another 2 minutes. Pour in the soy mixture and cook, tossing frequently, until only a small amount of glaze-like liquid remains, 1 to 2 minutes. Return the vegetables to the skillet and add the scallions. Cook, tossing, until the pan is dry and the noodles are tender but still quite chewy, about 2 minutes. If the noodles are still too firm, add another 1 to 2 tablespoons water and cook, tossing, until done. Taste and season with salt and pepper. Serve with lime wedges and sambal oelek.

No. 25

Caramelize Pasta for Deeper, Richer Flavor

Toasting dry pasta caramelizes some of the starches, producing nutty flavors similar to caramelized sugar.

HOW TO TOAST PASTA

1. Add the broken pasta to the skillet and stir to coat with the oil.

2. After a couple of minutes, the pasta will be golden brown.

3. The pasta is done when it is deep golden brown and has a toasty aroma.

Toasted Noodles with Shrimp
(Rossejat de Fideus)

Start to finish: **35 minutes**
Servings: **4**

½ cup mayonnaise

1 teaspoon grated lemon zest,
plus 2 tablespoons lemon juice

1 small garlic clove, finely grated, plus
2 medium garlic cloves, thinly sliced

1 pound extra-large (21/25 per pound)
shrimp, peeled and deveined

2 teaspoons smoked sweet paprika,
divided

Kosher salt and ground black pepper

3 tablespoons extra-virgin olive oil,
divided

6 ounces capellini pasta, broken into
rough 1-inch pieces (see note)

1 small yellow onion, finely chopped

1 plum tomato, cored and chopped

2 cups low-sodium chicken broth

1 pinch saffron threads

¼ cup lightly packed fresh flat-leaf
parsley, chopped

Rossejat de fideus is traditional to Spain's Catalonia region. It's similar to paella, but instead of rice it uses slender noodles that have been toasted until richly browned. We use capellini pasta (also called angel hair) and break it by hand into rough 1-inch pieces (do this over a bowl to catch the pieces as they fall). Toasting brings out the nutty-wheaty notes of the pasta, which then is simmered in broth instead of water. You will need a broiler-safe 12-inch skillet for this recipe, as the noodles are first cooked on the stovetop, then browned under the broiler. This dish traditionally is served with aioli, a garlicky mayonnaise; we make a quick, extra-lemony version using store-bought mayonnaise.

Don't use regular paprika. *Smoked paprika gives this dish a Spanish flavor profile. Before broiling the noodles, make sure most of the liquid has been absorbed; too much moisture in the pan will prevent the surface from crisping and browning. Don't forget that the skillet handle will be hot after broiling.*

In a small bowl, stir together the mayonnaise, lemon zest and juice and the grated garlic. Cover and refrigerate until ready to use.

Heat the broiler with a rack about 6 inches from the heat. In a medium bowl, toss the shrimp with 1 teaspoon paprika, ¾ teaspoon salt and ¼ teaspoon pepper; set aside.

In a broiler-safe 12-inch skillet over medium, heat 1 tablespoon of oil until shimmering. Add the pasta and cook, stirring frequently, until deep golden brown, about 5 minutes. Transfer to a medium bowl and set aside; wipe out the skillet with paper towels.

Return the skillet to medium-high, heat 1 tablespoon of the remaining oil until barely smoking. Add the shrimp in a single layer and cook without stirring until deep golden brown, 1 to 2 minutes. Flip the shrimp and continue to cook until opaque, another 20 to 30 seconds. Transfer to a plate, tent with foil and set aside.

In the same skillet over medium, combine the remaining 1 tablespoon oil, the onion, the remaining 1 teaspoon paprika and ½ teaspoon salt. Cook, stirring occasionally, until softened, about 5 minutes. Add the tomato and the sliced garlic and cook, stirring, until fragrant, about 30 seconds. Stir in the toasted pasta, the broth and the saffron. Bring to a boil over medium-high, then reduce to medium and cook, uncovered, stirring occasionally, until almost all of the liquid has been absorbed, 3 to 5 minutes.

Place the skillet under the broiler and cook until the surface is crisp and the tips of the noodles begin to brown, 3 to 5 minutes. Remove from the broiler, then top with the shrimp and drizzle with the accumulated juices. Spoon on some of the mayonnaise and sprinkle with the parsley; serve the remaining mayonnaise mixture on the side.

Middle Eastern Rice
with Toasted Pasta

4 tablespoons (½ stick) salted
butter, divided

1 ounce vermicelli pasta, broken into
1-inch pieces (generous ⅓ cup)

1 cup basmati rice, rinsed and drained

1⅔ cups low-sodium chicken broth

Kosher salt and ground black pepper

For this classic Middle Eastern dish, we preferred thin vermicelli pasta, but thin spaghetti or angel hair (capellini) work well, too. Toasting the pasta in butter gives it both color and a sweet, nutty flavor. Adding the vermicelli halfway through the cooking ensures the noodles don't overcook. For a different take, try our variation with almonds and herbs, recipe below.

Don't forget to rinse and drain the rice. *Rinsing removes excess starch that can make the cooked grains sticky instead of light and fluffy.*

In a large saucepan over medium, melt 2 tablespoons of butter. Add the pasta and cook, stirring frequently, until the noodles are deeply browned, about 5 minutes. Transfer to a small bowl and set aside.

In the pan, combine the rice and broth, then set over medium-high. Bring to a boil, then reduce to low, cover and cook for 8 minutes. Stir in the toasted pasta. Cover and continue to cook until all of the liquid has been absorbed, about another 7 minutes. Off heat, stir in remaining 2 tablespoons butter, then taste and season with salt and pepper.

MIDDLE EASTERN RICE WITH TOASTED PASTA, ALMONDS AND HERBS

Follow the recipe for Middle Eastern Rice with Toasted Pasta, adding 2 tablespoons each chopped fresh dill and chopped fresh flat-leaf parsley along with the remaining 2 tablespoons butter at the end. Taste and season with salt and pepper. Transfer to a bowl and sprinkle with an additional 2 tablespoons each chopped dill and parsley and ¼ cup toasted sliced almonds.

Toasted Pearl Couscous
with Chicken and Chickpeas

3 tablespoons extra-virgin olive oil, divided

1 cup pearl couscous

4 medium garlic cloves, chopped

1 medium yellow onion, chopped

3 large carrots, peeled, quartered lengthwise and cut into ½-inch pieces

Kosher salt and ground black pepper

1 tablespoon ground cumin

½ teaspoon ground allspice

1 pound boneless, skinless chicken thighs, trimmed and halved

2 bay leaves

15½-ounce can chickpeas, rinsed and drained

1 teaspoon pomegranate molasses, plus more to serve

1 cup lightly packed fresh flat-leaf parsley, roughly chopped

Palestinian maftoul, a pasta similar to pearl couscous, inspired this quick and easy one-pot meal. Before cooking the couscous pilaf-style, we toast the small bits to deepen their wheaty flavor and aroma. A sauté of browned garlic, onion, cumin and allspice creates a heady base for simultaneously poaching boneless chicken thighs and steaming the toasted couscous; the chicken gets a 5-minute head start before the couscous is added so everything finishes at the same time. A spoonful of tangy-sweet pomegranate molasses brightens the flavors while balancing the warm, earthy spices.

Don't worry if browned bits form on the bottom of the saucepan as you sauté the garlic, onion and carrots. These bits, called fond, help build rich flavor in the dish.

In a large Dutch oven over medium-high, heat 1 tablespoon of oil until shimmering. Add the couscous and cook, stirring, until golden brown, about 3 minutes. Transfer to a small bowl. In the same pot over medium-high, heat the remaining 2 tablespoons oil until shimmering. Add the garlic and cook, stirring, until beginning to brown, about 30 seconds. Add the onion, carrots, 2 teaspoons salt and 1 teaspoon pepper, then cook, stirring occasionally, until browned bits have developed on the bottom of the pan, 3 to 5 minutes. Add the cumin and allspice, and cook, stirring, until fragrant, about 30 seconds.

Stir in the chicken, bay, 1 teaspoon salt and 2 cups water. Bring to a boil, then cover, reduce to medium-low and simmer for 5 minutes. Stir in the couscous, cover and simmer until the chicken is opaque when cut into and the couscous is tender but not mushy, about 8 minutes.

Off heat, stir in the chickpeas, pomegranate molasses and half the parsley. Remove and discard the bay, then taste and season with salt and pepper. Transfer to a serving bowl and sprinkle with the remaining parsley. Serve with additional pomegranate molasses for drizzling.

Butternut Squash and Feta
with Toasted Pearl Couscous

Start to finish: **35 minutes**

Servings: **4**

4 tablespoons extra-virgin olive oil, divided

1 cup pearl couscous

1 pound butternut squash, peeled, seeded and cut into ½-inch cubes (about 3 cups)

Kosher salt and ground black pepper

1 medium yellow onion, chopped

4 medium garlic cloves, chopped

1 tablespoon ground cumin

2 bay leaves

15½-ounce can chickpeas, rinsed and drained

1 tablespoon lemon juice, plus lemon wedges, to serve

3 ounces feta cheese, crumbled (about ½ cup)

3 tablespoons chopped fresh dill, divided

For a vegetarian spin on our pearl couscous with chicken and chickpeas, we created a hearty version with subtly sweet butternut squash. A sprinkling of crumbled feta cheese balances the dish with sharp, salty notes and dill adds a fresh flavor and fragrance.

Don't stir the squash *during the first 3 to 5 minutes of cooking. This allows it to caramelize, adding to the flavor complexity of the finished dish.*

In a large Dutch oven over medium-high, heat 1 tablespoon of oil until shimmering. Add the couscous and cook, stirring, until golden brown, about 3 minutes. Transfer to a small bowl.

In the same pot over medium-high, heat 2 tablespoons of the remaining oil until shimmering. Add the squash, then stir in 1 teaspoon salt and ½ teaspoon pepper. Distribute in an even layer and cook without stirring until well browned, 3 to 5 minutes. Stir occasionally and continue to cook until a skewer inserted into the largest piece meets no resistance,

another 3 to 5 minutes. Transfer to a medium bowl and set aside.

Return the pot to medium-high. Add the remaining 1 tablespoon oil, the onion, garlic and 1 teaspoon salt, then cook, stirring occasionally, until the garlic begins to brown, 2 to 3 minutes. Add the cumin and bay, then cook, stirring, until fragrant, about 30 seconds. Stir in 2 cups water and the couscous. Cover and simmer until the couscous is tender but not mushy, about 7 minutes.

Off heat, remove and discard the bay. Stir in the chickpeas, squash, lemon juice and 2 tablespoons of dill. Taste and season with salt and pepper. Transfer to a serving bowl and sprinkle with the remaining 1 tablespoon dill and the feta. Serve with lemon wedges.

Spaghetti with Anchovies,
Pine Nuts and Raisins

12 ounces spaghetti

Kosher salt and ground black pepper

6 tablespoons extra-virgin olive oil, divided, plus more to serve

⅓ cup panko breadcrumbs, finely crushed or chopped (see note)

¼ cup pine nuts, finely chopped

3 tablespoons golden raisins, finely chopped

10 oil-packed anchovy fillets, patted dry

8 medium garlic cloves, finely chopped

2 tablespoons white wine vinegar

½ cup lightly packed fresh flat-leaf parsley, chopped

This pasta dish features the classic Sicilian flavor combination of savory, sweet and sour, while getting richness from a handful of pine nuts. Toasted breadcrumbs, sprinkled on just before serving, cling to the strands of pasta and provide pleasant crispness. We preferred fluffy panko breadcrumbs over regular powder-fine breadcrumbs, but crushing or chopping the panko before toasting ensured better blending with the pasta. Crush the panko in a zip-close plastic bag with a meat pounder or rolling pin, or simply chop it with a chef's knife on a cutting board. To be efficient, pile the pine nuts, raisins and garlic together on the cutting board and chop them all at once.

Don't overcook the pasta *after adding it to the sauce. The noodles should be al dente and slippery, not fully tender and dry. If needed, loosen them by tossing with additional reserved pasta water.*

In a large pot, bring 4 quarts water to a boil. Add the spaghetti and 2 tablespoons salt, then cook, stirring occasionally, until just shy of al dente. Reserve about 1½ cups of the cooking water, then drain the pasta.

While the pasta cooks, in a 12-inch skillet over medium, combine 2 tablespoons of oil and the panko. Cook, stirring frequently, until golden brown, 3 to 5 minutes. Transfer to a small bowl and set aside; wipe out the skillet.

Set the skillet over medium-high and add the remaining 4 tablespoons oil, the pine nuts, raisins, anchovies and garlic. Cook, stirring frequently, until the anchovies have broken up and the garlic is golden brown, about 2 minutes. Stir in the vinegar and cook until syrupy, 30 to 60 seconds. Add 1 cup of the reserved pasta water, ½ teaspoon salt and ¼ teaspoon pepper and bring to a simmer.

Add the pasta, reduce to medium, and cook, occasionally tossing to combine,

until the pasta is al dente and has absorbed most of the moisture but is still a little saucy, about 2 minutes. Remove from the heat. If the pasta is dry, add more cooking water, 1 tablespoon at a time. Stir in the parsley, then taste and season with salt and pepper. Transfer to a serving bowl. Sprinkle with the panko and top with additional oil and pepper.

No. 26

Parcook Pasta for Better Flavor

Boiling pasta until just shy of al dente, then finishing it directly in the sauce (fortified with some of the starchy cooking water), allows the pasta to better absorb other flavors

No. 27

Stop Pureeing Your Pesto

Processing the ingredients in a particular order—and only until grainy, not pureed—produces a dramatically better pesto with layers of texture and flavor.

Pasta with Pesto alla Genovese

1¾ ounces Parmesan cheese (without rind), chopped into rough 1-inch pieces

1 ounce pecorino Sardo cheese (without rind), chopped into rough 1-inch pieces (see note)

¼ cup pine nuts

2 medium garlic cloves, smashed and peeled

Kosher salt

⅓ cup extra-virgin olive oil

2½ ounces (about 5 cups lightly packed) fresh basil leaves

12 ounces dried pasta

We learned to make pesto alla Genovese in its birthplace—Genoa, Italy. It traditionally is made in a mortar and pestle of nothing more than basil, pine nuts, cheese, garlic, salt and olive oil, emphasis on the basil. Back at Milk Street, we felt a mortar and pestle simply weren't practical for U.S. home cooks. But we do follow the tradition of processing ingredients separately to ensure we preserve the appropriate texture of each. Seek out true Italian Parmesan cheese, as well as pecorino Sardo, a sheep's milk cheese from Sardinia. If you can't find pecorino Sardo use manchego, a Spanish sheep's milk cheese. To store pesto, press a piece of plastic wrap against its surface and refrigerate up to three days.

Don't toast the pine nuts. In Italy, the pine nuts for pesto are used raw. Don't be tempted to add all the ingredients at once to the food processor. Adding them in stages ensures the pesto has the correct consistency and texture, and that it won't end up thin and watery, the result of over-processing.

In a food processor, process both cheeses until broken into rough marble-sized pieces, about 10 seconds, then pulse until they have the texture of coarse sand, 5 to 10 pulses, scraping the bowl as needed. Transfer to a small bowl.

In the food processor, combine the pine nuts, garlic and ¾ teaspoon salt. Process until a smooth, peanut butter–like paste forms, about 1 minute, scraping the bowl as needed. Add the cheeses and about ½ of the oil and process until mostly smooth, 10 to 20 seconds, scraping the

bowl as needed; the mixture should hold together when pressed against the bowl with a rubber spatula.

Using a chef's knife, roughly chop the basil, then add to the food processor. Pulse about 10 times, scraping the bowl several times, until the basil is finely chopped and well combined with the cheese mixture. Add the remaining oil and pulse just until incorporated, about 2 pulses. The pesto should be thick, creamy and spreadable. Set the pesto aside.

In a large pot, bring 4 quarts water to a boil. Add the pasta and 2 tablespoons salt, then cook, stirring occasionally, until just shy of al dente. Reserve about ½ cup of the cooking water, then drain the pasta. Transfer the pasta to a large warmed bowl and top with the pesto. Pour in ⅓ cup of the reserved cooking water for long pasta shapes (such as spaghetti and linguine) or ¼ cup cooking water for short pasta shapes (such as penne and fusilli). Toss to combine.

No. 28

Punch Up Pasta and Noodles with Savory Flavors

Savory flavors are key to combatting the bland nature of noodles and pasta. It's why tomatoes, olives, anchovies, garlic and cheese are essential to Italian recipes, and mushrooms, fish sauce and soy sauce show up so often in Asian noodles.

Malaysian-Style Noodles
with Pork and Mushrooms

2 jalapeño chilies, stemmed, seeded and thinly sliced crosswise

½ cup unseasoned rice vinegar

¾ teaspoon white sugar

12 ounces dried Asian wheat noodles (see note)

2 tablespoons grapeseed or other neutral oil

6 medium garlic cloves, minced

8 ounces cremini mushrooms, finely chopped

12 ounces ground pork

3 tablespoons fish sauce

1 tablespoon soy sauce

3 scallions, thinly sliced on diagonal

This is our take on Malaysian hakka mee, a simple but flavorful dish of noodles topped with ground pork and minced mushrooms. To balance the deep, rich notes of the sauce, we make quick-pickled jalapeño chilies, which add bright heat to cut through the dish's richness; sliced scallions offer freshness. Almost any variety of Asian wheat or egg noodle works here so long as the strands are substantial enough to support the sauce. Because the pork and mushrooms tend to fall to the bottom of the bowl, it's best to portion the cooked noodles into individual bowls, then spoon sauce onto each.

Don't forget to reserve some of the cooking water before draining the noodles. *You'll need the starchy liquid to make the sauce.*

In a small bowl, stir together the jalapeños, vinegar and sugar; set aside. In a large pot, bring 4 quarts water to a boil. Add the noodles and cook until tender. Reserve 1 cup of the cooking water, then drain and rinse under cool water until no longer warm to the touch. Drain well, then divide evenly among individual serving bowls.

In a 12-inch skillet over medium, heat the oil until shimmering. Add the garlic and cook, stirring constantly, until fragrant, about 30 seconds. Add the mushrooms and cook, stirring frequently, until the moisture released by the mushrooms has mostly evaporated, 2 to 3 minutes. Add the pork and cook, stirring and breaking the meat into small bits, until only a little pink remains, another 2 to 3 minutes.

Add the fish sauce, soy sauce and reserved cooking water. Bring to a simmer over medium-high and cook, stirring occasionally, until the liquid is glossy and has reduced by about half, about 5 minutes. Spoon the sauce onto the noodles. Top with the scallions and serve with the pickled jalapeños.

Fettuccini with Olives
and Arugula

3 medium garlic cloves, minced

2 serrano or Fresno chilies, stemmed, seeded and minced

2 tablespoons lemon juice, plus lemon wedges to serve

Kosher salt and ground black pepper

12 ounces fettuccini or linguini

1 cup pitted black or green olives, or a mixture, finely chopped (see note)

2 tablespoons extra-virgin olive oil

4 cups lightly packed baby arugula, roughly chopped

Grated pecorino Romano, to serve (optional)

Meaty, flavor-packed olives require little effort to be transformed into a vegetarian no-cook sauce for pasta. We tame the bite of raw garlic and minced fresh chilies by steeping them in lemon juice, a combination that balances the olives' saltiness. You can use a food processor to pulse the olives until finely chopped or prep them by hand with a chef's knife—either way, make sure the pieces are evenly fine so they combine with the pasta rather than fall to the bottom of the bowl. Chopped baby arugula added at the end provides peppery notes as well as verdant color. Pecorino Romano is a delicious flourish, but you could omit it to make the dish vegan.

Don't use canned olives. *Their texture is mealy and soft, and their flavor tends to be weak and watery. Olives packed in jars or sold in bulk from the grocery store's deli section are the best choice for this dish.*

In a small bowl, stir together the garlic, chilies and lemon juice. Let stand for about 15 minutes. Meanwhile, in a large pot, bring 4 quarts water to a boil. Add 2 tablespoons salt and the pasta, then cook, stirring occasionally, until al dente. Reserve ½ cup of the cooking water, then drain.

While the pasta cooks, place the olives in a large bowl. Add the drained pasta to the olives, along with the oil, garlic-chili mixture, ¼ teaspoon pepper and 2 tablespoons of reserved cooking water. Toss, adding cooking water 1 tablespoon at a time as needed to create a silky sauce. Toss in the arugula and serve with lemon wedges and pecorino, if using.

No. 29

Super-Starch Your Pasta

Create silkier, thicker sauces by cooking pasta and noodles in less water than typically called for, concentrating the starches that leach out of the noodles and into the cooking water.

Spaghetti with Garlic,
Olive Oil and Chilies

⅓ cup extra-virgin olive oil

3 Fresno chilies, seeded, halved and thinly sliced crosswise

8 medium garlic cloves, smashed and peeled

12 ounces spaghetti

Kosher salt

½ ounce Parmesan or pecorino Romano cheese, finely grated (¼ cup), plus more to serve

¼ cup roughly chopped fresh flat-leaf parsley

This classic Roman dish, called pasta aglio, olio e peperoncino (pasta with garlic, oil and peppers), requires few ingredients, but packs big flavor. In our version, fresh Fresno chilies add vibrant color, a subtle fruitiness and chili heat that balance the intensity of the garlic. If you can't find Fresno chilies, use jalapeños. If you're a fan of spice, leave the seeds in one of the Fresnos, or add a pinch or two of red pepper flakes to the oil along with the chilies and garlic. Boiling the spaghetti for only 5 minutes in a relatively small amount of water (2 quarts) leaves the pasta only partly cooked and the water extra-starchy; we reserve some of the water to finish cooking the spaghetti in the same skillet in which we've made the garlic- and chili-infused oil.

Don't add the reserved pasta water to the skillet until the oil has had a chance to cool slightly. If the oil is very hot the mixture will splatter. After adding the pasta to the skillet, don't be afraid to cook at a rapid simmer; this helps ensure the water will be absorbed in 3 to 5 minutes, before the pasta overcooks.

In a 12-inch skillet over medium, combine the oil, chilies and garlic. Cook, stirring occasionally, until the garlic is golden brown, about 5 minutes. Remove from the heat, then transfer only the garlic to a small bowl. Use a fork to mash it to a coarse paste; set aside. Let the oil cool slightly.

In a large pot, bring 2 quarts water to a boil. Stir in the pasta and 1 tablespoon salt; cook for 5 minutes. Reserve about 2¼ cups of the cooking water, then drain the pasta.

Add 2 cups of the reserved cooking water and the pasta to the skillet. Bring to a vigorous simmer over medium-high and cook, stirring occasionally, until the pasta is al dente and most of the liquid has been absorbed, 3 to 5 minutes.

Off heat, add the cheese, 1 teaspoon salt and the smashed garlic. Toss, adding cooking water 1 tablespoon at a time as needed so the pasta is lightly sauced, not dry. Transfer to a serving bowl, then sprinkle with the parsley. Serve with additional grated cheese.

No. 30

Use Cornstarch to Smooth Out Lumpy Sauces

Some cheese-based sauces are notoriously difficult to make without clumping. Adding cornstarch to the mixture stabilizes the cheese as it melts, creating a silky-smooth sauce.

Cacio e Pepe

2 teaspoons cornstarch

6 ounces pecorino Romano cheese, finely grated (3 cups), plus more to serve

12 ounces linguini or spaghetti

Kosher salt and ground black pepper

We traveled to Rome to trace the family tree of three famous pastas, cacio e pepe, carbonara and gricia, and found all three were a study in the power of letting a few simple ingredients shine. Cacio e pepe is simple, made from just pecorino Romano cheese, lots of black pepper and a bit of pasta water. But it can be a challenge, easily turning into a broken, lumpy mess. The solution turns out to be starch, which stabilizes the cheese so it doesn't clump and separate. We stir finely grated pecorino into a mixture of cornstarch and water. Once heated, the mixture creates a light, creamy sauce that is stable enough to sit on the stove while we cook the pasta. Pecorino Romano, a salty, hard sheep's milk cheese, is traditional. We recommend looking for imported pecorino for the best flavor. This is the mother of classic Roman pastas. Add pancetta and it becomes pasta alla gricia (see p. 115). Add eggs and it's carbonara (p. 117).

Don't use pre-shredded cheese, *even if it's true pecorino Romano. And grate it finely; larger shreds won't melt. Don't pour the pecorino mixture onto the piping-hot, just-drained pasta; letting the pasta cool for a minute or so ensures the mixture won't break from overheating.*

In a large pot, bring 4 quarts water to a boil. Meanwhile, in a large saucepan, whisk 1½ cups water and the cornstarch until smooth. Add the pecorino and stir until evenly moistened. Set the pan over medium-low and cook, whisking constantly, until the cheese melts and the mixture comes to a gentle simmer and thickens slightly, about 5 minutes. Remove from the heat and set aside.

Stir the pasta and 2 tablespoons salt into the boiling water and cook until al dente. Reserve about ½ cup of the cooking water, then drain the pasta very well. Return the pasta to the pot and let cool for about 1 minute.

Pour the pecorino mixture over the pasta and toss with tongs until combined, then toss in 2 teaspoons pepper. Let stand, tossing 2 or 3 times, until most of the liquid has been absorbed, about 3 minutes. The pasta should be creamy but not loose. If it is too thick, toss in reserved pasta water 1 tablespoon at a time to adjust the consistency. Transfer to a warmed serving bowl and serve with more pecorino and pepper on the side.

Spaghetti with Pancetta
(Pasta alla Gricia)

3 ounces pancetta, finely chopped

2 teaspoons cornstarch

6 ounces pecorino Romano cheese, finely grated (3 cups), plus more to serve

12 ounces spaghetti or linguini

Kosher salt and ground black pepper

This classic Roman pasta dish relies on the quality of the pecorino Romano, a salty, hard sheep's milk cheese. The addition of cornstarch allowed us to overcome the tendency of lower-quality cheese to clump. But for flavor, we still suggest looking for imported pecorino. Guanciale (cured pork cheek) is traditional for gricia, but we used more widely available pancetta. Bacon was too smoky.

Don't use pre-shredded cheese. *Grate it finely and let the pasta cool before pouring the cheese mixture on.*

In a large pot, bring 4 quarts of water to a boil. Meanwhile, in a 10-inch skillet over medium, cook the pancetta until crisp, about 5 minutes. Using a slotted spoon, transfer the pancetta to a paper towel–lined plate; reserve 2 tablespoons of the rendered fat.

In a large saucepan, whisk 1½ cups water and cornstarch until smooth. Add the pecorino and stir until evenly moistened. Set the pan over medium-low and cook, whisking constantly, until the cheese melts and the mixture comes to a gentle simmer and thickens slightly, about 5 minutes. Remove from the heat, whisk in reserved pancetta fat and set aside.

Stir the pasta and 2 tablespoons salt into the boiling water and cook until al dente. Reserve about ½ cup of the cooking water, then drain the pasta very well. Return the pasta to the pot and let cool for about 1 minute.

Pour the pecorino mixture over the pasta and toss with tongs until combined, then toss in 2 teaspoons pepper and crisped pancetta. Let stand, tossing two or three times, until most of the liquid has been absorbed, about 3 minutes. The pasta should be creamy but not loose. If it is too thick, toss in reserved pasta water 1 tablespoon at a time to adjust the consistency. Transfer to a warmed serving bowl and serve, passing more pecorino and pepper on the side.

No. 31

Add Air to Your Carbonara

Classic carbonara can be heavy and dense. Whisking the egg-and-cheese sauce as it cooks slowly over gentle heat lightens it by pumping air into it.

Light and Creamy Spaghetti
Carbonara

Start to finish: **25 minutes**
Servings: **4**

3 ounces thinly sliced pancetta, chopped

6 large egg yolks

2 teaspoons cornstarch

6 ounces pecorino Romano cheese, finely grated (3 cups), plus more to serve

12 ounces spaghetti

Kosher salt and ground black pepper

This brighter take on carbonara came from Pipero Roma, a white-tablecloth restaurant in Rome. There, we saw that egg yolks were whisked until cooked and slightly foamy, creating a sauce that is much lighter than most carbonara recipes. Mixing the yolks with water and cornstarch ensures the cheese won't clump when tossed with the pasta.

Don't substitute bacon for the pancetta. *The smokiness of the bacon will overwhelm the cleaner flavors of the egg-based sauce.*

In a 10-inch skillet over medium, cook the pancetta, stirring, until crisp, about 5 minutes. Using a slotted spoon, transfer to a paper towel–lined plate. Measure out and reserve 3 tablespoons of the rendered fat; if needed, supplement with olive oil. Set the pancetta and fat aside.

In a large pot, bring 4 quarts water to a boil. Meanwhile, in a large saucepan, whisk 1¾ cups water, the egg yolks and cornstarch until smooth. Add the cheese and stir until evenly moistened. Set the pan over medium-low and cook, whisking constantly, until the mixture comes to a gentle simmer and is airy and thickened, 5 to 7 minutes; use a silicone spatula to occasionally get into the corners of the pan. Off heat, whisk in the reserved pancetta fat. Set aside.

Stir the pasta and 2 tablespoons salt into the boiling water and cook until al dente. Reserve about ½ cup of the cooking water, then drain the pasta very well. Return the pasta to the pot and let cool for about 1 minute.

Pour the pecorino-egg mixture over the pasta and toss with tongs until well combined, then toss in 2 teaspoons pepper. Let stand, tossing the pasta two or three times, until most of the liquid has been absorbed, about 3 minutes. Crumble in the pancetta, then toss again. The pasta should be creamy but not loose. If it is too thick, toss in up to 2 tablespoons reserved pasta water to adjust the consistency. Transfer to a warmed serving bowl and serve, passing more pecorino and pepper on the side.

No. 32

Beat Back Soggy Noodle Salads

Use Asian somen noodles for pasta salads that won't turn starchy and mealy when cooled.

Korean Spicy Chilled Noodles
(Bibim Guksu)

Start to finish: **30 minutes**

Servings: **4**

3 to 4 tablespoons gochujang

2½ tablespoons unseasoned rice vinegar, plus more as needed

2 tablespoons soy sauce

1½ tablespoons white sugar

1½ tablespoons toasted sesame oil

2 tablespoons sesame seeds, toasted, divided

1 cup drained cabbage kimchi, thinly sliced, plus 2 tablespoons kimchi juice

½ English cucumber

4 scallions, thinly sliced on the diagonal

8 ounces somen noodles

Ice

Kosher salt

This classic Korean dish is a pasta salad of sorts, with bold contrasting flavors and textures. Somen is the Japanese name for the type of dried wheat noodle to use here; in Korea they are called somyeon. The noodles are slender and creamy white; look for them, often packaged in bundles, in the Asian section of the grocery store or in Asian markets. Gochujang is a Korean fermented red pepper paste—it's an essential ingredient in this dish. Made with ¼ cup gochujang, the noodles are assertively spicy. To tone down the heat a bit, reduce the amount to 3 tablespoons. If you like, add a halved or quartered hard- or soft-cooked egg on top of each portion.

Don't overcook the noodles. *Somen cooks quickly—in a matter of minutes—and the delicate strands quickly go from tender to overdone.*

Bring a large pot of water to a boil. Meanwhile, in a large bowl, whisk together the gochujang, vinegar, soy sauce, sugar, sesame oil, 1 tablespoon sesame seeds and the kimchi juice. Set aside.

Thinly slice the cucumber on the diagonal. Stack several slices and cut lengthwise into matchsticks. Repeat with the remaining slices. Set aside.

Add the noodles to the boiling water and cook, stirring frequently, until tender, about 2 minutes. Drain in a colander, then add 1 cup ice cubes on top. Rinse the noodles under cold running water, tossing constantly, until completely cool to the touch. Remove any unmelted ice cubes, then drain well.

Add the drained noodles to the gochujang mixture, along with the kimchi. Toss, then taste and season with salt and additional vinegar. Transfer to a shallow serving bowl, then mound the scallions and cucumber on top. Sprinkle with the remaining 1 tablespoon sesame seeds. Toss together just before serving.

JAPANESE NOODLES 101

Don't Assume Italian Pasta Is Always Best

Japanese noodles come in a variety of thicknesses, lengths and textures, and have different uses than basic Italian pasta. Chewy varieties such as ramen are great in soups and stir-fries, while stretchy, delicate somen noodles make great salads. (In fact, they're a better choice than Italian pasta, which can turn mealy when cold.) In general, Japanese noodles should be cooked in a generous amount of water until tender—not al dente. Tasting for doneness is the best way to know when your noodles are ready. Some require rinsing after cooking to remove excess starch, and all are cooked without salt. Here are the varieties we reach for most often and how we like to cook them.

RAMEN

Chewy and stretchy, ramen noodles are made of wheat flour and an alkaline solution called kansui, which gives them their yellow hue. They usually are consumed in brothy soups or stir-fried with cabbage, pork and a sweet soy glaze. Most commonly sold in the U.S. in instant form, they also are available fresh and dried. We prefer dried, non-instant ramen, which typically come in straight bundles that cook in about 4 minutes. Drain and rinse in cold water, or drain and immediately add to soup.

Stir-Fried Ramen with Cabbage and Bean Sprouts

In a 12-inch nonstick skillet, toss **6 ounces dried ramen** (cooked and drained) with **1 tablespoon sake, 1 tablespoon grapeseed or other neutral oil** and **½ teaspoon soy sauce.** Set over medium-high and cook, without stirring, until the noodles begin to brown on the bottom, about 2 minutes. Add **2 cups mung bean sprouts, 2 cups thinly sliced green cabbage, 2 tablespoons sake** and 2 tablespoons water. Cover and cook until the vegetables are crisp-tender, 3 to 4 minutes. Uncover and stir in **2½ tablespoons oyster sauce, 4 teaspoons soy sauce,**

1 tablespoon neutral oil, ¼ teaspoon white sugar and ¼ teaspoon black pepper. If desired, top with **2 fried eggs.**

UDON

Chewy and well-kneaded, udon noodles are made from wheat flour, water and salt and are available in a variety of thicknesses. Usually served hot in soup, stir-fried or chilled with dipping sauce. They are sold dried, frozen and fresh (refrigerated and shelf-stable). We prefer the firm, springy texture of frozen udon, but dried is more widely available. Cooking times vary, depending on brand and thickness; check the cooking instructions on the package, but check for doneness a few minutes early. Drain and rinse with water to stop the cooking.

Udon Noodle Soup with Pork and Spinach

In a medium bowl, whisk together **1 tablespoon each white miso** and **soy sauce.** Cut one **1-pound pork tenderloin** (trimmed of silver skin) in half lengthwise, then slice each half crosswise about ¼ inch thick. Add the pork to the bowl and stir. In a large pot, bring 4 quarts of water to a boil. Add **4 ounces dried udon noodles** and cook until tender. Drain, rinse under lukewarm water, drain again, then divide among 4 serving bowls. In the same pot, bring **1½ quarts low-sodium chicken broth** to a boil over medium-high. In a small bowl, whisk **3 tablespoons white miso** with 2 tablespoons of the broth. Add the mixture to the pot along with **1 tablespoon soy sauce** and **1 tablespoon finely grated fresh ginger.** Reduce to medium and simmer gently for 10 minutes, then bring to a boil over medium-high. Add the pork and cook, stirring, for 2 minutes. Off heat, stir in **8 ounces baby spinach** and **3 tablespoons unseasoned rice vinegar.** Ladle the soup over the noodles, then sprinkle with **6 scallions** (thinly sliced).

SHIRATAKI

Bouncy, gelatinous and glassy, shirataki noodles have little flavor. Made from yam starch, water and pickling lime, they often are added to hot pots like sukiyaki, but also are used in stir-fries and noodle salads. Most commonly sold refrigerated and packed in liquid. Though they are pre-cooked, we prefer to drain and rinse the noodles, then blanch them in boiling water for about 3 minutes to improve the taste and texture. Drain and rinse with cold water.

Shirataki Noodles with Peanut Sauce

In a medium bowl, whisk together **5 tablespoons creamy peanut butter, 3 tablespoons soy sauce, 2 tablespoons white sugar, 1 tablespoon unseasoned rice vinegar, 1 small garlic clove** (finely grated) and **1 teaspoon finely grated fresh ginger.** Add **two 7-ounce packages shirataki** (blanched, drained and rinsed) and toss until evenly coated with the sauce. Serve topped with **4 scallions** (thinly sliced) and **pickled ginger.**

SOBA

Gray-brown and nutty, soba noodles are made from a blend of buckwheat and wheat flours or all buckwheat. Often served chilled with a dashi-soy dipping sauce or hot in a dashi-based broth, though we also like them in noodle salads. Sold dried and frozen fresh. Pale green cha soba is flavored with matcha tea. We prefer the clean, nutty flavor of dried, 100 percent buckwheat soba, but it can be difficult to find. Cook for 7 to 8 minutes, or until tender. Drain and rinse with cold water until cold to the touch.

Dipping Sauce for Cold Soba

In a small saucepan over medium, simmer **1 cup low-sodium chicken broth, ½ cup soy sauce, ½ cup mirin** and **¼ cup sake** for 3 minutes. Transfer to a bowl and refrigerate until cold. Divide the sauce between four bowls. Serve with **cold cooked and drained soba noodles,** along with **thinly sliced scallions, toasted sesame seeds** and **wasabi paste** for stirring into the dipping sauce.

SOMEN

Delicate, pale and thin, somen noodles are made from wheat flour dough that is oiled, then stretched several times. Usually served chilled in summer months with a soy dipping sauce. Sold dried, packaged in bundles. Add to boiling water and cook until tender, 2 or 3 minutes, stirring gently to prevent sticking, then drain and rinse with cold water until cool to the touch.

Somen Noodle Salad

In a small bowl, combine **⅓ cup soy sauce, ¼ cup unseasoned rice vinegar, 3 tablespoons white sugar, 1 tablespoon grapeseed or other neutral oil** and **2 teaspoons toasted sesame oil,** then whisk until the sugar dissolves. Top **cooked and drained somen noodles** with **shredded lettuce, cucumber matchsticks, thinly sliced radishes, thinly sliced scallions** and **toasted sesame seeds.** Serve with the dressing on the side.

Gemelli with Tomato-Almond Pesto and Croutons

Start to finish: **30 minutes**
Servings: **4**

¾ cup slivered almonds

12 ounces gemelli or other short pasta

Kosher salt and ground black pepper

4 medium garlic cloves, smashed and peeled

½ cup lightly packed fresh basil, torn if large

2 pints cherry tomatoes, divided

6 tablespoons extra-virgin olive oil, divided, plus more to serve

3 ounces crusty white bread, torn into rough ½-inch pieces (about 1¾ cups)

When we sampled this no-cook tomato sauce in Sicily, it was made the traditional way, with a large mortar and pestle. A food processor gets it done faster and more easily. Topped with crisp, olive oil-infused croutons and toasted almonds, the dish is served warm or at room temperature after the pasta has had a few minutes to soak in the flavorful sauce. Instead of blanched, slivered almonds, you also could use sliced or whole almonds that have been roughly chopped.

Don't overprocess the second addition of tomatoes. *The first half is pulsed to create a juicy sauce, but the rest are pulsed only until roughly chopped so the tomato chunks add bursts of bright color and texture.*

In a 10-inch skillet over medium-high, toast the almonds, stirring frequently, until golden brown and fragrant, 3 to 5 minutes. Transfer to a small bowl and set aside; reserve the skillet.

In a large pot, bring 4 quarts water to a boil. Add the pasta and 2 tablespoons salt, then cook, stirring occasionally, until al dente. Reserve about ½ cup of the cooking water, then drain the pasta.

Meanwhile, in a food processor, process ½ cup of the almonds, the garlic and

2 teaspoons salt until finely chopped, about 30 seconds. Add the basil and half of the tomatoes, then pulse until chopped and well combined, 4 to 6 pulses. Add the remaining tomatoes and 2 tablespoons of oil, then pulse just until the whole tomatoes are broken up, about 3 pulses. Transfer to a serving bowl, add the pasta and ¼ cup of the reserved cooking water, then toss. Let stand, tossing once or twice, for 10 to 15 minutes to allow the pasta to absorb some of the sauce.

While the pasta stands, in the same skillet used to toast the almonds, toss the bread, remaining 4 tablespoons oil, ½ teaspoon salt and ¼ teaspoon pepper. Cook over medium, stirring frequently, until the bread is crisp and golden brown, 5 to 7 minutes.

Scatter the toasted bread and the remaining ¼ cup almonds over the pasta. Drizzle with additional oil and sprinkle with pepper.

No. 33

Some Pasta Needs Nuts

Pasta can suffer from a singular, soft texture. So we borrow a trick from Sicily, where cooks add textural contrast—plus sweet and savory notes—with nuts, such as crushed pistachios and almonds.

Pasta with Pistachios,
Tomatoes and Mint

Start to finish: **20 minutes**
Servings: **4**

12 ounces pasta (see note)

Kosher salt and ground black pepper

¼ cup extra-virgin olive oil, plus more to serve

1 pint cherry tomatoes, halved

½ cup shelled roasted pistachios, finely chopped

1 tablespoon grated lemon zest

2 tablespoons roughly chopped fresh mint

Grated Parmesan or pecorino Romano cheese, to serve

Sicily is known for its pistachios, so it's no surprise that the colorful, subtly sweet nuts feature heavily in the region's cuisine. This recipe is our take on a pistachio- and tomato-dressed pasta we tasted in Siracusa. With lemon zest and mint as accent ingredients, the flavors are fresh and bright. Just about any variety of pasta worked well, but we particularly liked long strands, such as linguine and spaghetti.

Don't use raw pistachios; *opt for roasted, as they don't require toasting before chopping. Either salted or unsalted worked well.*

In a large pot, bring 4 quarts water to a boil. Add the pasta and 2 tablespoons salt, then cook, stirring occasionally, until just shy of al dente. Reserve about 2 cups of the cooking water, then drain the pasta.

In a 12-inch skillet over medium, combine the oil and tomatoes. Cook, stirring only once or twice, until the tomatoes have softened and the oil has taken on a reddish hue, 4 to 6 minutes. Stir in half the pistachios, 1½ cups of the reserved cooking water, ½ teaspoon salt and ¼ teaspoon pepper. Bring to a simmer and cook, stirring occasionally, until the mixture is slightly reduced and the tomatoes are completely softened, about 2 minutes.

Add the pasta and lemon zest, then cook, stirring frequently, until the pasta is al dente and has absorbed most of the liquid but is still quite saucy, 2 to 4 minutes. Off heat, stir in the mint, then taste and season with salt and pepper. If the pasta is dry, add more cooking water, 1 tablespoon at a time. Transfer to a serving bowl, then sprinkle with the remaining pistachios and drizzle with additional oil. Serve with cheese.

CHANGE THE WAY YOU COOK

No. 34

Add Yogurt to Make Dough Flavorful and Flexible

Adding tangy yogurt to dough is an easy way to boost flavor. It also makes the dough more tender and easier to work with.

SHAPING FLATBREAD (PIZZA) DOUGH

    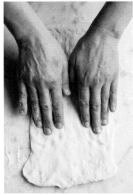

1. Place one ball of dough on a lightly floured counter.

2. Using your hands, begin patting and stretching the dough into an oval.

3. A ruler helps ensure that the dough reaches the correct dimensions.

4. Continue stretching the dough, making sure it is of even thickness.

5. The dough is properly shaped when it forms a 6- by 12-inch oval.

Flatbread (Pizza) Dough

Start to finish: **1½ hours**
(30 minutes active)

Makes two 12-inch pizzas or
flatbreads

241 grams (1¾ cups) bread flour, plus more for dusting

1½ teaspoons instant yeast

1¾ teaspoons kosher salt

¾ cup plain whole-milk Greek-style yogurt

1 tablespoon honey

This versatile dough is a breeze to make in a food processor and can be used for pizzas with various toppings or Middle Eastern-style flatbreads, which typically have simple toppings. The addition of Greek yogurt helps create a supple dough that's easy to work with and that bakes up with a chewy-soft crumb and subtle richness. For convenience, the dough can be made a day in advance. After dividing the dough in half and forming each piece into a round, place each portion in a quart-size zip-close bag that's been misted with cooking spray, seal well and refrigerate overnight. Allow the dough to come to room temperature before shaping.

Don't undermix the dough in the food processor; it needs a full minute of processing to build the gluten that provides structure and strength. When done, the dough may be warm to the touch; this is normal.

In a food processor, combine the flour, yeast and salt, then process until combined, about 5 seconds. Add the yogurt, honey and ¼ cup water. Process until the mixture forms a ball, about 30 seconds; the dough should be tacky to the touch and should stick slightly to the sides of the bowl. If it feels too dry, add more water, 1 tablespoon at a time, and process until incorporated. Continue to process until the dough is shiny and elastic, about 1 minute.

Transfer the dough to a lightly floured counter. Flour your hands and knead the dough a few times, until it forms a smooth ball. Divide the dough in half and form each half into a taut ball by rolling it against the counter in a circular motion under a cupped hand. Space the balls about 6 inches apart on a lightly floured counter, then cover with plastic wrap. Let rise until doubled in volume, 1 to 1½ hours.

About 1 hour before baking, heat the oven to 500°F with a baking steel or stone on the upper-middle rack. Working one at a time, gently stretch each ball on a lightly floured counter to an oval approximately 6 inches wide and 12 inches long. The dough is now ready to top and bake.

FLATBREAD (PIZZA) TOPPINGS

PIZZAS WITH PANCETTA, FIG JAM AND BLUE CHEESE

Start to finish: **30 minutes**

Makes **two 10-inch oval pizzas**

⅓ cup fig jam

2 teaspoons extra-virgin olive oil

Ground black pepper

Semolina, for dusting

Flatbread dough (p. 127)

3 to 4 ounces thinly sliced pancetta

4 ounces blue cheese, crumbled

½ cup lightly packed fresh sage leaves, torn if large

About 1 hour before baking, heat the oven to 500°F with a baking steel or stone on the upper-middle rack. In a small bowl, stir together the fig jam, oil and ½ teaspoon pepper; set aside.

Lightly dust a baking peel, inverted baking sheet or rimless cookie sheet with semolina. Transfer one portion of the shaped dough to the peel and, if needed, reshape into a 6-by-12-inch oval. Spread half the jam over the dough, then layer on half the pancetta, tearing the slices as needed to fit in a single layer. Sprinkle with half the blue cheese and half the sage. Slide the dough onto the baking steel and bake until golden brown, 9 to 11 minutes.

Using the peel, transfer the pizza to a wire rack. Top and bake the second portion of dough in the same way, then transfer to the wire rack.

PEPERONCINI AND CHEESE PIZZAS WITH GARLIC-HERB OIL

Start to finish: **30 minutes**

Makes **two 10-inch oval pizzas**

2 cups lightly packed fresh
flat-leaf parsley leaves

½ cup chopped fresh chives

¼ cup lightly packed fresh dill

1 large garlic clove, smashed
and peeled

⅔ cup extra-virgin olive oil

Kosher salt and ground black pepper

Semolina, for dusting

Flatbread dough (p. 127)

3 ounces fontina cheese,
shredded (1 cup)

2 ounces Parmesan cheese,
grated (1 cup)

1 cup drained peperoncini, stemmed,
patted dry and sliced into thin rings

About 1 hour before baking, heat the
oven to 500°F with a baking steel or
stone on the upper-middle rack. In a
food processor, combine the parsley,
chives, dill, garlic, oil, 1 teaspoon salt
and ½ teaspoon pepper. Process until
smooth, about 30 seconds, scraping
the bowl as needed. Transfer to a liquid
measuring cup and set aside.

Lightly dust a baking peel, inverted
baking sheet or rimless cookie sheet
with semolina. Transfer one portion of
the shaped dough to the peel and, if
needed, reshape into a 6-by-12-inch oval.
Sprinkle half the mozzarella and half
the Parmesan evenly over the dough,
then layer on half the peperoncini. Slide
the dough onto the baking steel and
bake until the edges are golden brown,
9 to 11 minutes.

Using the peel, transfer the pizza to a
wire rack. Top and bake the second

portion of dough in the same way, then
transfer to the wire rack. Stir the herb
oil to recombine, then drizzle over the
warm pizzas.

SHRIMP AND LEMONY RICOTTA PIZZAS WITH BABY ARUGULA

Start to finish: **35 minutes**

Makes **two 10-inch oval pizzas**

½ cup whole-milk ricotta cheese

1 ounce Parmesan cheese, grated
(½ cup)

2 tablespoons chopped fresh tarragon

2 tablespoons extra-virgin olive oil

1 tablespoon grated lemon zest, plus
2 tablespoons lemon juice, divided

Kosher salt and ground black pepper

Semolina, for dusting

Flatbread dough (p. 127)

12 ounces extra-large (21/25 per
pound) shrimp, peeled (tails removed),
deveined, halved crosswise and
patted dry

2 ounces baby arugula
(about 5 cups lightly packed)

About 1 hour before baking, heat the oven to 500°F with a baking steel or stone on the upper-middle rack. In a medium bowl, stir together the ricotta, Parmesan, tarragon, oil, lemon zest, 1 tablespoon of lemon juice, ¾ teaspoon salt and ½ teaspoon pepper.

Lightly dust a baking peel, inverted baking sheet or rimless cookie sheet with semolina. Transfer one portion of the shaped dough to the peel and, if needed, reshape into a 6-by-12-inch oval. Spread half the ricotta mixture evenly over the dough, then top with half the shrimp. Slide the dough onto the baking steel and bake until golden brown, 9 to 11 minutes.

Using the peel, transfer the pizza to a wire rack. Top and bake the second portion of dough in the same way, then transfer to the wire rack. In a medium bowl, toss the arugula with the remaining 1 tablespoon lemon juice and ¼ tea-

spoon each salt and pepper. Top the first pizza with half of the dressed arugula, mounding it on top; let the second pizza cool for a few minutes, then top with the remaining dressed arugula.

SPINACH AND FETA FLATBREADS

Start to finish: **40 minutes**

Makes **two 10-inch oval flatbreads**

1 pound baby spinach

1 medium shallot, finely chopped

4 tablespoons (½ stick) salted butter, room temperature

3 medium garlic cloves, finely grated

1 tablespoon grated lemon zest

1½ teaspoons sweet paprika

¼ teaspoon red pepper flakes (optional)

Kosher salt and ground black pepper

Semolina, for dusting

Flatbread dough (p. 127)

4 ounces feta cheese, crumbled (1 cup)

About 1 hour before baking, heat the oven to 500°F with a baking steel or stone on the upper-middle rack. Put the spinach in a large microwave-safe bowl. Cover and microwave on high until wilted, 2 to 4 minutes. Uncover and let cool slightly, then squeeze the spinach to remove excess moisture; wipe out the bowl. Roughly chop the spinach, then return it to the bowl and add the shallot, butter, garlic, lemon zest, paprika, pepper flakes (if using), 1 teaspoon salt and ½ teaspoon black pepper. Mix with your hands until well combined.

Lightly dust a baking peel, inverted baking sheet or rimless cookie sheet with semolina. Transfer one portion of the shaped dough to the peel and, if needed, reshape into a 6-by-12-inch oval. Spread half of the spinach mixture evenly over the dough, then top with half the feta. Slide the dough onto the baking steel and bake until the edges are golden brown, 9 to 11 minutes.

Using the peel, transfer the flatbread to a wire rack. Top and bake the second portion of dough in the same way, then transfer to the wire rack.

BUILD A BOLDER PIZZA

Wean Yourself off Delivery With Weeknight-Easy Flatbread

Our flatbread dough comes together quickly, making it a great way to get home-baked flavor into suppers without clocking hours in the kitchen. The flatbreads can be topped with just about anything, from a quick drizzle of olive oil and a dusting of spice to heartier meat-and-cheese mixes. Here are some of our favorite toppings for both before and after baking.

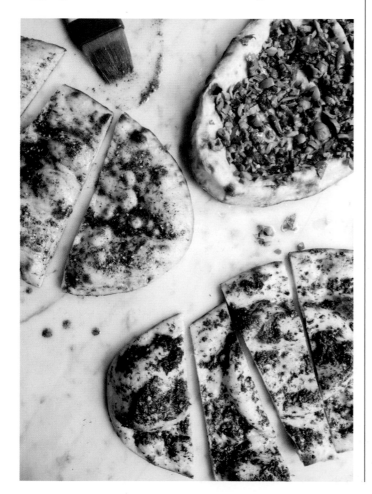

UNBAKED TOPPINGS

To bake plain flatbread—that is, dough minus the toppings—heat the oven and pizza steel or stone as you would if making pizza. If you plan to add toppings after baking, have them ready before baking the bread. Slide the shaped dough onto the hot pizza steel or stone and bake until slightly puffed and lightly browned, 7 to 9 minutes. Then spoon, brush, spread or otherwise apply toppings to the just-baked flatbread.

Za'atar butter: In a small saucepan, heat **salted butter** and **za'atar** until the butter is bubbling and the seeds are just beginning to color. Spoon the mixture onto warm baked flatbreads.

Garlic-chive-lemon butter: Using a silicone spatula, mash together **softened butter, finely chopped fresh chives, grated lemon zest, finely grated garlic,** kosher salt and ground black pepper until well combined.

Harissa butter: Stir together **harissa paste** and **melted butter.**

Honey-thyme butter: In a small saucepan, heat **honey, salted butter** and **chopped fresh thyme,** stirring until the honey dissolves and the mixture is bubbling.

Spicy garlic-herb oil: In a food processor, combine **2 cups lightly packed fresh flat-leaf parsley, ½ cup chopped fresh chives, ¼ cup chopped fresh dill, ⅓ cup extra-virgin olive oil, 1 tablespoon red pepper flakes, 1 medium garlic clove** (smashed and peeled), 1 teaspoon kosher salt and ½ teaspoon ground black pepper. Process until smooth, about 20 seconds.

Olive and roasted pepper relish: Stir together **½ cup chopped pitted green olives, ¼ cup chopped drained roasted red peppers, ¼ cup chopped fresh flat-leaf parsley, 1 tablespoon drained capers, 1 grated garlic clove, ½ teaspoon red pepper flakes** and **2 teaspoons red wine vinegar.**

Prosciutto, arugula and ricotta: Stir together **whole-milk ricotta cheese, grated lemon zest,** kosher salt and ground black pepper. Spread the ricotta mixture onto the baked flatbread, then top with **prosciutto slices** and **baby arugula** that's been tossed with lemon juice. Sprinkle with salt and drizzle with **extra-virgin olive oil.**

TOMATO SAUCE FOR PIZZA

This easy no-cook tomato sauce has bold, bright flavor to balance rich toppings.

In a food processor, process **a 14½-ounce can diced tomatoes, 1 small garlic clove** (finely grated) and **¼ teaspoon red pepper flakes** until smooth, about 30 seconds. Transfer to a fine mesh strainer set over a medium bowl. Let stand without stirring until liquid no longer drains off, about 15 minutes. Discard the liquid. Add the strained tomatoes to the now-empty bowl and stir in **1 tablespoon extra-virgin oil** and ½ teaspoon kosher salt.

BAKED AND BUBBLY

We offer a few recipes for delicious baked toppings on pp. 128-131, but topping options for pizza are endless, so here are a few more. Add the toppings to the shaped dough, then slide onto the hot baking steel or stone and bake until the edges are golden brown, 9 to 11 minutes.

Three cheese pizza: Top the shaped dough with **tomato sauce** (store-bought or see the recipe above). Sprinkle with **shredded whole-milk mozzarella, shredded fontina cheese and grated Parmesan,** then bake.

Tapenade, fresh mozzarella and arugula: Spread **homemade or store-bought tapenade** (black olive spread) onto the shaped dough and layer on slices of **fresh**
mozzarella cheese and **anchovy fillets** (if desired). Bake, then top with **baby arugula** and drizzle with **extra-virgin olive oil** and a squeeze of **lemon juice.**

Leeks, goat cheese and walnuts: In a skillet, cook **thinly sliced leeks** in **salted butter** until tender but not browned, then season with kosher salt and ground black pepper; let cool. Spread leeks onto the shaped dough, then top with **crumbled fresh goat cheese.** Bake, then top with **toasted walnuts** and **chopped fresh herbs** (we loved chives and mint).

Chorizo and roasted peppers: In a skillet, cook **Mexican chorizo** (casing removed) until no longer pink, breaking the meat into bite-size pieces, then drain on paper towels. Top the shaped dough with **tomato sauce** (store-bought or see the recipe above) and sprinkle with **shredded**
mozzarella. Layer on strips of **roasted red peppers** (patted dry) and the **chorizo,** then bake.

Red onion, olives and feta: Top the shaped dough with **tomato sauce** (store-bought or see the recipe above). Layer on **sliced red onion** and sprinkle with **chopped Kalamata olives** and **feta cheese.** Bake, then sprinkle with chopped fresh **oregano** or **mint.**

Smoked mozzarella, sun-dried tomatoes and basil: Arrange **oil-packed sun-dried tomatoes** (patted dry) in an even layer on the shaped dough. Add thinly sliced **garlic cloves** and sprinkle with **shredded smoked mozzarella.** Bake, then sprinkle with kosher salt and ground black pepper and top with **torn fresh basil.** Drizzle with some of the oil from the sun-dried tomatoes.

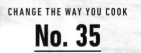

No. 35

Add Moisture Without Adding Liquid

Adding mashed potatoes to dough
yields a lighter, more tender crumb.
Using sweet potatoes multiplies
the impact, adding color and flavor
as well as tenderness.

Sweet Potato Rolls
Portuguese-Style

Start to finish: **3 hours**
(45 minutes active)
Makes eight 5-inch rolls

12 ounces orange-flesh sweet potatoes, peeled and cut into 1-inch chunks

3 tablespoons salted butter, cut into 3 pieces

1 tablespoon honey

1½ teaspoons kosher salt

411 grams (3 cups) bread flour, plus more for dusting

2 teaspoons instant yeast

The Portuguese sweet potato bread known as bolo de caco is a griddled bread that resembles an English muffin or a small, thick pita bread round. For our version, we use widely available orange-fleshed sweet potatoes rather than the white variety that's more traditional; the potatoes give the bread a saffron hue and a rich, moist crumb. The traditional way to cook bolos de caco is on a stone slab; we use a skillet set on the stovetop to brown the rounds, then finish baking them in the oven. The flatbreads typically are split while still warm, spread with garlic-chive butter (recipe below) and served as part of a meal, but you also could toast the halves and have them for breakfast or use them to make a sandwich.

Don't begin mixing the cooked sweet potato mixture until it has cooled for 30 minutes. Otherwise, the heat from the potatoes may kill the yeast. Don't worry if you don't own a digital thermometer for testing the breads. Simply bake them for the full 14 minutes. The sweet potato in the dough makes this a forgiving dough, so even if slightly overbaked, the crumb still will be moist and tender.

In a medium saucepan over medium-high, combine the potatoes, butter, honey, salt and ⅔ cup water. Bring to a boil, stirring to melt the butter, then reduce to low, cover and cook until a skewer inserted into the potatoes meets no resistance, 15 to 20 minutes. Transfer the potatoes and any liquid to the bowl of a stand mixer. Cool until just warm to the touch, about 30 minutes. Meanwhile, mist a medium bowl with cooking spray.

Using the paddle attachment, beat the mixture on low until smooth, about 1 minute. Switch to the dough hook and add the flour and yeast. Mix on low until a smooth dough forms, about 5 minutes. Increase to medium-high and knead for 1 minute to strengthen the dough. Transfer to the prepared bowl, cover with plastic wrap and let rise in a warm, draft-free spot until the dough is doubled in size, about 1 hour.

Heat the oven to 350°F with a rack in the middle position. Line a rimmed baking sheet with kitchen parchment. Turn the dough out onto a lightly floured counter, then divide into 8 pieces. Form each piece into a taut ball by rolling it against the counter in a circular motion under a cupped hand; place seam-side down on the prepared baking sheet. Using your hand, press and flatten each ball until it measures about 4 inches wide and ¼ inch thick. Cover with plastic wrap and let rise until doubled in size, about 30 minutes.

Heat a 12-inch skillet over medium until a drop of water sizzles immediately, about 2 minutes. Place 4 dough rounds seam-side up in the pan and cook until deep golden brown, 1 to 2 minutes. Using a wide metal spatula, flip and cook the second sides until golden brown, about 1 minute. Return to the baking sheet, then repeat with the remaining rounds, returning them to the baking sheet.

Bake the flatbreads in the oven until the centers reach 200°F, 12 to 14 minutes. Immediately transfer directly to a wire rack and cool for at least 15 minutes.

GARLIC-CHIVE BUTTER

Start to finish: **5 minutes**
Makes **½ cup**

This quick and easy compound butter is flavorful and versatile. Use to top steak, fish, bread or our Portuguese sweet potato rolls.

8 tablespoons (1 stick) salted butter, room temperature

3 tablespoons finely chopped fresh chives

1 small garlic clove, finely grated

¼ teaspoon ground black pepper

In a medium bowl, mix the butter with a rubber spatula until completely smooth. Stir in the chives, garlic and pepper.

No. 36

Change the Flour to Change the Chew

Different flours—such as starchy, sweet rice flour—can change the texture of breads for the better.

Chinese Sesame-Scallion Bread

Start to finish: **2 hours**
(30 minutes active)
Servings: **4**

217 grams (1⅔ cups) all-purpose flour, plus more if needed

40 grams (¼ cup) sweet (glutinous) rice flour

1 teaspoon instant yeast

1½ teaspoons kosher salt, divided

¾ cup warm (100°F) water

1 tablespoon honey

4 teaspoons toasted sesame oil, divided

1 bunch scallions, finely chopped (about 1 cup)

4 tablespoons sesame seeds, divided

2 tablespoons grapeseed or other neutral oil

This bread, known as zhima dabing—which translates as "sesame big bread"—is similar to Chinese scallion pancakes, but is larger, thicker and has a lighter, fluffier crumb. The addition of sweet (also called glutinous) rice flour gives the crust a unique crispness and the interior a satisfying chew. If you can't find sweet rice flour with the baking ingredients, check the Asian aisle for a white box labeled "mochiko," the Japanese term for the flour. Chop the scallions by thinly slicing them first, then running the knife over them a few times to further break them down. To keep the scallions fresh, prep them toward the end of the dough's one-hour rising time.

Don't use regular rice flour in place of the sweet rice flour, as it won't produce the same texture. Don't use pretoasted sesame seeds, as the seeds brown deeply as the bread cooks; already toasted seeds may end up scorched and bitter. Don't worry if some scallions are exposed on the surface of the dough as you flatten it into a round; this is normal.

In a stand mixer fitted with the dough hook, mix both flours, the yeast and 1 teaspoon of salt on low until combined, about 30 seconds. In a liquid measuring cup or small bowl, whisk the water and honey until dissolved. With the mixer on low, slowly pour the honey water into the flour mixture. Continue mixing on low until an evenly moistened dough forms, about 1 minute. Stop the mixer and check the dough; if it feels wet or very sticky, add an additional 1 to 3 tablespoons all-purpose flour. Continue mixing on low until smooth, about 4 minutes. The dough should feel tacky but not stick to your fingers.

Coat a medium bowl with 1 teaspoon of sesame oil. Place the dough in the bowl and turn to coat. Cover with plastic wrap and let rise in a warm, draft-free spot until the dough has doubled in size, about 1 hour.

Coat a rimmed baking sheet with 1 teaspoon of the remaining sesame oil. Turn the dough out onto the baking sheet and use your hands to press into a 12-by-9-inch rectangle. In a small bowl, toss the scallions with the remaining 2 teaspoons sesame oil, then distribute evenly over the dough. Sprinkle with the remaining ½ teaspoon salt. Starting from a long side, roll the dough into a cylinder and pinch the seam to seal. Roll the cylinder seam side down, then coil it into a tight spiral and tuck the end under. Using your hands, press the coil to slightly flatten, sprinkle with 2 tablespoons of sesame seeds and press to adhere. Flip the coil and sprinkle the second side with the remaining 2 tablespoons sesame seeds. Press and flatten into an even 10-inch round.

Add the grapeseed oil to a nonstick 12-inch skillet and swirl to evenly coat the bottom. Carefully transfer the dough to the skillet; reshape into a 10-inch round, if needed. Cover with a lid and let rise until about doubled in size, about 30 minutes.

Place the covered skillet over medium and cook until the bottom of the bread is deep golden brown, 5 to 6 minutes. Uncover and, using tongs and a wide metal spatula, carefully flip the bread. Cook until golden on the second side, about 3 minutes. Slide the bread onto a wire rack and let cool for at least 10 minutes. Cut into quarters to serve.

RECIPES & RULES

EGGS

EGGS

At Milk Street, we add interest to eggs by **changing their texture,** leaving yolks runny for a ready-made sauce or adding crunch with extra-crispy whites. We also **treat them gently, using steam or residual heat** to cook them perfectly and avoid rubbery whites. We **pair them with robust ingredients** like handfuls of fresh herbs. And we **keep them light,** adding leavener for lift.

We can be a bit unimaginative when it comes to eggs, corralling them mainly to breakfast and rarely venturing beyond frying and scrambling. So we looked for ways to break out of that shell, and found plenty of traditions elsewhere in the world that recognize eggs as the quick-cooking, versatile protein they are. And it turns out eggs are perfectly at home as lunch and dinner—and as the star of the plate, not an afterthought. Eggs can be bolstered by bold condiments and spices, or served with tangy sauces like the drizzle of garlicky yogurt that accompanies Turkey's classic çilbir.

For a one-stroke solution to saucing a dish, we **use tender poached eggs to add richness.** Poaching eggs can be intimidating, but not the way we do them. Rather than a saucepan, we use a shallow skillet, which cuts the risk of breaking the yolks when adding the eggs to the water. And we keep the heat low, which yields nice, neatly shaped whites. A simple way to turn poached eggs into a meal—add them to a quick and easy broth, as in our miso soup with poached eggs.

While a runny-yolked egg makes a great sauce, eggs don't have to be soft. We **use fried eggs to add texture,** as in our crispy fried eggs with piperade. We fry the eggs until the edges of the whites are crisp and brown, then pair them with onions, peppers and garlic cooked until meltingly tender.

We love a perfectly hard-cooked egg. But the traditional boiling method too often produces rubbery, overdone results. So **we hard cook our eggs with the gentler heat of steam.** Result: Perfectly tender eggs with firm whites. We use this technique for our curried eggs with coconut, tomatoes and spinach, as well as our take on Persian smashed potatoes and eggs served in flatbread.

We love the speed and simplicity of omelets, but they are fussy and easy to overcook. Our solution? **We pull the pan off the heat before the omelet is cooked through and let it finish with gentle residual heat.** We use a similar approach with flat omelets, starting them on the stovetop, then covering the pan and removing it from the heat.

Baked egg dishes with lots of vegetables are satisfying, but can cross the line from hearty to heavy. In our kuku, a vegetable-rich frittata-like dish popular in Persian cuisine, **we follow the lead of Iranian cooks and add baking powder to the eggs** to give a bit of extra lift. We came up with two versions, one with baked cauliflower and another with green beans.

To help you get started, we gathered all our basic egg techniques in one place, complete with simple serving suggestions. Check out our egg primer (pp. 142-143).

COOK PERFECT EGGS EVERY TIME

Put Down the Butter, Skip the Boil and Turn Off the Burner

We love the speed and versatility of eggs, but we don't love the bland or rubbery results we so often get. Eggs overcook in seconds and need seasonings that add flavor and texture to shine. While there's a place for butter in egg cookery, we **use olive oil to make the lightest, fluffiest scrambled eggs.** We **add simple, bold seasonings to fried eggs** that make them into a meal. We **poach eggs in shallow skillets and use residual heat to cook them perfectly.** Our hard-cooked eggs aren't boiled; **steam is better for producing perfect hard- or soft-cooked eggs.** And when we want an omelet, we have two ways to go. Open, with just a few ingredients piled on, or folded, which has the potential to be turned into a heartier meal with the addition of fillings such as roasted vegetables or chopped ham. **We take the worry out of folding omelets by sliding the cooked eggs onto a plate first.** A simple flip with the spatula is all that's needed to finish.

HOW TO
POACH AN EGG

We poach eggs in a skillet, not a saucepan; the low sides make it easier to get the eggs in without breaking the yolks. And we cook them mostly with gentle residual heat, a safeguard against overcooking. To make four poached eggs, fill a 10-inch skillet with at least 1 inch of water and bring to a simmer over medium-high. Line a large plate with paper towels. Crack **4 large eggs** into separate small bowls or cups. One at a time, carefully tip the eggs into the water near the edge of the pan. Once all eggs have been added, cover the pan and turn off the heat. Let stand until the whites are set but the yolks are still soft, 3 to 5 minutes. Using a slotted spoon, gently transfer each egg to the prepared plate to drain.

HOW TO
FRY EGGS

A few toppings easily transform the basic fried egg into a satisfying dinner. Our approach cooks four at a time. Don't worry if the whites run together a little. Simply use the edge of the spatula to separate them. In a nonstick 12-inch skillet over medium, melt **1 tablespoon salted butter,** swirling to coat the pan. One at a time, crack **4 eggs,** each into one quadrant of the pan. Use a silicone spatula to gently push the edges of the egg whites toward the yolks. Cover and cook until the whites are set but the yolks are still runny, about 1½ minutes. Using a thin metal spatula, transfer the eggs to serving plates, then season with kosher salt and black pepper.

FRIED EGG RECIPES

Fried Eggs with Arugula, Feta and Dukkah

The Egyptian seed, nut and spice blend known as dukkah is an excellent seasoning for simple fried eggs, and blooming it in butter coaxes out maximum flavor and fragrance. You can buy it ready-made or, for instructions on how to make your own, see p. 220. In a small bowl, toss **1 cup arugula** with **1 tablespoon lemon juice,** then divide between 2 serving plates. Sprinkle each with **1 tablespoon crumbled feta cheese.**

Top each portion with **2 fried eggs.** Add **2 tablespoons unsalted butter** to the still-hot skillet the eggs were cooked in and let melt with the pan's residual heat. Stir in **1 teaspoon dukkah,** then drizzle over the eggs and arugula on each plate.

Fried Eggs with Spinach and Tarka

For this recipe, we bloom mustard and cumin seeds in butter to create a topping with both texture and flavor. To make, divide **1 cup baby**

spinach between 2 serving plates. Top each portion with **2 fried eggs.** Return the skillet used to cook the eggs to medium-high. Add **2 tablespoons unsalted butter, ½ teaspoon mustard seeds** and **¼ teaspoon cumin seeds.** Cook until the butter is melted and gently sizzling, about 1 minute, occasionally swirling the pan. Add **1 clove garlic** (minced), **½ jalapeño chili** (seeded and minced) and **1 teaspoon finely grated fresh ginger** and cook, stirring, until fragrant, 30 to 60 seconds. Pour over the eggs.

HOW TO
MAKE A FOLDED OMELET

Folded omelets need just a few fillings to become satisfying meals. Try grated cheese, chopped ham and sliced scallions; leftover roasted or sautéed vegetables; or fresh herbs and crumbled soft cheese. For ease, we like to make large eight-egg omelets in a 12-inch skillet; one is enough to serve four. In a medium bowl, whisk together **8 large eggs,** 1 teaspoon kosher salt and ½ teaspoon black pepper. In a nonstick 12-inch skillet over medium, melt **2 tablespoons salted butter,** swirling to coat the pan. Pour in the egg mixture and, using a silicone spatula, draw the edges toward the center and gently stir, working your way around the perimeter of the pan. Cook this way until they form soft, pillowy curds but are still runny enough to pool on the surface, 1 to 2 minutes. Spread in an even layer, then cover, remove from the heat and let stand until the omelet is set, about 5 minutes. Run the spatula around the edge and under the omelet to loosen it, then slide it onto a plate. Place the filling on one half. Using the spatula, fold in half to enclose the filling. Cut into 4 wedges.

HOW TO
MAKE AN OPEN OMELET

Flat, thin, open-faced omelets are prepared throughout the Middle East. A few ingredients are cooked right in the pan, eggs seasoned with herbs are swirled in and the pan is covered to set the eggs in moments. No need to flip. We give a basic herb-and-onion version here with more flavoring suggestions below. In a large bowl, whisk together **8 large eggs, 1 cup finely chopped fresh soft herbs (such as cilantro, flat-leaf parsley, scallions and/or mint), 1 medium garlic clove** (finely grated) and 1 teaspoon kosher salt. In a 12-inch nonstick skillet over medium, melt **2 tablespoons salted butter.** Add **½ large red onion** (thinly sliced) and ¼ teaspoon salt and cook, stirring occasionally, until the onion has softened and just begun to brown, 3 to 5 minutes. Pour in the eggs and cook, stirring gently and taking care to scrape the sides of the pan, until soft curds form but are still loose and spreadable, 1 to 2 minutes. Spread the eggs to evenly cover the bottom of the pan. Cover, reduce to low and cook until the top is just set, 3 to 5 minutes.

.... **OPEN OMELET RECIPES** ....

Open Omelet with Mint and Feta

Make an open omelet using **¼ cup finely chopped fresh mint.** After spreading the eggs to cover the bottom of the pan, sprinkle evenly with **2 ounces crumbled feta cheese.** Cover, reduce to low and cook until the top of the eggs is just set, 3 to 5 minutes.

Open Omelet with Parsley and Roasted Peppers

Make an open omelet using **1 cup chopped fresh fresh flat-leaf parsley** and add **2 tablespoons finely chopped drained roasted red peppers** (patted dry) along with the **½ large red onion.**

HOW TO
SCRAMBLE EGGS

For scrambling eggs, we skip the butter and use olive oil, which contains compounds that help egg proteins form stronger links as they cook. Those links trap steam that results in moister, fluffier eggs that cook in seconds. The oil needs to heat for several minutes over medium. If not hot enough, the eggs won't puff properly. In a 12-inch nonstick skillet over medium, heat **2 tablespoons extra-virgin olive oil** until barely smoking, about 3 minutes. Meanwhile, in a bowl, use a fork to beat **8 large eggs** and ¾ teaspoon kosher salt until blended and foamy. Pour the eggs into the center of the pan. Using a silicone spatula, continuously stir, pushing the eggs toward the middle as they begin to set at the edges and folding the cooked egg onto itself. Cook until just set, 60 to 90 seconds. The curds should be shiny, wet and soft but not translucent or runny. Transfer to warmed plates and season with salt and black pepper.

HOW TO
STEAM SOFT- AND HARD-COOKED EGGS

To steam soft- or hard-cooked eggs, fill a large saucepan with 1 inch of water. Place a folding steamer basket in the pan, cover and bring to a boil over medium-high. Meanwhile, fill a medium bowl with ice water. Add **large eggs** to the steamer basket, cover and cook for 7 minutes for soft-cooked or 12 minutes for hard-cooked. Immediately transfer the eggs to the ice water and let stand until the eggs have cooled.

Turkish Poached Eggs
with Garlicky Yogurt (Çilbir)

2 small garlic cloves, finely grated

1¼ teaspoons lemon juice

4 tablespoons (½ stick) salted butter

1 tablespoon Aleppo pepper (see note)

2 cups plain whole-milk or low-fat Greek yogurt

Kosher salt

2 tablespoons lightly packed fresh cilantro

2 tablespoons lightly packed fresh mint, torn if large

1 tablespoon lightly packed fresh dill

4 large eggs

Flaky sea salt, to serve (optional)

This Turkish dish, called çilbir, nestles runny-yolked poached eggs in a creamy, garlic-spiked yogurt, then finishes with a spice-infused butter. We also add a handful of herbs for fresh flavor and bright color. Aleppo pepper gives the infused butter a vibrant red hue and subtle heat. If you can't find it, use 2 teaspoons sweet paprika plus ½ teaspoon red pepper flakes. Some wispy whites may float away from each egg as it is added to the poaching water, but a firm layer of white will set neatly around the yolk, forming picture-perfect poached eggs. Serve warmed bread alongside, either a crusty, country-style loaf or soft, tender flatbread.

Don't let the poaching water reach a full boil *before adding the eggs; aim for a full but gentle simmer with just a few bubbles breaking the surface every few seconds. The churn of boiling water will cause the eggs to break before they have a chance to set.*

In a medium bowl, stir together the garlic and lemon juice; set aside for 10 minutes. Meanwhile, in a small skillet over medium, heat the butter until bubbling. Add the Aleppo pepper and cook, swirling, until the butter is bright red and fragrant, about 1 minute. Remove from the heat and set aside.

To the garlic-lemon mixture, stir in the yogurt and ½ teaspoon salt. Divide among 4 serving bowls, then set aside at room temperature. In a small bowl, toss together the cilantro, mint and dill; set aside.

Fill a 10-inch skillet with at least 1 inch of water and bring to a simmer over medium-high. Line a large plate with paper towels. Crack each egg into a small bowl or cup. One at a time, carefully tip the eggs into the water near the edge of the pan. Once all eggs have been added, cover the pan and turn off the heat. Let stand until the whites are set but the yolks are still soft, 3 to 5 minutes.

Using a slotted spoon, gently transfer each egg to the prepared plate to briefly drain, then place 1 egg in each bowl, setting it on the yogurt. Drizzle each serving with 1 tablespoon of the Aleppo butter and top with the herb mixture, dividing it evenly. Sprinkle with sea salt, if using.

No. 37

Go Low for the Perfect Poached Egg

For the easiest poached eggs, use a low-sided skillet, not a tall saucepan. And once the eggs are in, turn off the burner. The residual heat will gently and perfectly poach the eggs.

HOW TO POACH EGGS

1. Fill a 10-inch skillet with at least 1 inch of water and bring to a simmer over medium-high. Crack each egg into a small bowl, then carefully tip them one at a time into the water near the edge of the pot.

2. Once all eggs have been added, cover the pan and turn off the heat. Let stand until the whites are set but the yolks are still soft, 3 to 5 minutes.

3. Using a slotted spoon, gently transfer each egg to a paper towel-lined plate to drain.

Miso Soup
with Shiitake Mushrooms and Poached Eggs

4 medium garlic cloves, smashed and peeled

2 tablespoons tomato paste

½ cup red miso

4 large eggs

5 ounces fresh shiitake mushrooms, stemmed and thinly sliced

14-ounce container silken (soft) tofu, drained and cut into rough ¾-inch cubes

2 cups cooked white rice, warmed

1 bunch scallions, thinly sliced

Shichimi togarashi, to serve

Toasted sesame oil, to serve

The backbone of this simple vegetarian soup is a quick and easy broth made with nothing more than water, red miso, garlic and tomato paste. It's made substantial and satisfying with the addition of fresh shiitake mushrooms, silken tofu and cooked rice. We float runny-yolked poached eggs on the soup to add flavor and richness. You can use any type of cooked white rice, but make sure it is warmed before portioning so it doesn't cool the soup. Shichimi togarashi is a fragrant Japanese spice blend. Sprinkled onto soups and broths, it adds a touch of chili heat; look for it in small jars in the Asian aisle of the supermarket.

Don't use white miso; *its flavor is too mild for this soup. Also, don't use dried shiitake mushrooms. We much preferred the taste and texture of fresh. Finally, don't bring the water to a full boil when poaching the eggs. The gentle simmer allows the eggs to retain their shape.*

In a large saucepan over medium, combine the garlic and tomato paste. Cook, stirring occasionally, until the tomato paste has browned, 2 to 3 minutes. Add 6 cups water, then whisk in the miso. Bring to a simmer, then reduce to medium-low and cook, uncovered, stirring occasionally, for 5 minutes.

Strain the broth through a fine mesh strainer set over a medium bowl. Return the broth to the pan; discard the solids in the strainer. Add the mushrooms and bring to a simmer over medium-high, then reduce to medium and cook, uncovered, until the mushrooms are tender, about 10 minutes.

While the mushrooms cook, fill a 10-inch skillet with at least 1 inch of water and bring to a simmer over medium-high. Line a large plate with paper towels. Crack each egg into a small bowl or cup. One at a time, carefully tip the eggs into the water near the edge of the pan. Once all eggs have been added, cover the pan and turn off the heat. Let stand until the whites are set but the yolks are still soft, 3 to 5 minutes. Using a slotted spoon, gently transfer each egg to the prepared plate to drain.

Add the tofu to the broth, leaving behind any liquid, and stir gently. Divide the rice evenly among 4 serving bowls, then ladle in the soup. Carefully place a poached egg on top of each serving. Sprinkle with the scallions and shichimi togarashi, then drizzle lightly with sesame oil.

Piperade with Fried Eggs

Start to finish: **40 minutes**

Servings: **4 to 6**

4 tablespoons extra-virgin olive oil, divided, plus more to serve

2 medium yellow onions, halved and thinly sliced

2 medium yellow or orange bell peppers, stemmed, seeded and cut into ½-inch strips

6 medium garlic cloves, thinly sliced

2 pints cherry or grape tomatoes, halved

2 large thyme sprigs

Kosher salt and ground black pepper

2 teaspoons sweet paprika

1 teaspoon packed light brown sugar

¼ to ½ teaspoon red pepper flakes

2 medium green bell peppers, stemmed, seeded and cut into ½-inch strips

2 teaspoons lemon juice

6 large eggs

Grated manchego or pecorino Romano cheese, to serve (optional)

Piperade—which originates in Spain's Basque country—is a silky, stew-like mixture of peppers, tomatoes and onions. Traditionally, the dish is spiced with piment d'Espelette, a ground red chili from southwestern France, but it's not easy to find. We approximate its heat and flavor with a combination of sweet paprika and red pepper flakes. Piperade can be used as a sauce or condiment, and it's commonly paired with eggs. We add textural contrast and richness with crisp-edged, runny-yolked fried eggs. We especially liked the sharp accent of an aged sheep milk cheese—such as Spanish manchego or Italian pecorino—sprinkled on top, but this is optional. Serve with crusty bread to soak up the juices.

Don't allow the moisture *to completely evaporate after uncovering the pot. If it does, add a few tablespoons of water to loosen; there should be just enough sauce to pool around the vegetables.*

In a large pot over medium, heat 2 tablespoons of oil until shimmering. Add the onions, yellow peppers and garlic, then cook, stirring frequently, until the peppers begin to soften, about 5 minutes. Stir in the tomatoes, thyme, 1½ teaspoons salt and ½ teaspoon black pepper. Cover and cook, stirring once or twice, until the tomatoes have released their juice, about 10 minutes.

Stir in the paprika, sugar, pepper flakes and green peppers. Increase to medium-high and cook, uncovered and stirring occasionally, until the green peppers are tender and the sauce has thickened, another 5 to 8 minutes. Remove and discard the thyme sprigs, then stir in the lemon juice. Taste and season with salt and black pepper. Cover and set aside to keep warm while you fry the eggs.

In a 12-inch nonstick skillet over medium, heat the remaining 2 tablespoons oil until shimmering. One at a time, crack the eggs into the pan, each in a different spot, then use a silicone spatula to gently push the edges of the egg whites toward the yolks to keep the eggs separate. Cook until the edges of the whites are browned and crisped, 5 to 7 minutes. Using a slotted spoon, transfer the eggs to a paper towel–lined plate to drain.

Transfer the piperade to a serving platter and top with the eggs. If you like, pierce each yolk with a knife so the yolks run. Drizzle with additional oil, then sprinkle with additional black pepper and cheese, if using.

No. 38

Add Crunch to Your Eggs

Eggs don't have to be soft. Crisp-edged whites can offer a pleasant contrast to tender yolks and vegetables.

No. 39

Steam, Don't Boil, Your Eggs

Safeguard soft- or hard-cooked eggs against rubbery whites and overdone yolks by steaming instead of boiling. Steam transfers less energy to the eggs, cooking them more gently.

Soft-Cooked Eggs
with Coconut, Tomatoes and Spinach

6 large eggs

3 tablespoons coconut oil, preferably unrefined

½ teaspoon yellow mustard seeds

2 teaspoons garam masala

½ teaspoon ground turmeric

½ cup unsweetened shredded coconut

1 small red onion, halved and thinly sliced

1 or 2 jalapeño chilies, stemmed, seeded and thinly sliced

1 pint cherry tomatoes, halved

Kosher salt and ground black pepper

1 bunch spinach, stemmed and thinly sliced (about 4 cups)

1 cup lightly packed fresh cilantro

This dish was inspired by mutta thoran from Kerala in southern India. It's typically made by scrambling eggs with coconut and spices, but we stir diced soft-cooked eggs into a fragrantly spiced mix of coconut, tomatoes and spinach to create a chunky, colorful curry. Either unrefined or refined coconut oil works here, though the stronger, richer coconut flavor from unrefined adds to the dish's complexity. The eggs can be steamed, cooled and even peeled a day ahead. Serve with steamed white rice or warmed flatbread.

Don't steam the eggs for longer than 9 minutes or they will be overcooked for this dish. Barely firm yolks are ideal because they blend with the other ingredients and create a rich, lightly thickened sauce. Also, don't use baby spinach, as it turns soggy and slippery when cooked; mature bunch spinach is the best choice.

Fill a large saucepan with about 1 inch of water. Place a folding steamer basket in the pan, cover and bring to a boil over medium-high. Meanwhile, fill a medium bowl with ice water. Add the eggs to the steamer basket, cover and cook for 9 minutes. Immediately transfer the eggs to the ice water and let stand until the eggs have cooled. Crack and peel the eggs, then chop into large bite-size pieces.

In a 12-inch skillet over medium, melt the coconut oil. Add the mustard seeds and cook, swirling the pan, until the seeds start to sizzle, about 30 seconds. Add the garam masala and turmeric and cook, stirring, until fragrant, about 30 seconds. Stir in the shredded coconut, onion, jalapeños, tomatoes and 2 teaspoons salt. Cook, stirring occasionally, until the liquid released by the tomatoes has almost evaporated and the onion is slightly softened, 7 to 10 minutes.

Stir in the spinach and cook until just beginning to wilt, 1 to 2 minutes. Pour in 1 cup water and bring to a simmer. Add the eggs and cook, stirring gently and occasionally, until the yolks begin to thicken the sauce and a spoon drawn through the mixture leaves a trail, 5 to 7 minutes. Off heat, stir in the cilantro. Taste and season with salt and pepper.

Smashed Potatoes

with Soft-Cooked Eggs and Mint (Yeralma Yumurta)

Start to finish: **30 minutes**

Servings: **4**

1 small red onion, quartered
and thinly sliced

2 tablespoons lemon juice, plus
lemon wedges to serve

Kosher salt and ground black pepper

6 large eggs

4 tablespoons extra-virgin olive oil,
divided, plus more to serve

1½ pounds Yukon Gold potatoes,
peeled and cut into ½-inch pieces

3 teaspoons ground sumac, divided

4 sheets lavash or 4 rounds pita
bread or naan (see note)

¼ cup chopped fresh mint, plus
½ cup lightly packed fresh mint, torn

Flaky salt, to serve (optional)

Yeralma yumurta, which translates simply as potato egg from the Azerbaijani language, is a popular street food in Tabriz, in northwestern Iran. Smashed potatoes and eggs are spread onto flatbread, which is rolled up for easy eating. For our version—inspired by a recipe from Naz Deravian's new cookbook, "Bottom of the Pot"—we soft-cook the eggs so the yolks stay moist and rich, and perk up the flavors and colors with lemon-pickled red onions, ground sumac and fresh mint. Thin, rectangular sheets of lavash are the best choice for bread, but if it's not available, use pita bread or naan instead; these types of bread are thicker than lavash and are especially good when warmed before topping.

Don't steam your eggs for longer than 9 minutes. Soft, barely set yolks add richness and a creamy texture to the dish. If you'd like your yolks very soft and rather runny, steam them for as little as 7 minutes. Don't mash the potatoes until smooth; leave them chunky so they add toothsome texture.

In a small bowl, stir together the onion, lemon juice and 1 teaspoon kosher salt. Set aside. Fill a large saucepan with about 1 inch of water. Place a folding steamer basket in the pan, cover and bring to a boil over medium-high.

Meanwhile, fill a medium bowl with ice water. Add the eggs to the steamer basket, cover and cook for 9 minutes. Immediately transfer the eggs to the ice water and let stand until cooled. Crack and peel the eggs, then cut each one lengthwise into 4 wedges.

While the eggs cook, in a 12-inch non-stick skillet over medium-high, heat 2 tablespoons of oil until shimmering. Add the potatoes in an even layer and cook, stirring once halfway through, until well browned, about 5 minutes. Reduce to medium and continue to cook, stirring frequently, until a knife inserted into the largest pieces meets no resistance, 5 to 10 minutes. Transfer to a medium bowl.

Using a potato masher or fork, roughly mash the potatoes with the remaining

2 tablespoons oil, 2 teaspoons of sumac, 1 teaspoon kosher salt and ½ teaspoon pepper; the mixture should remain quite chunky. Stir in the chopped mint. Taste and season with salt and pepper.

Spoon the potato mixture onto the bread, dividing it evenly. Place the egg wedges on top, then scatter over the torn mint and the pickled red onion. Sprinkle with additional kosher salt or flaky salt, if using, and the remaining 1 teaspoon sumac, then drizzle with additional oil.

No. 40

End the Cooking Early

Omelets are easily overcooked. To prevent this, we pull the pan off the heat when the curds are still slightly wet. The eggs finish cooking using just the residual heat in the pan.

Herbed Omelet
with Tomatoes and Blue Cheese

8 large eggs

1 tablespoon fresh thyme, finely chopped

Kosher salt and ground black pepper

3 tablespoons salted butter, divided

3 medium shallots, halved and thinly sliced

1 pint grape or cherry tomatoes, halved

2 ounces blue cheese, crumbled (½ cup)

2 tablespoons chopped fresh chives (½-inch pieces)

Sautéed shallots and tangy-sweet grape tomatoes fill this flavorful omelet, along with a scattering of rich, creamy blue cheese. If blue cheese is too funky for your taste, substitute an equal amount of feta cheese.

Don't be afraid *to use the tender tips of thyme sprigs. Though the woody parts of the stems are too tough and fibrous to chop (only the leaves attached to these stems are usable), the soft, flexible tips can be chopped with the leaves. Flowers are usable, too.*

In a medium bowl, whisk together the eggs, thyme and 1 teaspoon salt. In a nonstick 12-inch skillet over medium, melt 1 tablespoon of butter. Add the shallots, ½ teaspoon salt and ¾ teaspoon pepper. Cover and cook, stirring occasionally, until the shallots are lightly browned, about 5 minutes. Add the tomatoes and cook, uncovered and stirring occasionally, until the tomatoes have softened and started to brown, 5 to 7 minutes. Transfer to a small bowl and wipe out the pan.

In the same skillet over medium, melt the remaining 2 tablespoons butter, then swirl the pan to coat. Pour in the egg mixture and, using a silicone spatula, draw the edges toward the center and gently stir, working your way around the perimeter of the pan. Cook the eggs this way until they form soft, pillowy curds but are still runny enough to pool on the surface, 1 to 2 minutes. Spread the eggs in an even layer, then cover, remove from the heat and let stand until the omelet is set, about 5 minutes.

Run the spatula around the edge and under the omelet to loosen it, then slide it onto a plate. Scatter the tomato mixture over one half of the omelet, then top with the blue cheese and chives. Using the spatula, fold the omelet in half to enclose the filling. Cut the omelet into 4 wedges.

Zucchini and Goat Cheese Omelet

8 large eggs

Kosher salt and ground black pepper

3 tablespoons salted butter, divided

2 medium shallots, halved
and thinly sliced

1 medium zucchini (8 to 12 ounces),
quartered lengthwise, seedy core
removed, cut into ½-inch pieces

4 ounces fresh goat cheese (chèvre)

1 tablespoon finely chopped
fresh chives

3 tablespoons finely chopped
fresh flat-leaf parsley

In this simple omelet, lightly caramelized shallots and tender sautéed zucchini pair nicely with creamy, tangy fresh goat cheese. Rather than sprinkle crumbled goat cheese into the omelet, we mix it into the still-hot shallot-zucchini sauté so the cheese binds the filling and each bite is rich and flavorful.

Don't forget to remove the seedy core *from the zucchini, as the core turns soft and mushy when cooked. After cutting the zucchini lengthwise into quarters, use your knife to trim away the seedy section from each.*

In a medium bowl, whisk together the eggs and 1 teaspoon salt. In a non-stick 12-inch skillet over medium, melt 1 tablespoon of butter. Add the shallots and ½ teaspoon salt. Cover and cook, stirring occasionally, until lightly browned, about 5 minutes. Add the zucchini and cook, stirring often, until quite tender, 4 to 6 minutes. Transfer to a medium bowl and wipe out the pan. Add ½ teaspoon pepper and the goat cheese to the zucchini and stir until the cheese softens and the mixture is well combined; set aside.

In the same skillet over medium, melt the remaining 2 tablespoons butter, then swirl the pan to coat. Pour in the egg mixture and, using a silicone spatula, draw the edges toward the center and gently stir, working your way around the perimeter of the pan. Cook the eggs until they form soft, pillowy curds but are still runny enough to pool on the surface, 1 to 2 minutes. Spread the eggs in an even layer, then cover, remove from the heat and let stand until the omelet is set, about 5 minutes.

Run the spatula around the edge and under the omelet to loosen it, then slide it onto a plate. Spread the zucchini mixture over half of the omelet, then sprinkle with half of the chives and parsley. Using the spatula, fold the omelet in half to enclose the filling. Cut into 4 wedges, then sprinkle with the remaining chives and parsley.

Omelet with Mushrooms,
Mustard and Gruyère

8 large eggs

4 tablespoons finely chopped
fresh chives, divided

Kosher salt and ground black pepper

4 tablespoons (½ stick) salted
butter, divided

8 ounces cremini mushrooms,
trimmed and quartered

⅓ cup dry white wine

3 tablespoons whole-grain
Dijon mustard

4 ounces shredded Gruyère cheese
(1 cup packed)

Earthy cremini mushrooms, sautéed until lightly browned, are brightened with white wine and mustard. Gruyère cheese and fresh chives pair perfectly with the creminis, adding gooey richness and savory allium notes. A simple vinaigrette-dressed salad and warm crusty bread are ideal accompaniments.

Don't substitute smooth Dijon mustard *for whole-grain. Its stronger, sharper flavor will overwhelm the other ingredients, and its consistency will make the filling somewhat pasty and thick.*

In a medium bowl, whisk together the eggs, 2 tablespoons of chives and ½ teaspoon each salt and pepper. In a nonstick 12-inch skillet over medium, melt 2 tablespoons of butter. Add the mushrooms and cook, stirring occasionally, until well browned, 5 to 8 minutes. Stir in the wine and mustard, then cook, stirring, until the liquid has evaporated, about 2 minutes. Transfer to a small bowl and wipe out the skillet.

In the same skillet over medium, melt the remaining 2 tablespoons butter, then swirl the pan to coat. Pour in the egg mixture and, using a silicone spatula, draw the edges toward the center and gently stir, working your way around the perimeter of the pan. Cook the eggs this way until they form soft, pillowy curds but are still runny enough to pool on the surface of the pan, 1 to 2 minutes.

Spread the eggs in an even layer, then remove from the heat and sprinkle the cheese evenly over the eggs. Cover and let stand until the cheese is melted and the omelet is set, about 5 minutes. Run the spatula around the edge and under the omelet to loosen, then slide it onto a plate. Scatter the mushrooms over one half of the omelet. Using the spatula, fold the omelet in half to enclose the filling. Cut into 4 wedges, then sprinkle with the remaining 2 tablespoons chives.

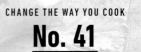

No. 41

Start on the Stovetop, Finish in the Oven

To ensure thicker flat omelets are perfectly done edge to edge, we start the cooking on the stovetop, then slide the pan into the oven, where the eggs finish cooking gently and evenly.

Southeast Asian-Style Mushroom
Omelet

Start to finish: **30 minutes, plus cooling**
Servings: **4**

8 large eggs

2 tablespoons chopped fresh cilantro, plus extra cilantro leaves, to serve

1 tablespoon chili-garlic sauce

1 teaspoon plus 1 tablespoon soy sauce, divided

3 tablespoons peanut oil

12 ounces fresh shiitake mushrooms, stemmed, caps finely chopped

2 teaspoons fish sauce

2 teaspoons white sugar

2 teaspoons finely grated fresh ginger

1 bunch scallions, finely chopped

Lime wedges, to serve

Made with a generous amount of mushrooms and seasoned with both soy sauce and fish sauce, this frittata-like omelet is so full of rich umami flavor you'll find it hard to believe it's meatless. Serve hot or at room temperature, with steamed jasmine rice.

Don't use a conventional skillet. *A nonstick pan is key to allow the omelet to easily slide out. Also, make sure the skillet, including its handle, is oven-safe, as the omelet finishes cooking in the oven at 400°F.*

Heat the oven to 400°F with a rack in the upper-middle position. In a medium bowl, beat the eggs, chopped cilantro, chili-garlic sauce and 1 teaspoon soy sauce. In an oven-safe nonstick 12-inch skillet over medium-high, heat the oil until shimmering. Add the mushrooms and cook, stirring frequently, until tender, 3 to 5 minutes. Stir in the remaining 1 tablespoon soy sauce, the fish sauce, sugar and ginger, then cook, stirring, until fragrant, 30 to 60 seconds. Add the scallions and cook, stirring, until fragrant, about 30 seconds.

Pour the egg mixture into the pan and cook, using a silicone spatula to stir from the edges to the center and evenly distribute the mushroom mixture in the pan, until soft curds form and the egg is no longer runny, about 2 minutes. Using the spatula, spread in an even layer, then transfer the skillet to the oven and bake until the surface is just set, 3 to 5 minutes.

Set the skillet on a wire rack and let cool for 5 minutes. Run the spatula around the edge and under the omelet to loosen, then slide the omelet onto a cutting board. Cut into 8 wedges and transfer to a serving platter. Serve with cilantro leaves and lime wedges.

Spanish Tortilla
with Roasted Red Peppers

Start to finish: **50 minutes**
(20 minutes active)
Servings: **4**

8 large eggs

¾ teaspoon smoked paprika

Kosher salt and ground black pepper

4 tablespoons extra-virgin olive oil, divided

1 medium yellow onion, chopped

1½ pounds Yukon Gold potatoes, peeled, halved if large, and sliced ¼ inch thick

1 cup drained roasted red peppers, patted dry and chopped

In Spain, a tortilla is a thick, hearty, frittata-like omelet made with potatoes, onions and plenty of olive oil. We whisk a little smoked paprika into the eggs, and also add some roasted red peppers for pops of color. If you prefer to stick with the simple and classic version, simply omit the paprika and peppers. And for an added Spanish touch, serve with aioli (garlicky mayonnaise) on the side. This recipe starts on the stovetop but finishes in the oven, so you will need an oven-safe nonstick 10-inch skillet.

Don't slice the potatoes thicker than ¼ inch or they may not cook through. Also, don't forget to pat the roasted red peppers dry before chopping. Excess moisture from the peppers can make the tortilla watery. Finally, don't forget that the skillet handle will be hot when you remove the pan from the oven.

Heat the oven to 350°F with a rack in the middle position. In a large bowl, whisk together the eggs, paprika and 1½ teaspoons salt. In an oven-safe nonstick 10-inch skillet over medium, heat 3 tablespoons of oil until shimmering. Stir in the onion, potatoes, 2 teaspoons salt and ½ teaspoon pepper. Cover and cook, stirring occasionally, until a fork inserted into the potatoes meets no resistance, 10 to 12 minutes. Stir in the roasted red peppers and cook, stirring, until the peppers are heated through, 1 to 2 minutes.

Fold the hot vegetables into the eggs, separating any potato slices that stick together. Add the remaining 1 tablespoon oil to the same skillet and heat over medium until shimmering. Pour in the egg-potato mixture and distribute in an even layer. Transfer to the oven and bake until the tortilla is set at the center, 25 to 30 minutes.

Transfer the pan to a wire rack (the handle will be hot) and let cool for about 10 minutes. Run a silicone spatula around the edge and under the tortilla to loosen it, then invert a large plate over the skillet. Invert both the skillet and plate, holding them together, then lift off the skillet. Serve the tortilla warm or at room temperature.

Baked Persian Cauliflower Omelet

1 tablespoon grapeseed
or other neutral oil

1 medium yellow onion, chopped

3 medium garlic cloves, finely chopped

1 small (about 2-pound) head
cauliflower, trimmed, cored and cut
into 1-inch florets

1 tablespoon all-purpose flour

2 teaspoons ground turmeric

2 teaspoons sweet paprika

1 teaspoon baking powder

¾ teaspoon dried mint

Kosher salt and ground black pepper

5 large eggs

1 teaspoon grated lemon zest

Kuku is a Persian frittata that's customarily flavored with an abundance of fresh herbs. In this version, we add sweet, buttery cauliflower, along with onion and garlic. A few earthy spices add depth of flavor and lemon zest keeps things bright. A small amount of flour helps keep the eggs tender, and baking powder provides lift. This is best served warm or at room temperature.

Don't add the flour *directly to the eggs; it will clump. Mixing it first with the seasonings will allow easy incorporation. When removing the skillet from the oven, don't forget that the handle will be hot.*

Heat the oven to 350°F with a rack in the middle position. In an oven-safe 10-inch nonstick skillet over medium, heat the oil until shimmering. Add the onion and garlic and cook, stirring occasionally, until the onion begins to soften, 3 to 5 minutes. Stir in the cauliflower and 2 tablespoons water, then cover and cook, stirring once or twice, until the cauliflower begins to soften, about 5 minutes.

Uncover and continue to cook, stirring once or twice, until the vegetables are lightly browned and a skewer inserted at the stem of the largest cauliflower floret meets only slight resistance, 3 to 5 minutes. Transfer to a medium bowl and set aside; reserve the pan.

In another medium bowl, whisk together the flour, turmeric, paprika, baking powder, mint, 2 teaspoons salt and 1 teaspoon pepper. Whisk in the eggs and lemon zest. Add to the still-warm vegetables and fold well with a silicone spatula. Pour into the skillet and distribute in an even layer. Bake until the eggs are set on top, about 30 minutes.

Carefully remove the pan from the oven (the handle will be hot). Run the spatula around the edge and under the omelet to loosen, then slide onto a serving plate. Serve warm or at room temperature.

PERSIAN GREEN BEAN OMELET WITH FETA

Heat the oven to 350°F with a rack in the middle position. In a 10-inch oven-safe nonstick skillet over medium, heat **1 tablespoon grapeseed or other neutral oil** until shimmering. Add the white parts from **1 bunch scallions** (thinly slice both white and green parts but reserve separately) and **3 medium garlic cloves** (finely chopped). Cook, stirring, until the scallions are softened, 1 to 2 minutes. Stir in **8 ounces green beans** (trimmed and cut into 1-inch pieces), 3 tablespoons water and ¼ teaspoon kosher salt. Cover and cook, stirring once or twice, until the beans begin to soften, 5 to 7 minutes. Uncover and cook, stirring, until the beans are crisp-tender, another 2 to 3 minutes. Transfer to a

plate and set aside; reserve the pan. In a small bowl, whisk together **1 tablespoon all-purpose flour, 1 teaspoon baking powder,** 1 teaspoon kosher salt and ¼ teaspoon ground black pepper. In a medium bowl, whisk **5 large eggs** and **¼ teaspoon saffron threads (crumbled)** until the saffron is evenly distributed, then whisk in the flour mixture and scallion greens. Add the egg mixture to the still-warm green beans and fold well with a silicone spatula. Pour into the skillet and distribute evenly. Sprinkle with **¼ cup crumbled feta cheese** and bake until the eggs are set on top, 15 to 20 minutes. Carefully remove the pan from the oven. Run the spatula around the edge and under the omelet to loosen, then slide onto a serving plate. Serve warm or at room temperature.

CHANGE THE WAY YOU COOK

No. 42

For Lighter Eggs, Borrow a Baking Ingredient

Baking powder can help lighten baked frittatas. Just as it does in traditional baking, the baking powder reacts with the heat of the oven to form carbon dioxide gas— or bubbles—that adds air to the frittata's structure.

RECIPES & RULES

SEAFOOD

At Milk Street, we cook delicate white fish in **gentle heat to preserve moistness and tenderness.** We **use sharp aromatics and bold spices to provide a punchy counterpoint** to mild flavors. And we do a **one-sided sear** to boost texture and flavor without overcooking.

Fast-cooking and packed with protein, seafood has plenty going for it as a weeknight staple. Except appeal. We probably were fed too many limp fish sticks as children or suffered through too many bland restaurant haddock fillets. And it doesn't help that seafood is particularly easy to overcook, making it rubbery and dry. The good news is there are easy solutions for nailing flawless cooking and fresh flavor.

To preserve the delicate texture of fish, **we cook with the gentle heat of steam and serve it with aromatic seasonings for flavorful contrast.** In our steamed fish with shiitake mushrooms, we pair perfectly steamed white fish with the fiery sweetness of Sriracha. We take the same approach with mussels, steaming them gently in residual heat and pairing them with spicy harissa.

We love well-seared seafood, and a good way to get it without overcooking is to **sear on just one side.** The fish or shellfish cooks undisturbed until a golden crust forms, then we turn off the burner and let residual heat finish the cooking. We use this technique in numerous recipes, including our Mexican shrimp in garlic sauce, our pan-seared halibut with spicy mint-lemon sauce and pan-seared salmon with red chili walnut sauce.

Pairing fish and assertive flavors like garlic requires a delicate touch. The sauce we use in our Mexican shrimp is rich and garlicky but **we soften the bite of raw garlic by first soaking it in lime juice.**

Stews are a satisfying, simple and flavorful way to cook seafood, but the small chunks of fish typically called for easily overcook. So we **use whole, thick fillets for easier control over cooking,** then break them up in the liquid just before serving. We do this in a Korean-style dish that flavors everything with spicy gochujang paste, as well as in Brazilian moqueca, which uses coconut milk, not heavy dairy cream, to add body and richness without masking spices and herbs.

Shrimp can be particularly easy to overcook. So in our shrimp satay, we marinate them in a sauce that promotes browning. This way we get bold caramelization on the outside before overcooking the insides.

And **since acidic marinades can toughen the texture of raw seafood, we wait until after cooking to season** our Italian-style swordfish steaks with a sweet-and-sour vinegar sauce.

No. 43

Cook Gentle, Season Strong

A gentle, even heat is best for keeping the delicate flesh of fish tender. Steaming is ideal because the heat surrounds the fish, cooking it from all sides without movement. We add an aromatic sauce to complement the mild fish.

Steamed Fish
with Shiitake Mushrooms

3 tablespoons oyster sauce

1 tablespoon Sriracha

1 tablespoon grapeseed or other neutral oil

8 medium garlic cloves, finely grated

1 tablespoon finely grated fresh ginger

3 tablespoons soy sauce, divided

Kosher salt and ground black pepper

Four 6-ounce skinless cod, haddock or halibut fillets (each about 1 inch thick)

8 ounces shiitake mushrooms, stemmed and thinly sliced

2 tablespoons unseasoned rice vinegar

1 tablespoon packed light or dark brown sugar

2 scallions, thinly sliced

Lean white fish is mild in flavor, so before steaming the fillets we season them boldly with garlic, ginger, oyster sauce and fiery-sweet Sriracha. For a little spice, drizzle the plated fish fillets with chili oil before sprinkling with the scallions. Or sprinkle with toasted sesame seeds. Serve with steamed or stir-fried greens and jasmine rice.

Don't uncover the pot *before 8 minutes of steaming has elapsed. Opening the lid releases steam and cools the pot.*

In a shallow bowl or pie plate, whisk together the oyster sauce, Sriracha sauce, oil, garlic, ginger, 2 tablespoons of soy sauce and ½ teaspoon each salt and pepper. Add the fillets and turn to coat, gently rubbing in the sauce. Add the mushrooms and toss until evenly coated. Marinate at room temperature for about 10 minutes.

Place a steamer basket in a large Dutch oven. Add enough water to fill the bottom of the pot without touching the basket. Remove the basket. Cover the pot and bring to a simmer over medium-high.

Meanwhile, mist the steamer basket with cooking spray. Arrange the fish in an even layer in the basket and top the fillets with the mushrooms, evenly arranging them. Return the basket to the pot, cover and steam over medium until the fish flakes easily, 8 to 12 minutes.

Meanwhile, in a small bowl, stir together the vinegar, sugar, the remaining 1 tablespoon soy sauce and ¼ cup water. When the fish is done, use a thin metal spatula to transfer the fillets and mushrooms to a platter. Sprinkle with the scallions and serve with the sauce on the side.

Steamed Mussels
with Harissa and Herbs

4 tablespoons (½ stick) salted
butter, divided

1 medium yellow onion, halved
and thinly sliced

6 medium garlic cloves, peeled
and thinly sliced

Kosher salt and ground black pepper

¼ cup harissa paste, plus more
to serve

15½-ounce can chickpeas,
rinsed and drained

½ cup dry white wine

1 teaspoon honey

3 pounds mussels, scrubbed

½ cup chopped fresh dill

½ cup chopped fresh cilantro

Cooking shellfish such as mussels and clams can seem like a bit of a project—most of us overcook them, then are disappointed when they turn out tough and flavorless. Our solution is to start with boiling liquid, but quickly turn off the heat, letting the gentler residual heat finish the cooking. We season the broth with earthy, spicy harissa balanced with a bit of honey to complement the briny mussels, then finish them with a generous amount of herbs for fresh flavor and color. Chickpeas make the dish more substantial and satisfying. Serve with warmed crusty bread for soaking up the delicious broth.

Don't forget to turn off the heat *as soon as the mussels begin to open. Cover the pot right away and allow the mussels to gently finish cooking in the residual heat. As you transfer the mussels to a serving bowl, discard any that haven't opened.*

In a large Dutch oven over medium, melt 2 tablespoons of butter. Add the onion, garlic, 1 teaspoon salt and ½ teaspoon pepper. Cook, stirring frequently, until the onion is golden brown, 5 to 8 minutes. Add the harissa and cook, stirring, until the paste begins to brown, about 1 minute.

Stir in the chickpeas, wine, honey and ½ cup water. Bring to a boil over medium-high, then stir in the mussels and return to a boil. Cover and cook just until the mussels begin to open, 2 to 3 minutes. Remove from the heat and let stand, covered, until the mussels fully open, 3 to 5 minutes, quickly stirring halfway through.

Using a slotted spoon, transfer the mussels to a serving bowl, discarding any that did not open. Bring the cooking liquid to a boil over medium-high, then stir in the remaining 2 tablespoons butter. Taste and season with salt and pepper. Off heat, stir in half of the dill and cilantro, then pour over the mussels. Sprinkle with the remaining herbs and serve with additional harissa.

No. 44

Stick with Single-Sided Searing

Fish and shellfish can quickly overcook. This makes it a challenge to develop a crisp, flavorful crust. So we sear seafood on just one side, then finish cooking off the burner with just residual heat.

Shrimp with Kerkennaise Sauce

Start to finish: **35 minutes**
(15 minutes active)
Servings: **4**

2 plum tomatoes, cored and cut into large chunks

1 Fresno chili, stemmed, quartered and seeded

1 medium garlic clove, smashed and peeled

½ teaspoon ground coriander

½ teaspoon caraway seed, coarsely ground

2 tablespoons white wine vinegar

3 scallions, white parts cut into 1-inch pieces, greens thinly sliced, reserved separately

¼ cup lightly packed fresh flat-leaf parsley, finely chopped

⅓ cup pitted green olives, chopped

1 tablespoon tomato paste

Kosher salt and ground black pepper

4 tablespoons grapeseed or other neutral oil, divided

1½ pounds extra-large (21/25 per pound) shrimp, peeled (tails left on), deveined and patted dry

On the Kerkennah Islands off the coast of Tunisia, seafood often is paired with sauce Kerkennaise, a spiced tomato sauce with subtle chili heat. The caraway seeds can be ground in a spice grinder, with a mortar and pestle, or even just chopped with a chef's knife. If you prefer a milder sauce, use just half of a seeded Fresno chili; if you like it hot and fiery, leave in all of the seeds. The sauce tastes best after the flavors have had a chance to mingle for about 20 minutes.

Don't forget to pat the shrimp dry *with paper towels. Removing as much moisture as possible helps ensure deep browning and reduces splatter.*

In a food processor, combine the tomatoes, chili, garlic, coriander, caraway, vinegar and the scallion whites. Pulse until finely chopped, about 10 pulses. Transfer to a small bowl and stir in the scallion greens, parsley, olives, tomato paste and 2 tablespoons of oil. Set aside at room temperature for about 20 minutes. Taste and season with salt and pepper.

Season the shrimp with ½ teaspoon each salt and pepper. In a 12-inch nonstick skillet over medium-high, heat 1 tablespoon of the remaining oil until barely smoking. Add half of the shrimp in an even layer and cook without stirring until deep golden brown, about 2 minutes. Stir, remove the pan from the heat and continue stirring, allowing the pan's residual heat to finish the cooking, until the shrimp are opaque on both sides, another 20 to 30 seconds. Transfer to a serving dish. Repeat with the remaining 1 tablespoon oil and the remaining shrimp. Spoon the sauce over the shrimp or serve the sauce on the side.

Pan-Seared Salmon
with Red Chili-Walnut Sauce

1 teaspoon ground coriander

½ teaspoon dry mustard

½ teaspoon fennel seeds, crushed

Kosher salt

Four 6-ounce skin-on center-cut salmon fillets (each 1 to 1¼ inches thick), patted dry

¼ cup walnuts

2 Fresno chilies, stemmed and quartered

2 medium garlic cloves, peeled

1 plum tomato, cored and quartered

¼ cup drained roasted red bell peppers, patted dry

1 tablespoon grapeseed or other neutral oil

In the country of Georgia, pepper-based pastes known as adjika are slathered on roasted meats and sometimes vegetables to punch up both flavor and color. Red adjika may be made from garlic, chilies, spices, tomato and walnuts. Green varieties start with handfuls of herbs, most often mint. We like the pastes as a way to balance the richness of well-seared fish. We use a sauce based on red adjika for our pan-seared salmon and a green adjika for halibut, (see recipe p. 181). Heating a skillet over medium-high, then lowering the temperature once the salmon is in the pan ensures a nice sear without the risk of scorching. Finishing the cooking off heat, using just the pan's residual heat, ensures the fish stays moist and won't overcook. Try to purchase fillets of the same thickness so they cook at the same rate.

Don't place the salmon in the skillet with the skin facing down. Make sure they go in flesh side down, and don't fuss with them once they're in. Cooking them undisturbed allows the fish to develop flavorful browning.

In a small bowl, whisk together the coriander, mustard, fennel and 2 teaspoons salt. Season the flesh side of the salmon fillets with 2 teaspoons of the spice mixture and set aside.

In a food processor, combine the remaining spice mixture, the walnuts, chilies, garlic, tomato and roasted peppers. Pulse until the mixture is finely chopped, 10 to 15 pulses, scraping down the bowl as needed.

In a nonstick 12-inch skillet over medium-high, heat the oil until shimmering. Place the salmon flesh side down in the pan, then immediately reduce to medium. Cook, undisturbed, until golden brown, 4 to 6 minutes. Using a wide metal spatula, carefully flip the fillets, then cover the pan and remove from the heat. Let stand until the thickest part of the fillets reach 120°F or are nearly opaque when cut into, about another 5 minutes for 1-inch-thick fillets or about 8 min-utes if 1¼ inches thick. Transfer the salmon to a platter.

Return the skillet to medium-high and add the walnut-chili puree. Cook, stirring often, until the liquid released by the puree has evaporated and the sauce is thick, 2 to 3 minutes. Spoon about 1 tablespoon of the sauce on top of each fillet, then serve with the remaining sauce on the side.

USE CHILIES FOR MORE THAN HEAT

How to Harness the Smoky, Spicy, Sweet and Savory Flavors of Dried Chilies

Beyond basic heat, dried chilies also add deep, complex flavors reminiscent of dried fruits, bittersweet chocolate, red wine, warm spices and smoke. They do require some preparation before use; we often toast them to enhance flavor. First, remove the chili stems and shake out the seeds. The pods can be left whole or torn into pieces, then toasted in a dry skillet or in a moderately hot oven just until fragrant and beginning to darken; don't allow them to scorch. At this point, the chilies can either be ground to a powder in a spice grinder or soaked in hot water to soften and puree. Here are suggested uses and recipes for the varieties we use most.

ANCHO

Earthy and warm, ancho chilies taste of dried fruits, red wine and bittersweet chocolate. The dried version of ripe poblanos, anchos are perfect with rich braised meats or creamy pinto beans. Use them in chili con carne, or in our simple salsa roja that can be used as a marinade for meats, as a drizzle for tacos or quesadillas, or as a dip for tortilla chips.

Ancho Chili Salsa Roja

In a microwave-safe bowl, combine **3 medium ancho chilies** (stemmed, seeded, torn into pieces and toasted), with enough hot water to cover. Microwave on high until the chilies are slightly softened, 1 to 2 minutes. Let stand until fully softened, about 5 minutes, then drain. In a food processor or blender, combine the drained chilies, **1 large garlic clove** (smashed and peeled), **1 medium shallot** (roughly chopped), **1 medium vine-ripened tomato** (cored and roughly chopped), 1 teaspoon kosher salt, **2 teaspoons white sugar** and ½ cup water. Process until finely chopped and well combined, scraping the sides as necessary, about 20 seconds.

ÁRBOL

Árbols can pack a real wallop of bright, bracing heat. We use them whole to add subtle heat and chili flavor to dishes. Or for direct spiciness, we break them into pieces and use as we would red pepper flakes. Process them with peanuts and salt for a spicy spread for toast drizzled with honey. Grind to a powder and use instead of cayenne pepper (they are related). Or make our fiery chili sauce, then toss a little of it with cooked rice; brush some onto seared or grilled fish, chicken or pork. Add to vinaigrettes to dress starchy salads, such as bean or potato. Keep in mind that a little goes a long way.

Chili de Árbol Sauce

In a microwave-safe bowl, combine **16 árbol chilies** (stemmed, seeded, torn into pieces and toasted), with enough hot water to cover. Microwave on high until the chilies are slightly softened, 1 to 2 minutes. Let stand until fully softened, about 5 minutes, then drain. In a blender, combine the drained chilies, **½ cup grapeseed or other neutral oil**, ¼ teaspoon kosher salt and **¼ teaspoon white sugar**. Pulse until only small pieces of chili remain, about 10 pulses.

CALIFORNIA

The ripe and dried version of fresh green Anaheim chilies, Californias have a light, bright flavor reminiscent of golden raisins and red peppers. When toasted and ground to powder, they can be used in place of mildly spicy paprika. Or use them to add complexity to a salsa like our chunky fresh salsa for tacos, burritos and nachos.

Chunky Fresh Salsa with California Chilies

In a microwave-safe bowl, **combine 6 California chilies** (stemmed, seeded, cut into ⅛- to ¼-inch pieces and toasted) with enough hot water to cover. Microwave on high until the chilies are slightly softened, 1 to 2 minutes. Let stand until fully softened, about 5 minutes, then drain. In a medium bowl, combine the drained chilies, **2 medium tomatoes** (cored and chopped), **1 small white onion** (finely chopped), **1½ cups lightly packed fresh cilantro** (chopped), 2 teaspoons kosher salt and **2 tablespoons lime juice.**

GUAJILLO

Fruity, bright and moderately hot, guajillo chilies pair well with tomatoes and balance the earthier flavors of New Mexico or ancho chilies. Blend them into pasta sauces, or puree them with peanuts to spoon over grilled meats, or serve as a dip for grilled vegetables.

Peanut-Guajillo Sauce

In a microwave-safe bowl, combine **4 guajillo chilies** (stemmed, seeded, torn and toasted) with enough hot water to cover. Microwave on high until the chilies are slightly softened, 1 to 2 minutes. Let stand until fully softened, about 5 minutes, then drain. In a blender, combine the drained chilies, **2 medium garlic cloves** (smashed and peeled), **¾ cup roasted unsalted peanuts, 2 tablespoons extra-virgin olive oil, 2 teaspoons white sugar, 1 tablespoon lime juice,** 2 teaspoons kosher salt and 1 cup water. Puree until smooth, scraping the sides as needed, 1 to 2 minutes. Add **2 tablespoons fresh oregano** and pulse until roughly chopped, 2 to 3 pulses.

CHIPOTLE

Chipotle chilies are dried smoked jalapeños. Their assertive heat, smokiness and deep flavor notes make them good additions to dark sauces, such as mole negro, as well as hearty soups, meaty stews and bean dishes. We use dried chipotles to prepare homemade chipotles in adobo sauce, our fresher, more flavorful take on the canned version.

Smoky Chipotle Chili Sauce

In a 12-inch skillet over medium, toast **8 chipotle chilies** (stemmed, seeded, torn into pieces) and **4 large garlic cloves** (unpeeled) until fragrant and the garlic skins are blackened in spots, 2 to 4 minutes. Remove the garlic cloves and set aside. Transfer the chilies to a medium bowl and add enough boiling water to cover, then let stand until the chilies are softened, about 10 minutes. Drain the chilies and peel the garlic, then add both to a blender along with **½ cup chopped drained roasted red bell peppers, 2 teaspoons dark brown sugar,** ½ teaspoon kosher salt and ½ cup water. Puree until completely smooth, scraping the sides as needed, 1 to 2 minutes.

NEW MEXICO

On the sweet side and slightly earthy, these brick-red chilies have a subtle dried cherry flavor and moderate heat. They are used widely in Southwestern cooking, most famously in the braised pork dish carne adovada. They pair equally well with beef, in sauces or salsas and can enhance a pot of pinto beans. They also can be substituted for similarly mild California chilies, as in our chunky salsa.

Pan-Seared Halibut
with Spicy Mint-Lemon Sauce

Start to finish: **25 minutes**
Servings: **4**

4 cups lightly packed fresh mint

4 serrano chilies, stemmed, seeded and quartered

2 medium garlic cloves, smashed and peeled

1 teaspoon honey

1 teaspoon ground coriander

Kosher salt

1 tablespoon grated lemon zest, plus 2 tablespoons lemon juice

¼ cup extra-virgin olive oil

Four 6-ounce skinless halibut fillets (each ¾ to 1 inch thick), patted dry

1 tablespoon grapeseed or other neutral oil

Lean, mild-tasting halibut is a blank canvas for a sauce inspired by Georgian green adjika, a garlicky chili-herb condiment. The freshness of the mint and lemon and the fruitiness of the olive oil give the dish richness without overwhelming the halibut's delicate flavor.

Don't fuss with the halibut fillets once they're in the skillet. Allow them to cook undisturbed so they develop a deep, golden-brown crust. And while the fillets finish cooking in the residual heat, keep the pan covered for at least a full 2 minutes to prevent loss of heat.

In a food processor, combine the mint, chilies, garlic, honey, coriander and 1 tablespoon salt. Process until finely chopped, 1 to 2 minutes, scraping the bowl as needed. Transfer to a small bowl and stir in the lemon zest and juice and the olive oil; set aside.

Season the halibut fillets on all sides with salt. In a nonstick 12-inch skillet over medium-high, heat the grapeseed oil until shimmering. Place the fillets in the pan, then immediately reduce to medium. Cook, undisturbed, until golden brown, 5 to 8 minutes. Using a wide metal spatula, carefully flip the fillets, then cover the pan and remove from the heat. Let stand until the thickest parts of the fillets reach 115°F to 120°F, or are almost opaque when cut into, another 2 to 4 minutes.

Transfer the fillets to a platter and spoon about 1 tablespoon of the sauce on top of each. Serve with the remaining sauce on the side.

SEAFOOD   181

Tame Garlic with an Acid Touch

Briefly soaking garlic in an acid, such as lime juice, tames its bite and mellows its pungency without sacrificing flavor.

Mexican Shrimp in Garlic Sauce
(Camarones al Mojo de Ajo)

Start to finish: **30 minutes**
Servings: **4**

1½ pounds extra-large (21/25 per pound) shrimp, peeled (tails left on), deveined and patted dry

Kosher salt and ground black pepper

10 medium garlic cloves, finely chopped

2 tablespoons lime juice

3 tablespoons grapeseed or other neutral oil, divided

1 small jalapeño chili, stemmed, seeded and finely chopped

¼ cup lightly packed fresh cilantro, finely chopped

2 tablespoons salted butter, cut into 2 pieces

There are many versions of this coastal Mexican dish, but its defining characteristics are a bold use of garlic and a bright citrus flavor. Though traditional recipes may require roasting or slow-cooking whole heads of garlic, we first mellow the allium's pungency by steeping it in lime juice for a few minutes. We then coax out its sweet, nutty notes by gently pan-frying it in a little oil. A knob of butter—also traditional—tossed in at the end balances the garlic and lime and creates a silky sauce that clings lightly to the shrimp. Rice is classic accompaniment, but crusty bread is delicious, too.

Don't add the garlic–lime juice mixture without first allowing the skillet to cool for about 5 minutes. This will prevent splattering and help ensure that the garlic browns evenly without scorching.

Season the shrimp with ½ teaspoon each salt and pepper. In a small bowl, stir together the garlic and lime juice; set aside. In a nonstick 12-inch skillet over medium-high, heat 1 tablespoon of oil until barely smoking. Add half the shrimp in an even layer and cook without stirring until deep golden brown, about 2 minutes. Stir, remove the pan from the heat and continue stirring, allowing the pan's residual heat to finish the cooking, until the shrimp are opaque on both sides, another 20 to 30 seconds.

Transfer to a medium bowl. Repeat with 1 tablespoon of the remaining oil and the remaining shrimp, adding them to the first batch.

Allow the empty skillet to cool for about 5 minutes, then add the remaining 1 tablespoon oil, the garlic-lime mixture and ½ teaspoon salt. Set the pan over medium-low and cook, stirring frequently and scraping up any browned bits, until the garlic is softened and golden brown, about 5 minutes.

Add the jalapeño and any accumulated shrimp juices, then cook until the chili is softened, 1 to 2 minutes. Taste and season with salt and pepper. Off heat, add the shrimp, cilantro and butter, then stir until the butter has melted and mixed into the sauce.

Spicy Korean-Style Fish Stew

Four 6-ounce skinless cod fillets

2 tablespoons sake

3 tablespoons soy sauce, divided

Kosher salt and ground black pepper

1 tablespoon grapeseed or other neutral oil

1 bunch scallions, white parts finely chopped, green parts thinly sliced on the diagonal, reserved separately

6 medium garlic cloves, minced

2 teaspoons minced fresh ginger

¼ cup gochujang

4 ounces shiitake mushrooms, stemmed and thinly sliced

8 ounces daikon radish, peeled, halved lengthwise and sliced ¼-inch thick

3 cups low-sodium chicken broth

4 ounces baby spinach (about 4 cups lightly packed)

1½ teaspoons toasted sesame oil

Korean maeuntang usually is made with anchovy stock, chrysanthemum greens and bone-in chunks of fish. And it's typically brought to the table simmering in a wide, shallow pot. Our simplified version uses store-bought broth, baby spinach and cod fillets, all cooked in a Dutch oven. It still gets fiery notes and lots of umami from gochujang, a Korean fermented chili paste. Soy sauce, sesame oil and plenty of garlic and ginger round out the flavors. Serve with steamed white rice.

Don't worry *that the chicken broth will make the stew taste like chicken. The soy sauce, gochujang and other high-impact flavorings will cover any poultry notes.*

In a medium bowl, combine the cod with the sake, 1 tablespoon of soy sauce and ½ teaspoon pepper. Turn to coat on all sides, then set aside at room temperature until ready to use.

In a large Dutch oven over medium, combine the grapeseed oil, scallion whites, garlic and ginger. Cook, stirring occasionally, until beginning to soften, about 5 minutes. Stir in the gochujang and remaining 2 tablespoons soy sauce, then stir in the mushrooms, daikon, broth and 1 cup water. Bring to a simmer, then reduce to medium-low and cook, uncovered and stirring occasionally, until the radish is almost tender, about 10 minutes.

Add the fish with its marinade. Bring to a gentle simmer and cook for about 5 minutes. Stir in the spinach and continue to cook until the fish is opaque throughout and flakes easily with a fork, about another 3 minutes. Stir in the sesame oil, breaking the fish into chunks as you stir. Taste and season with salt and pepper. Ladle the stew into bowls and top each serving with scallion greens.

No. 46

For Tender Fish Stews, Think Big

Small chunks of fish are easy to overcook, turning them dry and tasteless. So when making fish stew, we use thick fillets and leave them whole so we can better control their rate of cooking.

Brazilian Fish Stew
(Moqueca)

2 tablespoons coconut oil, preferably unrefined

1 medium yellow onion, halved and thinly sliced

1 medium yellow, red or orange bell pepper, stemmed, seeded and thinly sliced

1 serrano chili, stemmed and sliced into thin rounds

4 medium garlic cloves, minced, divided

¾ teaspoon sweet paprika

14½-ounce can diced tomatoes, drained

Kosher salt and ground black pepper

Four 6-ounce skinless cod fillets

1 tablespoon grated lime zest, plus 2 tablespoons lime juice, plus more juice if needed

8-ounce bottle clam juice

1 cup coconut milk

14-ounce can diced hearts of palm, drained and diced

½ cup roughly chopped fresh cilantro

In Brazil, the fish stew called moqueca traditionally is made with red palm oil, which lends the dish an orange-red hue. We opted for easier-to-find coconut oil that reinforces the flavor of the coconut milk, and we give the broth some color with sweet paprika. By poaching large pieces of cod, it's easier to keep the fish from overcooking. When you stir in the cilantro at the end, simply break the fish into smaller bits. Any type of boneless, skinless firm white fish works well in this recipe, but if the fillets are thin, they will cook more quickly than cod, so make sure to adjust the timing accordingly. Serve with steamed rice.

Don't marinate the cod *for more than 20 minutes in the lime juice or the acid will degrade the texture of the fish.*

In a Dutch oven, heat the coconut oil over medium until shimmering. Add the onion, bell pepper and chili, then cook, stirring occasionally, until the vegetables begin to soften, about 10 minutes. Stir in half the garlic, the paprika, tomatoes and 1 teaspoon salt. Cook, stirring occasionally, for about 5 minutes.

Meanwhile, in a medium bowl, combine the fish, lime zest and juice, the remaining garlic, 1 teaspoon salt and ½ teaspoon pepper. Turn to coat on all sides, then set aside at room temperature until ready to use.

Add the clam juice, coconut milk and ½ cup water to the pot. Bring to a simmer, then cook for about 10 minutes. Stir in the hearts of palm and the fish with its marinade. Bring to a gentle simmer and

cook for about 5 minutes. Gently flip the fish and continue to cook until the fish is opaque throughout and flakes easily with a fork, about another 3 minutes.

Remove from the heat and stir in the cilantro, breaking the fish into chunks as you stir. Taste and season with salt, pepper and lime juice.

No. 47

Use Marinades to Help Brown Shrimp

Shrimp tend to overcook on the inside before the outside has time to develop flavorful browning and caramelization, especially when grilling. To help with this, we briefly marinate shrimp in ingredients that speed browning, such as sugar and fat.

Grilled Shrimp Satay

½ cup roasted cashews, plus 2 tablespoons finely chopped roasted cashews

5 tablespoons coconut milk, divided

1 ounce fresh ginger, peeled and roughly chopped

4 medium garlic cloves, smashed and peeled

1 tablespoon grated lime zest

2 serrano chilies, stemmed, halved and seeded, divided

3 tablespoons packed light or dark brown sugar, divided

4 teaspoons fish sauce, divided

1½ pounds extra-large (21/25 per pound) shrimp, peeled and deveined, tails left on

2 medium shallots, finely chopped

½ cup unseasoned rice vinegar

There are myriad versions of Southeast Asian satay, or grilled skewers of seasoned meats or seafood. This is our simplified version of Singapore-style shrimp satay. A fragrant blend of cashews and coconut milk gives the shrimp richness and cloaks them with bold flavor. The shallot-vinegar dipping sauce is a perfect accent.

Don't use shrimp smaller than the size specified. *They will overcook before they have a chance to take on the flavorful char that is a hallmark of satay. And don't use light coconut milk. The fat from regular coconut milk is needed for flavor.*

In a food processor, combine the ½ cup cashews and 3 tablespoons of coconut milk. Process until almost smooth, about 1 minute, scraping the bowl as needed. Add the ginger, garlic, lime zest, 2 chili halves, 1 tablespoon of sugar and 2 teaspoons fish sauce; process until finely chopped, 1 to 2 minutes. Transfer to a medium bowl. Add the shrimp, rubbing to coat them thoroughly. Marinate at room temperature while you make the sauce and prepare the grill.

Thinly slice the remaining 2 chili halves and add to a small bowl along with with the remaining 2 tablespoons sugar, the remaining 2 teaspoons fish sauce, the shallots and vinegar. Stir until the sugar dissolves; set aside.

Prepare a charcoal or gas grill for high-heat cooking. For a charcoal grill, ignite a large chimney of coals, let burn until lightly ashed over, then distribute evenly over one side of the grill bed; open the bottom grill vents. Heat the grill, covered, for 5 to 10 minutes, then clean and oil the grate. For a gas grill, turn all burners to high and heat, covered, for 15 minutes, then clean and oil the grate.

While the grill heats, thread the shrimp onto eight 10- to 12-inch skewers, dividing them evenly. Skewer each shrimp in a C shape, piercing through two points.

When the grill is ready, brush one side of the skewered shrimp with some of the remaining 2 tablespoons coconut milk.

Place the skewers brushed side down on the grill (directly over the coals if using charcoal) and cook until the shrimp are well charred, 2 to 3 minutes. Brush the skewers with the remaining coconut milk, then flip and cook until the second sides are well charred and the shrimp just turn opaque, about another 2 minutes. Sprinkle with chopped cashews and serve with the dipping sauce.

No. 48

Keep Seafood Tender by Saving Acids for the End

Acids can toughen the texture of raw seafood. So when we want to add tangy flavor, we add them after cooking as a sauce.

Sweet-and-Sour Swordfish

Two 12-ounce skinless swordfish steaks (each about 1 inch thick), patted dry

Kosher salt and ground black pepper

2 tablespoons grapeseed or other neutral oil, divided

3 medium red onions, halved and thinly sliced

2 bay leaves

1 cup plus 1 tablespoon white wine vinegar, divided

¼ cup white sugar

3 tablespoons yellow mustard seeds

In Italy, agrodolce (literally, sour-sweet) is a sweet-and-tangy flavor combination made by reducing vinegar with sugar or honey. We drew inspiration from the tradition and paired sugar and vinegar-seasoned red onions to add tangy contrast to mild and meaty swordfish. We also borrowed a technique from Spanish escabeche and marinate the fish after cooking so the steaks absorb the flavors and don't toughen up. The fish should be served barely warm or at room temperature, or it can be prepared ahead, refrigerated overnight and served chilled. Simple braised or sautéed greens, stewed white beans or crusty bread are great served alongside.

Don't use a metal baking pan for marinating the fish, as metal may react with the acidity of the marinade and leave the dish with an off metallic taste. And don't slice the fish until ready to serve. If sliced before marinating, the acid will cause the fish to turn an unappealing gray color.

Season the fish on all sides with salt and pepper. In a 12-inch nonstick skillet over medium-high, heat 1 tablespoon of oil until barely smoking. Add the fish and cook without disturbing until well browned, 5 to 7 minutes. Flip, reduce to medium and continue to cook until the fish is opaque throughout and the centers reach about 130°F, about another 5 minutes. Transfer to a small glass or ceramic baking dish and set aside; wipe out the pan.

In the same pan over medium, heat the remaining 1 tablespoon oil until shimmering. Add the onions, bay and ½ teaspoon salt. Cook, stirring occasionally, until the onions are very soft, 5 to 7 minutes. Stir in 1 cup of vinegar, the sugar and the mustard seeds. Bring to a simmer and cook, stirring occasionally, until the liquid has thickened to a light syrup consistency, 5 to 7 minutes. Off heat, stir in the remaining 1 tablespoon vinegar.

Immediately pour the onion mixture over the fish. Marinate for about 30 minutes at room temperature or cover and refrigerate up to overnight. To serve, remove the fish from the marinade, then slice each piece and transfer to a platter. Discard the bay from the marinade and spoon the onions and liquid around and over the fish.

RECIPES & RULES

CHICKEN

CHICKEN

Instead of chasing the impossible—a whole, bronzed, perfectly cooked bird—at Milk Street, **we break down the chicken into manageable portions, add flavor fast with layers of spices and condiments** and **use liquid,** not air, to cook it fast and keep it tender.

Americans spend some $95 billion a year on chicken—a lot of money for a protein that's become a byword for bland. There's plenty of great restaurant chicken—like the sauce-slicked, low-and-slow barbecued birds of Kansas City and the brick oven roasted chicken of San Francisco's Zuni Café. But for home cooks it's a different story. We marinate, grill, roast and go to extraordinary lengths in pursuit of crisply golden skin, only to end up with pink thighs, dry breasts and dull dinners.

Happily, the rest of the world has figured out it is possible to get better, easier results with bolder flavors. We just need to let go of the aspirational notion of the picture-perfect, golden brown, whole-roasted bird.

The challenge of cooking a whole bird is that breasts are done at 160°F while thighs need to reach 175°F to 180°F. One solution is to **flatten birds to put the breasts and thighs on the same plane so they cook more evenly.** In our chicken under a brick, we follow the lead of cooks in the country of Georgia and weigh the flattened chicken down to render sizzling, golden skin. Another option is to break the chicken down into parts for quicker cooking and easier seasoning. When we roast chicken parts on shallow sheet pans to speed up cooking and add vegetables alongside, as British cooks do with their traybakes, we get a one-pan solution to supper.

Skewers, with their flavorful, charred crusts, are popular around the world, from Nigerian beef suya to Singaporean satay. For our Turkish-inspired version, we **make skewers with thin strips, not thick chunks, for faster and more flavorful cooking.** We also change the shape of chicken intended for salad. In our Vietnamese chicken salad, we **shred the cooked meat for faster, bolder seasoning.**

We like to **amplify flavor by layering ingredients.** In our Thai-style fried chicken, seasonings used in the crust are repeated in a mixture used to dust the cooked pieces. Likewise, we layer flavors in our lemon-lime lacquered grilled chicken, using leftover marinade to make a basting and serving sauce. In our Iraqi spice-crusted grilled chicken we **slide spices under the skin** to better season the meat and help them stay put. For our skinless chicken cutlets, we **use boldly seasoned breadcrumbs inspired by the Egyptian nut-and-spice blend dukkah for a crunchy, flavorful crust. And we balance rich, fried foods with bright, acidic counterpoints,** serving a tangy carrot salad with the cutlets. Similarly, our Japanese-style cutlets are paired with a brightly acidic cabbage slaw.

Marinades often are disappointing. They add little flavor because they can't penetrate deeply. And acidic marinades tend to leave meat tough and mushy. In our chicken escabeche, we avoid that and **skip the marinade, saucing the chicken after it's cooked.**

When we do want to cook a bird whole, we **use moist heat for more effective and gentler cooking.** This helps solve the white meat-dark meat temperature differential. And we have no skin in this game. Rather than focus on ideal bronzing, we focus on the flavor of the meat and toss the skin before serving. For inspiration, we look to Hainan, in southern China, where chicken is poached silky smooth and paired with vibrant dipping sauces. In our chicken soup, inspired by Peruvian flavors, we **focus on a few high-impact ingredients,** using a whole bunch of fresh cilantro and spicy ají amarillo paste.

French cooks solve the whole-bird cooking challenge with chicken en cocotte. They **cook chicken in a covered pot with a relatively small amount of liquid, creating richly concentrated juices.** We came up with a few flavorful variations, including one rich with apricots, saffron and tarragon.

Flat Birds Cook Faster, Crisp Better

Spatchcocking puts the breasts and thighs on an even plane so they cook at the same time. Flattening the bird also exposes all of the skin to heat, resulting in crisper skin.

HOW TO SPATCHCOCK A CHICKEN:

1. Set the chicken breast side down on a cutting board. Using sturdy kitchen shears, cut along one side of the backbone from top to bottom.

2. Repeat the cut on the other side of the backbone, then remove and discard the backbone.

3. Spread the sides of the chicken, opening it like a book and flattening it as much as possible.

4. Flip the chicken breast side up, then use your hands to press firmly on the highest point of the breast to flatten the bird. The breast bone may crack.

5. If desired, the skin of the thighs and breasts can be loosened from the edges to allow seasoning to be rubbed underneath.

Crispy Chicken Under a Brick
(Tsitsila Tabaka)

Start to finish: **2 hours**
(50 minutes active)
Servings: **4**

1½ teaspoons ground coriander

½ teaspoon granulated garlic

Kosher salt and ground black pepper

3½- to 4-pound whole chicken, spatchcocked

1 tablespoon grapeseed or other neutral oil

2 tablespoons salted butter

8 medium garlic cloves, peeled and chopped

2 cups low-sodium chicken broth

⅛ to ¼ teaspoon cayenne pepper

2 tablespoons lemon juice

¼ cup lightly packed fresh cilantro, chopped

For this recipe, we find inspiration in Georgia, set at the crossroads of Europe and Asia and known for dishes that benefit from both traditions. The chicken is spatchcocked, which puts thighs and breasts on the same plane for even cooking. Georgian cooks use a brick to keep their chickens truly flat (you'll find the same technique in Italy's pollo al mattone). The weight presses the chicken down, ensuring the bird makes good contact with the hot surface. The skillet in which the chicken is cooked must be oven-safe, as the bird roasts in the oven after the initial stovetop sear. For the "brick," we use a second heavy skillet or a large, sturdy pot (such as a Dutch oven); it's easier and works fine. If crisp skin is what you're after, this is the way to get it. The hot pan renders the fat and crisps the skin. If you have them on hand, you could instead use one or two clean bricks wrapped in heavy-duty foil. Niortskali, a Georgian garlic sauce with lemon and cilantro, is the perfect pan sauce to complement the chicken.

Don't use a chicken *much larger than 4 pounds, as it may not fit comfortably in the skillet. Don't forget to pat the chicken dry before searing (after it has stood for 45 minutes). The drier the skin, the better it crisps. After searing, drain off the fat in the pan before putting the bird in the oven; this helps reduce splatter. Finally, don't forget that the skillet's handle will be hot when taken out of oven.*

In a small bowl, stir together the coriander, granulated garlic, 1 tablespoon salt and ½ teaspoon black pepper. Place the spatchcocked chicken, skin-side up, on a cutting board. Season the chicken all over with the spice mixture, rubbing it into the skin. Let stand uncovered at room temperature for 30 to 45 minutes.

Heat the oven to 450°F with a rack in the lowest position. Thoroughly pat the chicken dry with paper towels.

In a 12-inch oven-safe skillet over medium-high, heat the oil until barely smoking. Place the chicken breast down

in the pan. Lay a small sheet of foil over the chicken, then place a second heavy skillet or pot on top. Reduce to medium and cook until the skin is golden brown, 10 to 15 minutes, removing the weight and foil and checking every 4 to 5 minutes to ensure even browning.

Using tongs, carefully transfer the chicken to a large plate, turning it breast up. Pour off and discard the fat in the skillet. Slide the chicken breast up back into the pan and place in the oven. Roast until the thickest part of the breast reaches 160°F, 25 to 35 minutes. Carefully transfer the chicken to a cutting board and let rest while you make the sauce.

Set the skillet (the handle will be hot) over medium-high and cook the butter and garlic, stirring occasionally, until the garlic is lightly browned, about 2 minutes. Add the broth and bring to a simmer, scraping up any browned bits, then cook until the garlic is softened and the mixture is lightly thickened and reduced to about ¾ cup, 10 to 15 minutes. Using a silicone spatula, mash the garlic until almost smooth and mix it into the sauce. Off heat, stir in the cayenne, lemon juice and cilantro, then transfer to a serving bowl. Carve, then serve with the sauce.

No. 50

Roast on Baking Sheets, Not Roasting Pans

Roasting on a low-rimmed baking sheet rather than in a deep pan allows for better air circulation around the food, accelerating cooking and boosting browning.

Chicken and Cremini Mushroom
Traybake with Roasted Red Pepper Sauce

Start to finish: **50 minutes**
Servings: **4**

1 tablespoon ground fennel seeds

1 tablespoon granulated garlic

Kosher salt and ground black pepper

1½ pounds cremini mushrooms, trimmed, kept whole

2 roasted red peppers, kept whole

¼ cup extra-virgin olive oil

3 pounds bone-in, skin-on chicken parts, trimmed and patted dry

1 tablespoon firmly packed light or dark brown sugar

1 tablespoon dried oregano

10 medium garlic cloves, peeled

2 teaspoons unseasoned rice vinegar

4 scallions, thinly sliced

Cooking dinner on a shallow pan in the oven is a technique that's become more popular in recent years. Called a traybake or sheetpan supper, it's all about pairing meat and vegetables with seasonings and tossing and roasting everything together. We build flavor by adding the ingredients for a sauce, strategically positioning more delicate items such as garlic cloves so they don't burn. Once the cooking is done, we deglaze the fond on the pan and chop or mash the roasted aromatics into a sauce. We use bone-in, skin-on chicken parts for these dishes. If the quicker-cooking breasts reach 160°F before the thighs and drumsticks hit 175°F, simply remove them and continue cooking the dark meat. Cooking at 450°F gives us crisp skin without drying out the meat. We frequently use chicken leg quarters, which include the thigh and drumstick. In this take on the traybake, we look to the flavors of Provence in southern France, pairing mushrooms and roasted red peppers with the delicate, anise-like flavor of ground fennel. The peppers—we save time and start with the jarred variety—cook a bit more in the pan, then go into a subtly sweet scallion-accented pan sauce. If you can't find ground fennel seed at the supermarket, grind your own by processing a generous 1 tablespoon whole fennel seeds in a spice grinder until fine and powdery.

Don't remove the stems from the mushrooms. *Simply trim off the ends, which tend to be dry and discolored.*

Heat the oven to 450°F with a rack in the middle position. In a small bowl, stir together the fennel, granulated garlic and 2 teaspoons salt. In a medium bowl, toss the mushrooms and red peppers with 1 tablespoon of the spice mixture and the oil; set aside. Into the remaining spice mixture, stir the brown sugar, oregano, 1 tablespoon salt and 2 teaspoons pepper.

On a rimmed baking sheet, evenly season both sides of the chicken parts with the spice mixture. Place the garlic cloves in the center of the baking sheet, then arrange the chicken parts, skin up, around the garlic; this prevents the garlic from scorching during roasting. Place the roasted peppers around the chicken, then scatter the mushrooms in an even layer over them.

Roast until the thickest part of the breast (if using) reaches about 160°F and the thickest part of the largest thigh/leg (if using) reaches about 175°F, 30 to 40 minutes.

Using tongs, transfer the chicken and mushrooms to a platter and transfer the roasted peppers to a cutting board; leave the garlic on the baking sheet. Carefully pour ¼ cup water onto the baking sheet, then use a wooden spoon to scrape up any browned bits. Pour the liquid, along with the garlic cloves, into a medium bowl. Roughly chop the roasted peppers and add to the bowl, then use a fork or potato masher to mash the mixture until almost smooth. Stir in the vinegar and half the scallions, then spoon the sauce over the chicken. Sprinkle with the remaining scallions.

MAKING TRAYBAKE WITH ROASTED POBLANO AND TOMATO SALSA

1. In a large bowl, toss together the poblanos, onion wedges, tomatoes, habanero, 1 tablespoon of the chili powder mixture and the oil.

2. Place the garlic cloves in the center of the baking sheet, then arrange the chicken parts, skin up, around the garlic; this prevents the garlic from scorching during roasting.

3. Arrange the vegetables around the chicken, taking care to not overlap for even cooking.

4. After roasting, remove the chicken and tilt the pan to pour the garlic, the remaining vegetables and any liquid on the baking sheet into a medium bowl.

5. Using a fork or potato masher, mash the mixture until broken down but slightly chunky.

6. Stir in half of the cilantro and the vinegar, then spoon the salsa over the chicken. Sprinkle with remaining cilantro.

Chicken Traybake
with Roasted Poblano and Tomato Salsa

1 tablespoon chili powder

Kosher salt and ground black pepper

2 poblano chilies, stemmed, seeded and roughly chopped

1 medium yellow onion, root end intact, cut into 8 wedges

1 pint cherry or grape tomatoes

1 habanero chili, stemmed halved and seeded (optional)

¼ cup extra-virgin olive oil

1 tablespoon firmly packed light or dark brown sugar

1 tablespoon dried oregano

3 pounds bone-in, skin-on chicken parts, trimmed and patted dry

10 medium garlic cloves, peeled

1 tablespoon white vinegar

¼ cup lightly packed fresh cilantro, roughly chopped

In Mexico, salsas start with charring chilies, tomatoes, onions and garlic on a steel or clay comal (a flat griddle used to make tortillas) to soften and deepen their flavors. We adapt that concept in this traybake, roasting chilies alongside chicken parts. Glossy, dark green poblano peppers have an earthy, minerally flavor and moderate heat level. Habanero adds a burst of bright, fruity heat that sharpens the tomatoes' flavor. The tomatoes release their juice during cooking, so deglazing the baking sheet with water after roasting isn't necessary. If you want a lot of heat in your salsa, include the optional habanero chili.

Don't forget to leave the root end *of the onion intact so the wedges don't separate into layers. If the layers separate, they tend to scorch during roasting.*

Heat the oven to 450°F with a rack in the middle position. In a small bowl, stir together the chili powder and 2 teaspoons salt. In a large bowl, toss together the poblanos, onion wedges, tomatoes, habanero (if using), 1 tablespoon of the chili powder mixture and the oil. Into the remaining chili powder mixture, stir the sugar, oregano, 1 tablespoon salt and 2 teaspoons pepper.

On a rimmed baking sheet, evenly season both sides of the chicken parts with the chili powder mixture. Place the garlic cloves in the center of the baking sheet, then arrange the chicken parts, skin up, around the garlic; this prevents the garlic from scorching during roasting. Arrange the vegetables evenly around the chicken.

Roast until the thickest part of the breast (if using) reaches about 160°F and the thickest part of the largest thigh/leg (if using) reaches about 175°F, 30 to 40 minutes.

Using tongs, transfer the chicken to a platter and transfer the onion wedges and habanero to a cutting board. Pour the garlic, the remaining vegetables and any liquid on the baking sheet into a medium bowl. Roughly chop the onion and habanero, then add to the bowl. Using a fork or potato masher, mash the mixture until broken down but slightly chunky. Stir in half of the cilantro and the vinegar, then spoon the salsa over the chicken. Sprinkle with the remaining cilantro.

Chicken and Cauliflower Traybake
with Roasted Garlic–Yogurt Sauce

2 teaspoons ground turmeric

2 teaspoons sweet paprika

Kosher salt and ground black pepper

1 small head cauliflower (about 2 pounds), leaves trimmed, cored and cut into 3-inch florets

¼ cup extra-virgin olive oil

1 tablespoon firmly packed light or dark brown sugar

1 tablespoon dried oregano

3 pounds bone-in, skin-on chicken parts, trimmed and patted dry

10 medium garlic cloves, peeled

⅓ cup whole-milk Greek yogurt

2 tablespoons lemon juice

¼ cup lightly packed fresh mint, chopped

The cauliflower in this simple Indian-inspired traybake serves two purposes: it's a delicious side to the roasted chicken and it's the base for the creamy sauce that accompanies the dish. We use sweet paprika in the spice mixture, but if you like you could use smoked paprika for an earthy, woodsy flavor or hot paprika to add heat.

Don't use a large head of cauliflower because there won't be enough space on the baking sheet for both the chicken and cauliflower. Don't cut the cauliflower into small florets, which will overcook in the time it takes the chicken to roast.

Heat the oven to 450°F with a rack in the middle position. In a small bowl, stir together the turmeric, paprika and 2 teaspoons salt. In a large bowl, toss the cauliflower with 1 tablespoon of the spice mixture and the oil. Into the remaining spice mixture, stir the brown sugar, oregano, 1 tablespoon salt and 2 teaspoons pepper.

On a rimmed baking sheet, evenly season both sides of the chicken parts with the spice mixture. Place the garlic cloves in the center of the baking sheet, then arrange the chicken parts, skin up,

around the garlic; this prevents the garlic from scorching during roasting. Arrange the cauliflower evenly around the chicken.

Roast until the thickest part of the breast (if using) reaches about 160°F and the thickest part of the largest thigh/leg (if using) reaches about 175°F, 30 to 40 minutes.

Using tongs, transfer the chicken and cauliflower to a platter, then transfer the garlic along with 2 cauliflower florets to a medium bowl. Using a fork,

mash the garlic and cauliflower mixture to a coarse paste. Carefully pour ¼ cup water onto the baking sheet, then use a wooden spoon to scrape up any browned bits. Pour the water into the garlic-cauliflower mixture, then whisk in the yogurt, lemon juice and half the mint. The mixture should have the consistency of thin yogurt; if it is too thick, whisk in additional water 1 tablespoon at a time. Drizzle the sauce over the chicken and cauliflower and sprinkle with remaining mint.

Build Better Skewers with Strips, Not Chunks

Think thin strips rather than thick chunks when making meat skewers. They cook faster and provide plenty of surface area for applying flavorful rubs and sauces.

Chili–Red Pepper Chicken Kebabs
(Tavuk Şiş)

Start to finish: **1 hour, plus marinating**

Servings: **4**

½ cup drained roasted red bell peppers, patted dry

6 medium garlic cloves, smashed and peeled

2 Fresno chilies, stemmed, seeded and roughly chopped

¼ cup extra-virgin olive oil

2 tablespoons dried mint

2 tablespoons Aleppo pepper (see note)

1 tablespoon honey

1 tablespoon tomato paste

Kosher salt

1½ tablespoons lemon juice

2 pounds boneless, skinless chicken thighs, trimmed and cut crosswise into 1-inch strips

3 tablespoons chopped fresh mint

For our take on kebabs, we draw inspiration from Turkey, the country that gave shish kebabs their name. Shish (or şiş) means skewers or small swords, while kebab means roasted meat. There, biber salçası, or Turkish red pepper paste, is used to flavor kebabs. We use easier to find Fresno chilies, which we puree, along with roasted bell peppers and a touch of tomato paste. Our puree also includes Aleppo pepper; look for it in well-stocked markets and spice shops. If Aleppo pepper is not available, substitute 1 tablespoon sweet paprika plus ¼ teaspoon cayenne pepper or red pepper flakes. We prefer chicken thighs over breasts for their richer flavor. Plus, dark meat is more forgiving when it comes to doneness.

Don't forget to scrape excess marinade off the chicken as you thread the pieces onto skewers. This prevents a sticky buildup on the grill grates.

In a food processor, combine the roasted red peppers, garlic, chilies, oil, dried mint, Aleppo pepper, honey, tomato paste and 2 teaspoons salt. Process until almost smooth, 45 to 60 seconds, scraping the sides as needed. Measure 3 tablespoons of the puree into a small bowl, then stir in the lemon juice; cover and refrigerate. Transfer the remaining puree to a medium bowl, add the chicken and toss to coat. Cover and refrigerate for at least 1 hour or up to 12 hours.

Prepare a charcoal or gas grill for direct, medium-high heat. For a charcoal grill, ignite a large chimney three-quarters full of coals, let burn until lightly ashed over, then distribute evenly over one side of the grill bed; open the bottom grill vents and the lid vent. For a gas grill, turn all burners to high. Heat the grill, covered, for 5 to 10 minutes; clean and oil the grate. Remove the reserved puree from the refrigerator.

While the grill heats, thread the chicken onto eight 10- to 12-inch metal skewers, evenly dividing the pieces and scraping off excess marinade. If using a gas grill, turn all burners to medium-high. Place the skewers on the grill, on the hot side if using charcoal, and cook, uncovered, turning every 2 to 3 minutes, until evenly charred on all sides and the thickest piece is opaque when cut into, 10 to 12 minutes. Transfer to a serving platter. Stir the fresh mint into the reserved puree and serve with the kebabs.

ESSENTIAL SPICES

The 18 Spices You Need to Build a Better Spice Cabinet

Dried spices have a limited shelf life because the essential oils they contain are volatile. For best flavor, we recommend buying whole spices in small volumes. It's quick work to grind them as needed in a spice mill (a cheap blade-style coffee grinder works well) or a mortar and pestle. If purchasing ground spices, choose amounts that can be used up within six months or so. Older, flat-tasting spices can be perked up somewhat with a quick toast in a hot skillet (see tips on p. 55).

ALEPPO PEPPER

Fruity and only moderately spicy, coarsely ground Aleppo pepper is used throughout Middle Eastern cooking. We use it frequently and consider it a valuable flavoring for all manner of dishes that benefit from a little spark of heat. Aleppo pepper can be found at most Middle Eastern shops and spice dealers. It's typically processed with a little salt and safflower oil. We like Aleppo pepper on roasted salmon and chicken, and it's particularly good when combined with walnuts and pomegranate molasses on braised greens, green beans, broccoli or roasted sweet potatoes. It's good with dairy, too, such as a yogurt-based dip, grilled cheese sandwich, even macaroni and cheese. If a recipe calls for Aleppo pepper but you don't have it, for a quick substitute mix one part cayenne with four parts sweet paprika.

ALLSPICE

With a flavor tasting subtly of clove, cinnamon, nutmeg and black pepper, allspice works in both sweet and savory dishes. We typically buy whole allspice berries and grind fresh for the best flavor. We also use whole allspice berries when pickling.

BAY LEAVES

We think of bay leaves as we do vanilla—it's a flavor noticed mostly by omission. Bay leaves, technically an herb, lend a certain aroma and savory notes to soups, stews and pickles. They're also great tossed with roasting vegetables. We even use them in sweet dishes, such as syrups for glazing baked goods. Turkish bay leaves have the best flavor (California bay leaves actually are a variety of laurel and don't taste the same). Buy in bulk for economy's sake and store the leaves in the freezer to maintain flavor and aroma.

CARDAMOM

We use cardamom widely in both sweet and savory recipes. It is sold whole in pods (white, black and green—each with a slightly different flavor), corticated (removed from the papery husk) and ground. More often than not, we use ground, as the seeds can be difficult to grind finely. We like to make Arabic coffee by grinding the whole pods into our coffee beans, then brewing as normal. Use 1 tablespoon of cardamom pods per 1 cup of whole coffee beans.

CUMIN SEEDS

One of our more liberally used spices, cumin packs an earthy flavor and pungency that lends backbone to all manner of Latin, Middle Eastern and even Chinese dishes. Buy whole and grind fresh, if possible.

FENNEL SEEDS

We use both whole and ground fennel seed to add a licorice-like flavor to vegetables, meats and sauces. Fennel pairs particularly well with a little spiciness from chilies and the pungency of garlic. To make a fennel-rosemary rub, in a small bowl, stir together 2 tablespoons kosher salt, 1 tablespoon ground black pepper, **2 tablespoons packed light brown sugar, 1 tablespoon fennel seeds** (ground), **1 teaspoon red pepper flakes, 1 teaspoon granulated garlic** and **4 teaspoons minced fresh rosemary.** Rub the mixture between your fingertips until well combined and the rosemary is fragrant. This rub is especially good on pork that will be roasted or grilled.

BLACK PEPPER

Black pepper adds depth and a nominal amount of heat. We use it to give a mild kick and not always paired with salt. For best flavor, buy whole peppercorns and grind as needed (find a good-quality, adjustable pepper mill). Preground pepper lacks the aroma and much of the flavor of freshly ground. Consider tasting different varieties of black pepper to see which you prefer, as some are more assertive than others.

CORIANDER SEEDS

Coriander is the seed of the cilantro plant. It has a bright, citrusy flavor with a hint of mint. The seeds are tender enough to use whole—we like them with cracked potatoes—though it typically is used ground. We prefer to buy it whole and grind as needed.

GROUND GINGER

We love the sharp, spicy flavor and aroma of ground ginger and use it frequently in both sweet and savory applications. It's a spice with oils that are particularly volatile, so we recommend purchasing smaller amounts that you can use up within a few months.

MUSTARD SEEDS

Whether the yellow, brown or black variety, we pickle mustard seeds or stir them into curries and the occasional bean dish for a pop of flavor. Their flavor blossoms in hot oil so we almost always bloom them before using. To pickle mustard seeds, in a small saucepan over high, combine **¼ cup yellow mustard seeds** and enough water to cover by 2 inches. Bring to a boil, then reduce to medium-low and simmer until the seeds are tender, about 8 minutes. Strain the seeds in a fine mesh strainer and transfer to a small bowl. To the same pan, add **½ cup cider vinegar, ¼ cup white sugar, ¼ cup water, 1½ teaspoons black peppercorns, ½ teaspoon coriander seeds, 3 allspice berries, 1 bay leaf and ⅛ tea-**

spoon red pepper flakes. Bring to a boil over high, then reduce to medium-low and simmer, stirring, until the sugar has dissolved, 3 to 5 minutes. Strain over the mustard seeds; discard the solids. Let cool to room temperature. Use immediately or cover and refrigerate for up to 1 month. Sprinkled drained seeds onto salads or rich pork or beef braises to add pops of bright flavor.

PAPRIKA

Paprika comes in two styles: plain and smoked. The best-known sources of plain paprika are Hungary and Spain. Spain also is home to smoked paprika; pimentón de la Vera, produced only in the La Vera region of Spain, is regarded as the finest quality. Both plain and smoked paprika are available in sweet and hot versions. We typically use sweet, choosing to add a few red pepper flakes or cayenne to ratchet up the heat if the dish needs it.

RED PEPPER FLAKES

We use the sharp chili bite of red pepper flakes to punctuate many dishes. We don't

aim for spicy food per se, just balanced dishes with a compelling range of flavors to keep things interesting start to finish. Red pepper flakes are produced from various dried peppers and intensity can vary by brand. Age affects heat level as well; the older the flakes, the less intense they will be. To make a chili-sesame oil with red pepper flakes, in a small skillet over medium, heat **¼ cup grapeseed or other neutral oil, 1 tablespoon toasted sesame oil, 1½ tablespoons sesame seeds and 2 teaspoons red pepper flakes,** stirring, until fragrant and the seeds begin to brown, 3 to 5 minutes. Pour into a small bowl and let cool to room temperature. Drizzle the oil over stir-fries or hot or cold Asian noodle dishes, or use salad dressings.

SAFFRON

Warm, deep and aromatic, saffron is an essential flavoring and coloring agent for many Spanish and Middle Eastern dishes. It's the defining ingredient in Italy's risotto milanese. Saffron is predominantly grown in Spain, Iran and Afghanistan (our favorite comes from Afghanistan). To make the most of this expensive seasoning, either soak it in a little hot water before use or crumble it with your fingers to release its essential oils.

SICHUAN PEPPERCORNS

Not technically pepper, Sichuan peppercorns have a high, sharp, slightly resinous flavor and unique ability to "numb" the mouth. They are used broadly in Sichuan cooking in tandem with whole chilies in a combination known as "ma la." Sichuan peppercorns are almost always sold whole and require grinding before use; toasting heightens their flavor and aroma. To make a Sichuan seasoning, in a small, dry skillet over medium, toast **3 tablespoons Sichuan peppercorns** until fragrant, about 2 minutes. Transfer to a bowl and let cool, then finely grind in a spice grinder. Sift through a fine mesh strainer to remove any fibrous pieces, then mix with **2 teaspoons white sugar** and 1 teaspoon kosher salt. Sprinkle onto fried or grilled foods of any type.

SUMAC

Deep red and bursting with tangy zest, sumac has been an essential flavoring of Middle Eastern cooking—and closer to home, Native American cooking—for centuries. It's made from the berries of the sumac bush and usually is sold ground. You can find it online, at Middle Eastern markets and at some larger grocers. (Though they're related, this is not the poison sumac you've been warned to stay away from.) Sumac has a sour, lemony flavor and is a good way to add a tart note of citrus without the liquid of lemon juice, as well as a bright pop of color. It works well as a condiment and can be dusted over just about anything— hummus and baba ghanoush are traditional, but it's also great on avocado toast with extra-virgin olive oil, salt and ground black pepper. In cooking, it works well in dry rubs for chicken and fish. To make sumac dressing, in a small bowl, whisk **¼ cup whole-milk Greek yogurt**, 1 tablespoon water, **1¼ teaspoons ground sumac, 1 teaspoon Dijon mustard, 1 teaspoon honey, 1½ teaspoon red wine vinegar** and **2 tablespoons finely chopped fresh flat-leaf parsley**. Season with salt and ground black pepper.

TURMERIC

Earthy and bittersweet, turmeric is broadly used to add both depth to dishes and a bright marigold coloring—it's a potent pigment. It's one of the anchor ingredients in most Indian curry powders and some southeast Asian curry blends. It is most commonly used in powdered (ground) form, though is increasingly available fresh (and looks like a yellow-tinted, smaller version of fresh ginger). When used fresh, it must be grated or otherwise reduced to a pulp before cooking. Be careful handling turmeric: It can stain whatever it touches.

URFA PEPPER

Smoky, earthy and moderately spicy, mahogany-colored Urfa pepper is one of our favorite dried chilies. It has notes of dark chocolate and wine tannins with mild aromas of bitter orange. The moist texture of the coarse-ground flakes—preserved through a slow-and-steady drying process—make it ideal for finishing a dish.

WHITE PEPPER

Though we use white pepper far less than black, its unique flavor and aroma make it an important pantry staple for some Asian and Scandinavian dishes. It's often used in place of black pepper to season light-colored dishes so that the grounds are not quite as noticeable. White pepper comes from the same berry (piper nigrum) as black, but is processed differently. Like black pepper, white is best when freshly ground. For a complex flavor, consider using a blend of black and white peppercorns in your pepper mill.

Vietnamese Chicken Salad
with Sweet Lime-Garlic Dressing (Goi Gà)

Start to finish: **15 minutes**
Servings: **6**

⅓ cup lime juice, plus lime wedges, to serve

3½ tablespoons fish sauce

1½ teaspoons white sugar

2 medium garlic cloves, finely grated

1 small red onion, quartered lengthwise and thinly sliced

3 cups shredded cooked chicken

½ medium head green or red cabbage (14 ounces), cored and shredded (about 4 cups)

4 medium carrots, peeled and shredded on the large holes of a box grater (about 2 cups)

3 medium jalapeño chilies, stemmed, halved lengthwise and thinly sliced

1 cup lightly packed fresh basil, torn

1 cup lightly packed fresh cilantro leaves and tender stems, roughly chopped

1½ cups roasted, salted peanuts, roughly chopped

For this recipe, we turn cooked and cooled chicken into a refreshing salad by way of a bright and flavorful dressing. Fish sauce, known as nuoc mam in Vietnam, gives the dressing savory, umami-rich underpinnings, while lime juice, sugar and garlic punch up the flavors. The jalapeños add moderate spiciness; if you prefer milder heat, seed the jalapeños before slicing them. We call for about 3 cups of shredded meat, the yield of a small to average size bird (3 to 4 pounds). The finished salad can be covered and refrigerated for up to an hour.

Don't tear the basil *too far in advance or it will discolor. When preparing the herbs, leave them on the larger side. Bigger pieces punctuate the salad with color, flavor and texture. Marinating the sliced onion in the dressing for about 10 minutes tames its raw bite, so don't skip this step.*

In a small bowl, stir together the lime juice, fish sauce, sugar and garlic, until the sugar dissolves. Add the onion and let stand for 10 minutes, stirring occasionally.

In a large bowl, toss together the chicken, cabbage, carrots, chilies, basil and cilantro. Pour on the red onion–dressing mixture and toss. Toss in half of the peanuts, then transfer to a serving bowl. Sprinkle with the remaining peanuts and serve with lime wedges on the side.

No. 52

Shred Your Chicken for Bolder Flavor

Shredding cooked chicken not only makes the meat more tender, it also can result in better flavor. Shredded chicken has more surface area to better absorb seasonings and sauces.

CHANGE THE WAY YOU COOK

No. 53

Hit Repeat for Better, Bigger Flavor

Repeating flavors is a signal-boosting tactic that creates bold layers of flavor. We often use the same spice mixture twice—first to coat chicken before cooking, then again to dust the finished dish.

Southern Thai–Style Fried Chicken

Start to finish: **40 minutes, plus marinating**

Servings: **4**

3 tablespoons ground cumin

3 tablespoons ground coriander

3 tablespoons ground white pepper, divided

1 large egg white

¼ cup fish sauce

1 bunch fresh cilantro, finely chopped

2 serrano chilies, stemmed and finely chopped

2 pounds boneless, skinless chicken thighs, trimmed, each cut crosswise into 3 strips

2 cups cornstarch

Kosher salt

2 quarts peanut oil, plus more if needed

Lime wedges, to serve

Sweet chili sauce, to serve (see note; optional)

In this recipe, the spices (toasted for intensity) go both into the crust and over it after frying, keeping flavors clear and distinct. Gai tod hat yai, fried chicken from the southern region of Thailand, inspired this recipe, but we made it quicker by using boneless, skinless thighs cut into strips instead of the typical bone-in, skin-on parts. The chicken is customarily sprinkled with crisp fried shallots after cooking, but we opted out of this garnish, as the spices themselves provide plenty of bold flavor. If you like, you can purchase fried shallots in most Asian grocery stores; scatter them over the chicken just before serving. If you're not up for making our extra-easy version of Thai sweet chili sauce, serve with store-bought sweet chili sauce, or simply offer lime wedges for squeezing.

Don't marinate the chicken for longer than an hour or it will be too salty. Don't crowd the pot when frying. Cook only a third of the chicken at a time so the temperature of the oil won't drop drastically, which results in greasy chicken.

In a 10-inch skillet over medium, toast the cumin and coriander until fragrant and just beginning to color, 2 to 3 minutes. Transfer to a small bowl and stir in 1 tablespoon of white pepper; set aside.

In a large bowl, whisk together the egg white, fish sauce and ¼ cup water. Stir in the cilantro, chilies and 3 tablespoons of the spice mixture. Add the chicken and stir to thoroughly coat, then cover and refrigerate for 30 to 60 minutes.

Set a wire rack in a rimmed baking sheet. In a large bowl, whisk together the cornstarch, the remaining 2 tablespoons white pepper and 2 teaspoons salt.

Drain the chicken in a colander. Scraping off excess marinade, add ⅓ of the chicken to the cornstarch mixture and toss to coat completely, then firmly press the pieces into the cornstarch. Transfer the pieces to the prepared rack in a single layer, shaking to remove excess coating. Repeat with the remaining chicken and cornstarch mixture, working in two more batches.

Set another wire rack in a rimmed baking sheet. In a large Dutch oven over medium-high, heat the oil to 350°F (the oil should be at least 2 inches deep; add more if needed). Add ⅓ of the chicken pieces and cook, stirring occasionally to prevent sticking, until golden brown, about 5 minutes. Using a slotted spoon or wire skimmer, transfer the chicken to the second rack and season on all sides with about ⅓ of the reserved spice mixture. Allow the oil to return to 350°F, then repeat with the remaining chicken and spice mixture, working in two more batches. Serve with lime wedges and sweet chili sauce (if using).

TANGY-SWEET CHILI SAUCE

Start to finish: **10 minutes**

Makes about **¾ cup**

1 cup white vinegar

½ cup white sugar

Kosher salt

3 tablespoons chili-garlic sauce

In a small saucepan over medium-high, bring the vinegar, sugar and ¼ teaspoon salt to a boil, stirring to dissolve the sugar. Cook until the mixture thickens and is reduced to about ¾ cup, 10 to 12 minutes. Off heat, stir in the chili-garlic sauce. Cool to room temperature.

Lemon-Lime Lacquered Grilled
Chicken (Inihaw Na Manok)

Start to finish: **50 minutes, plus marinating**

Servings: **4**

¾ cup cider vinegar

½ cup ketchup

⅓ cup soy sauce

6 tablespoons packed light or dark brown sugar

6 medium garlic cloves, peeled

4 bay leaves

1 tablespoon black peppercorns

Kosher salt

1 cup lemon-lime soda, such as Sprite or 7Up

3 pounds bone-in, skin-on chicken breasts, thighs and/or drumsticks, trimmed and patted dry

1 tablespoon lime juice

The core flavors of Filipino adobo—vinegar, garlic, soy sauce and bay leaves—get the layering treatment in this take on Filipino chicken barbecue. Inihaw na manok (which translates simply as "grilled chicken") commonly includes multiple sweet ingredients, the most intriguing being lemon-lime soda such as Sprite or 7Up. The soda adds a touch of acidity and helps produce nicely lacquered skin. Its sweetness is balanced by tangy vinegar, salty soy sauce and savory garlic and black pepper. We reinforce those flavors by straining and reducing the marinade to use as a basting sauce, with extra served at the table. Gas grills vary in heat output; check the browning on the chicken when you uncover the grill for the first basting—if the bottoms threaten to scorch, shut off the burners under the chicken. If you cook both breasts and legs, make sure to take the internal temperatures of the different parts and remove the pieces as they are done cooking, as white meat is done at about 160°F and dark meat at about 175°F.

Don't flip the chicken *or place the pieces directly over the fire until the final minutes of cooking. The basting sauce contains a good dose of sugar and will burn if it gets too much direct heat.*

In a blender, combine the vinegar, ketchup, soy sauce, sugar, garlic, bay, peppercorns and 1½ teaspoons salt. Blend until well combined and the bay leaves are broken into tiny bits, 15 to 30 seconds. Pour the mixture into a large bowl, then stir in the soda.

If using chicken breasts, use a sturdy chef's knife to cut each in half crosswise. Cut 2 or 3 diagonal slashes about ½ inch deep through the skin and meat of each piece of chicken. Add the chicken to the marinade and turn to coat. Cover and refrigerate for at least 2 hours or up to 10 hours.

Prepare a charcoal or gas grill for indirect high-heat cooking. For a charcoal grill, spread a large chimney of hot coals evenly over one side of the grill bed; open the bottom grill vents and the lid vent. Heat the grill, covered, for 5 to 10 minutes, then clean and oil the grate. For a gas grill, turn all burners to high and heat, covered, for 15 minutes, then clean and oil the cooking grate; leave the primary burner on high and turn the remaining burner(s) to low.

While the grill heats, transfer the chicken to a large plate, allowing the marinade to drip off. Pour the marinade into a medium saucepan, bring to a simmer over medium and cook, stirring occasionally, until reduced to 1 cup, about 20 minutes. Stir in the lime juice and set aside. Set aside ⅓ cup for serving; use the remainder as a basting sauce.

Place the chicken skin side up on the cooler side of the grill. Cover and cook for 15 minutes. Generously brush the pieces with basting sauce, then re-cover and cook until the thickest part of the breast, if using, reaches 160°F or the thickest part of the thighs and drumsticks, if using, reach 175°F, another 15 to 20 minutes.

Brush the chicken with the reduced sauce, then flip the chicken skin side down onto the hot side of the grill. Cook until deeply browned, about 1 minute. Brush the bone side with basting sauce, then flip a final time and cook until deeply browned, about 1 minute. Transfer skin side up to a platter and let rest for about 5 minutes. Serve with the reserved sauce.

No. 54

Spice Under the Skin

When seasoning chicken with spices, we often apply them under the skin where they can directly flavor the meat and stay in place better.

Iraqi Spice-Crusted Grilled Chicken

Start to finish: **1½ hours** (**1 hour active**), plus resting
Servings: **4**

2½ tablespoons extra-virgin olive oil, divided

3 medium garlic cloves, finely grated

1 tablespoon ground sumac

2 teaspoons ground coriander

2 teaspoons curry powder

1 teaspoon garam masala

1 teaspoon sweet or hot paprika

¾ teaspoon ground cumin

½ teaspoon ground cardamom

Kosher salt and ground black pepper

3½- to 4-pound whole chicken, spatchcocked (instructions, p. 196)

Lemon wedges, to serve

This dish, based on an Iraqi spice rubbed chicken, uses two of our techniques, spatchcocking for even cooking (see p. 196 for instructions) and robust spicing. For maximum impact, those spices get rubbed under and over the skin. That's because while chicken skin can be a good thing—it reduces moisture loss during cooking by drip and evaporation—it also can make it hard for seasoning and meat to meld. To save time, we shorten the very long list of spices that make up the traditional rub by reaching for both curry powder and garam masala, two Indian seasoning blends that add up to about a dozen different spices. Ground sumac in the rub lends the chicken earthy, citrusy notes and, along with the paprika, a deep, brick-red hue. The bird cooks in under an hour and is rich and complexly flavored, with smokiness from the grill. Serve with basmati rice or warmed flatbread.

Don't forget to open the grill vents, *both on the bottom of the grill and on the lid, if you're using charcoal. This allows airflow so the fire does not extinguish during the covered cooking time.*

In a small skillet over low, combine 1½ tablespoons of oil and the garlic. Cook, stirring frequently, until fragrant and sizzling, but not browned, about 2 minutes. Transfer to a small bowl and set aside. In another small bowl, stir together the sumac, coriander, curry powder, garam masala, paprika, cumin, cardamom, 1 tablespoon salt and 1 teaspoon pepper. Add 2 tablespoons of the spice mixture to the garlic oil and stir to form a paste.

Place the chicken skin side up, on a cutting board. Loosen the skin over the chicken's breasts and thighs by gently working your fingers between the skin and the flesh. Using your fingers, evenly distribute the garlic-spice paste under

the skin and rub it into the flesh. Sprinkle the remaining spice mixture evenly on both sides of the chicken, patting gently to help it adhere. Tuck the wing tips to the back. Let stand uncovered at room temperature for about 45 minutes.

Prepare a grill for high-heat cooking. For a charcoal grill, spread a large chimney of hot coals evenly over one side of the grill bed; open the bottom grill vents and the lid vent. For a gas grill, turn all burners to high. Heat the grill, covered, for 5 to 10 minutes, then clean and oil the cooking grate.

If using a gas grill, leave the primary burner on high and turn off the other burners. Set the chicken skin up on the

cooler side of the grill, legs facing the heat. Cover and cook for 25 minutes.

Using tongs, rotate the chicken to bring the breast side closest to the heat. Cover and cook until the thickest part of the breast reaches 160°F and the thighs reach 175°F, another 25 to 35 minutes.

Brush the skin of the chicken with the remaining 1 tablespoon oil. Using tongs and a wide spatula, flip the chicken skin down onto the hot side of the grill. Cook until the skin is lightly charred, about 5 minutes. Transfer skin up to a cutting board and let rest for 15 minutes. Carve and serve with lemon wedges.

No. 55

Season Crumbs for Better Crust

Breading often is bland. But seasoning the breadcrumb coating itself—rather than just the meat— is an easy opportunity to build flavor into a dish.

Dukkah-Crusted Chicken Cutlets
with Carrot-Cashew Salad

2 tablespoons sesame seeds

1 tablespoon coriander seeds

1 tablespoon cumin seeds

1½ teaspoons caraway seeds

½ teaspoon dried oregano

½ cup roasted unsalted cashews, chopped, divided

Kosher salt and ground black pepper

4 medium carrots, peeled and shredded

3 tablespoons white wine vinegar

⅓ cup all-purpose flour

2 tablespoons cornstarch

2 large eggs

1¼ cups panko breadcrumbs

Four 5- to 6-ounce chicken breast cutlets, pounded to an even ¼-inch thickness

10 tablespoons grapeseed or other neutral oil, divided

Originally from Egypt, dukkah is a varying blend of seeds, nuts and spices used as a seasoning, garnish and dip (its high fat and protein content made it the original trail mix for Egyptian laborers). Adding the mix to the breading for pan-fried cutlets is an easy way to boost the flavor of mild-tasting chicken breasts. We prefer the uniformity of home-sliced cutlets. To make your own cutlets, start with breasts that weigh about 7 ounces each and use kitchen shears to remove the tenderloin (save for another use). Trim away any fat, then lay on a cutting board under plastic wrap. Use a meat mallet or small, heavy skillet to gently but firmly pound the meat until ¼ inch thick. If you do buy precut cutlets, make sure they are the same size to ensure even cooking. A tangy shredded carrot salad studded with cashews and sesame seeds is a savory-sweet counterpoint to these cutlets. If your carrots seem aged and a little lacking in natural sugar, add ⅛ to ¼ teaspoon sugar to sweeten them.

Don't overprocess the nut and seed mixture. Pulse until coarsely ground so the individual ingredients retain texture and flavor even after being combined with the panko.

In a 12-inch skillet over medium, toast the sesame seeds, stirring, until golden and fragrant, 1 to 2 minutes. Transfer to a small bowl and set the skillet aside.

In a food processor, combine the coriander, cumin, caraway, oregano, ¼ cup of cashews, 1 tablespoon of the toasted sesame seeds and ¼ teaspoon each salt and pepper. Pulse until coarsely ground, 12 to 15 pulses.

In a medium bowl, combine the carrots, vinegar, the remaining ¼ cup cashews, the remaining 1 tablespoon toasted sesame seeds and 1 teaspoon salt. Toss, then set aside.

Set a wire rack in each of 2 rimmed baking sheets. In a pie plate or wide, shallow bowl, stir together the flour and cornstarch. In a second similar dish, use a fork to beat the eggs and 1 tablespoon water until well combined. In a third, stir together the spice blend, the panko, ½ teaspoon salt and ¼ teaspoon pepper.

Season each cutlet on both sides with salt and pepper. One at a time, dredge the cutlets through the flour mixture, turning to coat and shaking off any excess, then coat both sides with egg, and finally dredge through the panko, pressing so the crumbs adhere. Place the cutlets on one of the prepared racks.

In the same 12-inch skillet over medium-high, heat 6 tablespoons of oil until shimmering. Add 2 cutlets and cook undisturbed until golden brown, 1 to 2 minutes. Using tongs, flip and cook until the second sides are golden brown, about 1 minute. Remove the skillet from the heat. Transfer the cutlets to the second prepared rack. Repeat with the remaining 4 tablespoons oil and the remaining cutlets, adjusting the heat as needed if the cutlets brown too quickly. Serve immediately with the carrot salad.

ESSENTIAL SPICE BLENDS

Six One-Stroke Solutions to Supper Seasonings

Spice blends are used around the world to add complexity with a simple sprinkle. Many are associated with particular regions, though within those regions the formula of ingredients can vary widely for each blend. With the exception of five-spice powder, shichimi togarashi and za'atar—which have finicky ingredient lists—we like the freshness and control we get from making our own blends.

BAHARAT

In Syria, this Middle Eastern blend is rich with allspice, while Persian Gulf variations emphasize dried limes. All versions generally are anchored by black pepper, paprika and dried chilies. Nutmeg, coriander, cumin, cardamom, cinnamon and cloves are common, too.

How to Make: Stir together **1½ tablespoons each ground black pepper, toasted ground coriander** and **toasted ground cumin, 1 tablespoon each ground cinnamon** and **ground cardamom,** and **½ teaspoon each cayenne pepper** and kosher salt.

How to Use: Baharat pairs well with red meat, salmon and vegetables. Rub it onto meat or fish before cooking, mix it into hot oil or butter for drizzling over everything from bulgur or couscous to popcorn and roasted sweet potatoes. Stir into lentil soups or add a spoonful to hamburgers or ground lamb patties.

BERBERE

Fiery hot and brick-red, berbere (bur-bur-ree) is the defining spice blend of Ethiopia. It contains red chilies, salt, fresh or dry aromatics (ginger, garlic and onion), and often fenugreek, allspice, cardamom, cloves, black pepper and turmeric. With its powerful heat, a little goes a long way.

How to Make: In a small skillet over medium-low, toast **1 tablespoon smoked paprika, 1 teaspoon each ground coriander** and **ground ginger, ½ teaspoon cayenne pepper** and **¼ teaspoon ground cardamom,** stirring constantly, for 1 to 2 minutes. Off heat, stir in ½ teaspoon kosher salt.

How to Use: Use it as a spice rub or as a final dusting for lentils and stews. It also works well with the savory-sweet flavor of tomatoes, such as a simple sauté of diced tomatoes and garlic to accompany plain roasted meats or seared steaks. Or, mix with lime juice and extra-virgin olive oil to use as a dressing that is especially good on a chickpea, radish and red onion salad.

DUKKAH

Dukkah is a mixture of sesame, cumin and coriander seeds blended with nuts (usually hazelnuts), herbs and whole or crushed spices. In Egypt, it is sprinkled on hard-boiled eggs, oiled flatbreads and roasted vegetables and meats. We use it to boost the flavor and texture of soups, stews and salads, or as a way to spice up olive oil for dipping. We also process it with panko for breading chicken cutlets.

How to Use: While shichimi is sprinkled on finished dishes, it is not typically used in cooking. The lively spice blend adds heat and depth to noodle dishes, soups, sauces and grilled meats.

How to Make: In a large skillet over medium, toast **½ cup cashews** for 3 to 4 minutes. Add **2 tablespoons sesame seeds** and toast for 1 to 2 minutes. Add **2 tablespoons each coriander seeds** and **cumin seeds** and **1 tablespoon caraway seeds,** then toast for 1 minute. Remove from the heat and let cool, then pulse in a food processor with **1 teaspoon dried oregano** and ½ teaspoon each kosher salt and ground black pepper until coarsely ground.

How to Use: Add to soups, stews and salads, or sprinkle over olive oil for dipping. Add textural contrast to salads and vegetables or create a crust on roasted meat, chicken or fish. We also use it as a topping for hearty toast smeared with goat cheese, cream cheese or smashed avocado.

FIVE-SPICE POWDER

Five-spice powder comes from China, where it's used in braising, stir-fries and roasting. It's a blend of star anise, fennel, cloves, tongue-tingling Sichuan pepper and cinnamon (or cassia, sometimes called Chinese cinnamon). Black pepper, ground ginger and/or cardamom some-

times find their way into the mix as well.

How to Use: Five-spice is particularly good with roasted meats like pork, beef and duck—star anise can boost the "browned" flavor in these dishes. The blend also can add dimension to sweets and baked goods, where its warmth can balance the sugar. Try adding a pinch to hot chocolate.

SHICHIMI TOGARASHI

Japan's seven-ingredient answer to Chinese five-spice, Japanese shichimi togarashi is a fine mixture of chili flakes, seaweed, ground ginger or garlic, dried citrus peel, Sichuan pepper and sesame, poppy and/or hemp seeds.

ZA'ATAR

In the Middle East, za'atar is the name of a fresh herb—reminiscent of thyme, marjoram and oregano—as well as a spice blend that often includes it. Though highly variable, the blend often includes sesame seeds and sumac, as well as dried herbs. It often is mixed with olive oil and used as a seasoning for flatbread, stews and vegetables.

How to Use: Rub za'atar onto meat and vegetables, or stir it into yogurt to make a quick dip or sauce. Try pairing with a drizzle of pomegranate molasses on roasted vegetables or fold into buttered couscous or rice.

No. 56

Tangy Sides Lighten and Brighten Heavy Mains

Fried and other oily foods often taste heavy. But serving them with sides spiked with acidic ingredients like slaws and quick pickles balances the richness.

Japanese-Style Chicken Cutlets
with Cabbage Slaw and Tonkatsu Sauce

3 tablespoons unseasoned
rice vinegar

½ teaspoon oyster sauce

Kosher salt and ground black pepper

½ small head green cabbage,
cored and shredded (about 3 cups)

2 scallions, thinly sliced on
the diagonal

⅓ cup all-purpose flour

2 tablespoons cornstarch

2 large eggs

1¾ cups panko breadcrumbs

Four 5- to 6-ounce chicken breast
cutlets, pounded to an even ¼-inch
thickness

10 tablespoons grapeseed or other
neutral oil, divided

Fried chicken usually is bone-in pieces in the U.S. But in Japan boneless chicken is the norm. Japanese panko-breaded chicken cutlets known as katsu cook quickly so the meat retains moisture and flavor, and the broad surface area offers lots of crisp, golden brown crust. Katsu traditionally are deep-fried and served with an intensely savory-sweet tonkatsu sauce. We opt for the ease of pan-frying. You could use store-bought tonkatsu sauce, but it's easy to make your own; ours is a little lighter and brighter than sauces from a bottle. A tangy cabbage slaw livens up the plate and balances the richness of the cutlets. Serve with steamed rice or, to make a chicken katsu sandwich, put a cutlet, sauce and slaw between slices of bread.

Don't use regular breadcrumbs. *The crisp, light texture of Japanese panko breadcrumbs is key to getting the crunchy coating on chicken katsu.*

In a medium bowl, combine the vinegar, oyster sauce and ½ teaspoon salt. Add the cabbage and scallions, then toss until the cabbage begins to wilt, about 1 minute. Set aside.

Set a wire rack in each of 2 rimmed baking sheets. In a pie plate or wide, shallow bowl, stir together the flour and cornstarch. In a second similar dish, use a fork to beat the eggs and 1 tablespoon water until well combined. In a third, stir together the panko, ½ teaspoon salt and ¼ teaspoon pepper.

Season each cutlet on both sides with salt and pepper. One at a time, dredge the cutlets through the flour mixture, turning to coat and shaking off any excess, then coat both sides with egg, and finally dredge through the panko, pressing so that the crumbs adhere. Place the cutlets on one of the prepared racks.

In a 12-inch skillet over medium-high, heat 6 tablespoons of oil until shimmering. Add 2 cutlets and cook undisturbed until golden brown, 1 to 2 minutes. Using tongs, flip and cook until the second sides are golden brown, about 1 minute. Remove the skillet from the heat. Transfer the cutlets to the second prepared rack. Repeat with the remaining 4 tablespoons oil and the remaining cutlets, adjusting the heat as needed if the cutlets brown too quickly. Serve immediately with the sauce and slaw.

TONKATSU SAUCE

This versatile dipping sauce is the classic accompaniment to fried chicken or pork cutlets, but it's also great blended with mayonnaise to make a sandwich spread.

Start to finish: **5 minutes**
Makes about **½ cup**

¼ cup ketchup

2½ tablespoons Worcestershire sauce

1 teaspoon granulated garlic

2 tablespoons unseasoned rice vinegar

4 teaspoons oyster sauce

In a small bowl, stir together all ingredients. Can be covered and refrigerated for up to 5 days.

Peruvian-Style Tangy Chicken
with Red Onions and Bell Pepper

2 pounds bone-in chicken thighs, skin removed, trimmed and patted dry

Kosher salt and ground black pepper

2 tablespoons grapeseed or other neutral oil, divided

2 cups low-sodium chicken broth

4 medium garlic cloves, minced

2 tablespoons ají amarillo paste (or 1 to 2 seeded and finely minced jalapeños)

1 tablespoon ancho chili powder

¼ teaspoon ground cumin

3 medium red onions, halved and sliced ¾-inch thick

1 large orange bell pepper, stemmed, seeded and sliced into ¼-inch strips

⅓ cup white wine vinegar

This dish is based on Peruvian chicken escabeche—escabeche roughly translates to pickled—and it's made by soaking meat or seafood in an acidic marinade after cooking, allowing the addition of bright flavors without altering the texture of the meat. A key component of the seasoning is ají amarillo, an orange-yellow chili ubiquitous to Peruvian cooking. In the U.S., the chilies are difficult to find fresh, but ají amarillo paste, sold in jars, is available in some well-stocked markets and specialty stores. The fruity, yet earthy flavor of ají amarillo is an important part of this dish, but if you can't find the paste, use 1 or 2 seeded and finely minced jalapeños. Serve with garlic rice, slices of steamed sweet potato and peeled and halved hard-cooked eggs.

Don't use regular chili powder *instead of pure ancho chili powder. Regular chili powder is a spice blend, whereas ancho chili powder contains only ancho chilies.*

Season the chicken all over with salt and pepper. In a large Dutch oven over medium-high, heat 1 tablespoon of oil until barely smoking. Add the chicken in a single layer and cook on each side, without disturbing, until deep golden brown, 3 to 5 minutes per side. Add the broth and bring to a boil. Cover, reduce to low and simmer until a skewer inserted into the largest thigh meets no resistance, 10 to 15 minutes.

Transfer the chicken to a serving dish and cover with foil. Bring the cooking liquid to a boil over high and cook until reduced to 1 cup, about 5 minutes. Transfer to a small bowl or measuring cup and set aside.

In the same pot, heat the remaining 1 tablespoon oil over medium until shimmering. Add the garlic, ají amarillo paste, ancho chili and cumin, then cook, scraping the bottom, until browned and fragrant, about 1 minute. Stir in the onions, bell pepper, 2 teaspoons salt and ¼ teaspoon pepper, then add the vinegar. Cook, stirring, until the onions have begun to soften and the sauce is just thick enough to coat the vegetables,

2 to 3 minutes. Add the reduced broth, bring to a simmer over medium-high and cook, stirring, until thickened to a glaze, about 5 minutes.

Pour the sauce and vegetables over the chicken. Let rest for 10 minutes, then serve.

No. 57

Cook First,
Flavor Last

Marinades rarely deliver much
flavor. They don't penetrate deeply
enough and the heat of cooking
can dull their flavors. So we instead
turn them into sauces we apply
at the end.

Hainanese Chicken and Rice

Start to finish: **1½ hours**
(30 minutes active)
Servings: **4**

2 quarts low-sodium chicken broth

6 medium garlic cloves, smashed and peeled, plus 4 medium garlic cloves, finely grated

5 ounces ginger, peeled and thinly sliced, plus 1 tablespoon finely grated ginger

1 tablespoon white peppercorns

Four 10- to 12-ounce bone-in, skin-on chicken breasts, skin removed and reserved

2 shallots, halved and thinly sliced

1½ cups jasmine rice, rinsed and drained

3 scallions, thinly sliced on the diagonal

Sliced cucumbers or shredded iceberg lettuce, to serve

Dipping sauce and/or sweet soy sauce (kecap manis), to serve (see note)

Though this dish is named for Hainan province in China, it's popular in several Southeast Asian countries and is widely regarded as one of Singapore's national foods. It's a humble preparation but is exceptional when done well. Ultra-tender, super-silky poached chicken served with rice cooked in a rich, fragrant chicken broth, with Indonesian sweet soy sauce (kecap manis) and additional condiments offered alongside such as our ginger-chili sauce, see following recipe. Skin-on chicken cooks gently in the broth, yielding moist, tender meat. Then the skin is removed and its fat rendered to flavor the rice, which is cooked with the liquid used to poached the chicken. Rather than use a whole chicken, which is traditional, we use breasts to keep the cooking as brief as possible. A digital thermometer is the best way to test the chicken's doneness. If you can't find sweet soy sauce but would like to offer it for serving, you can make your own (recipe p. 271).

Don't use boneless, skinless chicken breasts, as both the bones and skin are needed to give the rice rich, chicken flavor. When cooking the chicken, don't allow the broth to boil or even reach a vigorous simmer; this toughens the meat. A bare simmer keeps it tender and succulent.

In a large pot over medium-high, combine the broth, smashed garlic cloves, sliced ginger and peppercorns. Bring to a simmer, then submerge the chicken breasts, meat side down. Cover, reduce to low and cook, adjusting the heat as needed to maintain a bare simmer, until the thickest part of the breast reaches 160°F, 20 to 25 minutes.

Transfer the chicken, meat side down, to a medium bowl. Pour 1 cup of the hot cooking liquid over the chicken and set aside until cool enough to handle, about 30 minutes.

Meanwhile, strain the cooking liquid through a fine mesh strainer set over a large bowl; discard the solids. Reserve 2½ cups of the liquid; the remainder can be saved for another use. Reserve the pot.

When the chicken breasts are cool enough to handle, remove the meat from the bones, keeping each breast in a single piece. Discard the bones. Return

the meat to the bowl.

Set the pot over medium and add the chicken skin. Cook, stirring and scraping often to prevent sticking, until the skin is rendered and crisp, 3 to 5 minutes. Add the shallots, the grated garlic and grated ginger and cook, stirring, until they begin to brown, 1 to 2 minutes. Add the rice and cook, stirring, until the grains are coated with fat, 2 to 5 minutes. Carefully stir in 2 cups of the reserved cooking liquid (reserve the remaining ½ cup liquid for the dipping sauce), scraping the bottom of the pot. Cover and bring to a boil, then reduce to low and cook until the rice absorbs the liquid, about 12 minutes.

Remove the pot from the heat and let stand, covered, for 10 to 15 minutes. Fluff the grains with a fork and discard the chicken skin. Transfer the rice to a serving bowl and sprinkle with scallions. Cut the chicken breasts crosswise

into ½-inch slices and arrange on a platter with the cucumbers or lettuce. Serve with the rice, dipping sauce and/or kecap manis.

GINGER-CHILI DIPPING SAUCE

Start to finish: **5 minutes**

Makes about **¾ cup**

½ cup reserved chicken cooking liquid, warmed

¼ cup soy sauce

1 teaspoon finely grated fresh ginger

1 teaspoon white sugar

1 teaspoon chili-garlic sauce

¼ teaspoon ground white pepper

1 tablespoon finely chopped scallion greens

In a medium bowl, whisk together the chicken cooking liquid, soy sauce, ginger, sugar, chili-garlic sauce and white pepper. Stir in the scallions.

No. 58

Use a Low, Slow Simmer to Keep Meat Moist

Cooking meat in liquid that's kept at a gentle simmer makes for moister meat. The liquid itself doesn't add moisture, but the milder heat cooks the meat more gently, keeping it tender and moist.

No. 59

Stop Tossing Your Stems

Don't trash your cilantro stems; they are full of flavor. We frequently puree them into sauces, salsas and moles, and use them to flavor rice dishes and soups.

Peruvian Chicken, Rice
and Cilantro Soup (Aguadito de Pollo)

1 tablespoon grapeseed or other neutral oil

4 medium garlic cloves, minced

1 medium white onion, finely chopped

1 bunch fresh cilantro, stems minced, leaves left whole, reserved separately

¼ cup ají amarillo paste (see note)

Kosher salt and ground black pepper

1½ pounds bone-in, skin-on chicken breasts, thighs or legs

1 cup long-grain white rice, rinsed and drained

3 medium carrots, peeled and cut crosswise into ½-inch pieces

1 medium red or yellow bell pepper, stemmed and cut into ½-inch pieces

1 cup frozen peas

2 tablespoons lime juice

Chicken soup too often turns out blandly insipid—or a muddle of flavors with too many seasonings added to compensate. We avoid that trap in this version, inspired by Peru's aguadito de pollo. Bright, green seasonings take center stage with a full bunch of cilantro, stems and all, and a cup of peas; we use frozen for convenience. Traditional aguadito includes starchy Peruvian corn. Rather than substitute sweet corn, which is far more sugary, we opted to omit it. The soup gets mild spiciness from ají amarillo, an orange-yellow chili with a fruity yet earthy flavor that is ubiquitous in Peruvian cuisine. In fresh form, the chilies are difficult to find in the U.S., but ají amarillo paste, sold in jars, is available in some well-stocked markets and specialty stores, as well as online. If you can't find it, use 2 or 3 seeded and finely minced jalapeños.

Don't use boneless, skinless chicken parts in this soup. Both the bones and skin give the broth rich flavor, as well as body. Don't make this soup in advance; it's best served right away. As it sits, the rice continues to absorb liquid and eventually the grains become mushy.

In a large pot over medium-high, heat the oil until shimmering. Add the garlic, onion, cilantro stems, ají amarillo paste and 2 teaspoons salt. Cook, stirring occasionally, until the paste begins to brown on the bottom of the pot, about 8 minutes. Add 7 cups water and bring to a simmer, scraping up the browned bits. Add the chicken in an even layer, then return to a simmer. Cover and cook, adjusting heat to maintain a simmer, until a skewer inserted at the thickest part of the meat meets no resistance, about 40 minutes. Transfer the chicken to a plate and set aside until cool enough to handle.

In a blender, combine the cilantro leaves, a pinch of salt and ⅓ cup water. Blend, scraping the sides as needed, until smooth, about 1 minute. You should have about ½ cup puree. Set aside.

To the pot, add the rice, carrots, bell pepper, and ½ teaspoon each salt and pepper, then stir to combine. Bring to a simmer over medium-high, then cover, reduce to low and cook without stirring until the rice and vegetables are tender, about 10 minutes. Meanwhile, shred the chicken into bite-size pieces, discarding the skin and bones.

When the rice and vegetables are tender, stir the shredded chicken and peas into the soup. Cook until the peas are heated through, about 1 minute. Stir in the cilantro puree and lime juice, then taste and season with salt and pepper.

Put a Lid on It for Richer Low-Liquid Cooking

Cooking chicken in a covered pot with a small amount of liquid cooks the meat mainly in its own juices, keeping flavors rich and concentrated.

Mushrooms, Leeks and Chives
Chicken en Cocotte

Start to finish: **1¾ hours
(30 minutes active)**
Servings: **4**

4- to 4½-pound whole chicken, wings tucked and legs tied

Kosher salt and ground black pepper

5 tablespoons salted butter, divided

1½ pounds cremini mushrooms, quartered

3 large leeks, white and light green parts sliced crosswise, rinsed and dried

8 medium garlic cloves, peeled and halved

1½ cups dry white wine

10 thyme sprigs

3 tablespoons lemon juice

2 tablespoons whole-grain Dijon mustard

6 tablespoons finely chopped fresh chives, plus more to serve

We came up with three variations on this Dutch oven-cooked chicken, one with a classic French pairing of mushrooms with leeks and chives, a second with fennel and spicy North African harissa, and a third flavored with dried apricots and saffron threads. In this first version, the flavors of Provence are highlighted. Mushrooms add umami flavor and lemon juice and whole-grain mustard perk up the butter-enriched wine sauce with bright acidity. To be efficient, chop the chives while the chicken cooks. Serve with mashed potatoes, egg noodles or steamed rice.

Don't be lax about washing the leeks. Their many layers trap dirt and sand. It's best to rinse them after slicing so you can get between the layers, then drain and pat them dry to remove excess moisture.

Heat the oven to 400°F with a rack in the lower-middle position. Using paper towels, pat the chicken dry, then season on all sides with salt and pepper. Set aside.

In a large (at least 7-quart) Dutch oven over medium-high, melt 1 tablespoon of butter. Add the mushrooms, leeks and garlic, then cook, stirring occasionally, until the mushrooms have released their liquid and most of it has evaporated, about 12 minutes. Add the wine and bring to a simmer. Lay the thyme sprigs on top, then place the chicken breast down in the pot. Cover and bake until the thickest part of the breast reaches 160°F

and the thighs reach 175°F, 55 to 65 minutes. Using tongs inserted into the cavity, carefully transfer to a baking dish, turning the chicken breast up. Let rest for 15 minutes.

While the chicken rests, remove and discard the thyme sprigs from the pot. Bring the cooking liquid to a simmer over medium and cook until thick enough to lightly coat a spoon, about 5 minutes. Off heat, add the remaining 4 tablespoons butter, the lemon juice and mustard, then stir until the butter melts. Taste and season with salt and pepper. Stir in the chives.

Transfer the chicken to a cutting board. Remove the legs from the chicken by cutting through the hip joints. Remove and discard the skin from the legs, then separate the thighs from the drumsticks by cutting through the joints. Remove the breast meat from the bone, remove and discard the skin, then cut each breast half crosswise into thin slices. Arrange the chicken in a serving dish. Spoon the sauce and vegetables over and around the chicken. Sprinkle with additional chives.

Fennel, Tomatoes and Harissa
Chicken en Cocotte

Start to finish: **1 hour 35 minutes**
(15 minutes active)
Servings: **4**

4- to 4½-pound whole chicken, wings tucked and legs tied

Kosher salt and ground black pepper

5 tablespoons salted butter, divided

1 large yellow onion, cut into ½-inch wedges

1 large fennel bulb, trimmed, halved, cored and sliced crosswise ½ inch thick

6 medium garlic cloves, chopped

¼ cup harissa

2 teaspoons ground turmeric

28-ounce can whole tomatoes, lightly crushed

1½ cups dry white wine

½ cup chopped pimento-stuffed green olives

1 tablespoon grated lemon zest

¼ cup finely chopped fresh mint

The sweetness of onion and fennel are balanced by the spiciness of harissa and the tanginess of tomatoes and white wine in this dish inspired by the blending of French and North African culinary traditions. If you like, offer additional harissa at the table for extra heat. Couscous, crusty bread or warmed flatbread are excellent accompaniments for this dish.

Don't drain the juice from the tomatoes*. Add them to the pot along with the tomatoes. They lend color, acidity and a little sweetness to the sauce.*

Heat the oven to 400°F with a rack in the lower-middle position. Using paper towels, pat the chicken dry, then season on all sides with salt and pepper. Set aside.

In a large (at least 7-quart) Dutch oven over medium, melt 1 tablespoon of butter. Add the onion and fennel, then cook, stirring occasionally, until lightly browned, about 8 minutes. Stir in the garlic and cook until fragrant, about 30 seconds. Stir in the harissa, turmeric and tomatoes, then bring to a simmer and cook until the mixture thickens, 5 to 7 minutes. Add the wine and return to a simmer, then place the chicken breast-side down in the pot. Cover and bake until the thickest part of the breast reaches 160°F and the thighs reach 175°F, 55 to 65 minutes. Using tongs inserted into the cavity, carefully transfer to a baking dish, turning the chicken breast up. Let rest for 15 minutes.

While the chicken rests, stir the olives into the vegetable mixture, then bring to a simmer over medium-high. Cook until the liquid is thick enough to lightly coat a spoon, about 15 minutes. Off heat, add the remaining 4 tablespoons butter and the lemon zest; stir until the butter melts. Taste and season with salt and pepper.

Transfer the chicken to a cutting board. Remove the legs from the chicken by cutting through the hip joints. Remove and discard the skin from the legs, then separate the thighs from the drumsticks by cutting through the joints. Remove the breast meat from the bone, remove and discard the skin, then cut each breast half crosswise into thin slices. Arrange the chicken on a serving dish. Stir the mint into the sauce, then spoon the sauce and vegetables over and around the chicken.

Apricots, Saffron and Tarragon
Chicken en Cocotte

Start to finish: **1 hour 35 minutes**
(15 minutes active)
Servings: **4**

4- to 4½-pound whole chicken, wings tucked and legs tied

Kosher salt and ground black pepper

5 tablespoons salted butter, divided

8 large shallots, peeled and halved

8 medium garlic cloves, peeled and halved

½ teaspoon red pepper flakes

½ cup dried apricots, thinly sliced

¼ teaspoon saffron threads

1½ cups dry white wine

6 thyme sprigs

1 tablespoon lemon juice

¼ cup finely chopped fresh tarragon

This chicken en cocotte evokes the rich flavor, fragrance and colors of Persian cuisine. Dried apricots and silky braised shallots balance the tender mildness of the chicken. Saffron threads give the sauce a golden hue and a slightly minerally, subtly floral flavor and aroma. Serve the chicken with couscous, egg noodles or rice pilaf.

Don't use unsulfured dried apricots. *Their brown color will make the dish appear drab and dull. Use regular dried apricots instead.*

Heat the oven to 400°F with a rack in the lower-middle position. Using paper towels, pat the chicken dry, then season on all sides with salt and pepper. Set aside.

In a large (at least 7-quart) Dutch oven over medium, melt 1 tablespoon butter. Add the shallots and garlic and cook, stirring occasionally, until lightly browned, about 5 minutes. Stir in the red pepper flakes, apricots and saffron, then cook until fragrant, about 30 seconds. Add the wine and bring to a simmer. Lay the thyme sprigs on top, then place the chicken breast down in the pot. Cover and bake until the thickest part of the breast

reaches 160°F and the thighs reach 175°F, 55 to 65 minutes. Using tongs inserted into the cavity, carefully transfer to a baking dish, turning the chicken breast up. Let rest for 15 minutes.

While the chicken rests, remove and discard the thyme sprigs from the pot. Bring the cooking liquid to a simmer over medium and cook until thick enough to lightly coat a spoon, about 10 minutes. Off heat, add the remaining 4 tablespoons butter and lemon juice, then stir until the butter melts. Taste and season with salt and pepper.

Transfer the chicken to a cutting board. Remove the legs from the chicken by cutting through the hip joints. Remove and discard the skin from the legs, then separate the thighs from the drumsticks by cutting through the joints. Remove the breast meat from the bone, remove and discard the skin, then cut each breast half crosswise into thin slices. Arrange the chicken in a serving dish. Stir the tarragon into the sauce, then spoon the sauce, apricots and vegetables over and around the chicken.

PORK

RECIPES & RULES

PORK

At Milk Street, we pair **pork with warm spices** and aromatic sauces. We **chill chewy cuts to make it easy to slice them extra-thin for tenderness.** And we **use marinades two ways, as an initial seasoning and as a serving sauce.**

Pork comes with a learning curve. While we're generally comfortable tossing bacon or sausage into a skillet, or smothering pork chops with onions, other cuts get trickier. Lean tenderloins are easy to overcook and lack flavor. Cheaper cuts like pork shoulder can take hours to cook, and even then there's no guarantee they won't be tough or fatty.

So we looked to Asia, where pork is prized, as well as India, Mexico and Italy, and found plenty of ideas for tender, flavorful, simple dishes. There's no one-size-fits-all solution; some techniques call for fast-cooking; others rely on low-and-slow. But key to all is flavoring with a bold hand and keeping a close eye on balance—rich meets tangy, robust marries mild.

Tenderness can be a problem with some cuts of pork. In our skewers inspired by the popular Thai street food moo ping, we **partially freeze meat for easier slicing, then cut it thin to shorten muscle fibers, making them less chewy.** For our Tuscan pork ribs, we use thicker St. Louis-style spareribs and **add water to the pan to create a steamy environment that cooks the meat gently and effectively.**

If we do go to the trouble of marinating, we make sure it counts. In our ginger pork, based on Japanese shogayaki, we **use a marinade two ways—as an initial flavoring and later as a serving sauce.** And we **balance the richness of pork with tangy ingredients,** like the tamarind sauce we use with our Indian-inspired curry.

Tenderloins live up to their name and are quick-cooking, too, though they are inclined to be bland. To add flavor and texture, we **coat tenderloins in flavorful rubs and briefly sear them on the stovetop to enhance the flavor of the spices.** Chilies and cocoa powder bring depth to our Mexican stew, a simplified version of the celebratory wedding dish known as asado de bodas.

No. 61

Cut Meat Cold for Thin, Tender Slices

Tough cuts of meat can be made more tender by thinly slicing them, shortening the otherwise chewy muscle fibers. Sometimes we freeze the meat to make the slicing easier.

Thai Grilled Pork Skewers
(Moo Ping)

Start to finish: **1 hour, plus chilling and marinating**
Servings: **4 to 6**

2 pounds boneless pork shoulder, trimmed of surface fat

6 medium garlic cloves, minced

2 tablespoons finely minced fresh cilantro stems

⅓ cup firmly packed light or dark brown sugar

3 tablespoons fish sauce

2 tablespoons peanut oil

1 tablespoon soy sauce

Ground white pepper

⅓ cup coconut milk

Chili-lime sauce (jaew), to serve

In Thailand, moo ping is sold by street vendors who cook the skewers on grills set out on crowded sidewalks. Pork shoulder is the best cut to use as it has a generous amount of fat, which is essential for flavor and juiciness. Partially freezing the meat firms it so it is easier to slice. Aim for ⅛-inch-thick slices to minimize the chewiness. And if the pork doesn't wind up in neat strips, don't worry—they can be folded or pieced together as they're threaded to make neat-looking skewers. Though moo ping is tasty on its own, a dipping sauce is customary and adds a whole other flavor dimension. We liked ours with a chili-lime sauce called jaew; see following recipe.

***Don't thread the meat loosely** on the skewers. The pieces should be scrunched together somewhat tightly. This helps guard against overcooking. If you're using a charcoal grill, don't push the meat all the way to the bottom of the skewers; the protruding handle end of the skewers may prevent you from being able to position the meat directly over the coals.*

Place the pork on a large plate and freeze until the meat is firm and partially frozen, 1 to 1½ hours. Meanwhile, in a medium bowl, stir together the garlic, cilantro, sugar, fish sauce, oil, soy sauce and ½ teaspoon white pepper.

Using a sharp chef's knife, slice the partially frozen pork into pieces about ⅛ inch thick. The slices will be irregularly shaped; cut them into strips 1 to 1¼ inches wide (it's fine if the strips are not uniform). Add the pork to the marinade and mix with your hands until evenly coated. Cover and refrigerate for at least 2 hours or up to 12 hours.

Thread the pork onto ten 10- to 12-inch metal skewers, evenly dividing the meat and scrunching it together and packing it quite tightly. If some pieces are too wide, too wispy or awkwardly shaped, fold the meat or tuck in the edges as you skewer. Place on a rimmed baking sheet or in a large baking dish, cover and refrigerate while you prepare the grill.

Prepare a charcoal or gas grill. For a charcoal grill, ignite a large chimney of coals, let burn until lightly ashed over,

then distribute the coals evenly over one side of the grill bed; open the bottom grill vents. Heat the grill, covered, for 5 to 10 minutes, then clean and oil the grate. For a gas grill, turn all burners to high and heat, covered, for 15 minutes, then clean and oil the grate.

Place the skewers on the hot side of the grill (if using charcoal) and cook until lightly charred, about 3 minutes. Using tongs, flip the skewers, then brush with some of the coconut milk. Cook until the second sides are lightly charred, about another 3 minutes. Flip the skewers again and continue to cook, occasionally brushing with coconut milk and turning every couple of minutes, until deeply charred on both sides, about another 5 to 6 minutes. Transfer to a platter and serve with the sauce.

CHILI-LIME SAUCE (JAEW)

This sauce strikes a balance of salty and tangy with a touch of sweet and heat. The toasted rice adds a unique flavor and gives the sauce clingability.

Start to finish: **20 minutes**
Makes about **¾ cup**

1½ tablespoons jasmine rice

¼ cup fish sauce

3 tablespoons lime juice

1 medium shallot, minced

2 tablespoons finely chopped fresh cilantro

1 tablespoon packed light or dark brown sugar

2 teaspoons red pepper flakes

In a small skillet over medium, toast the rice, occasionally shaking the pan, until golden brown, about 5 minutes. Transfer to a spice grinder and let cool completely, then pulse to a coarse powder, 8 to 10 pulses. Transfer to a small bowl.

Into the rice powder, stir in the remaining ingredients and 1 tablespoon water. Cover and refrigerate for at least 1 hour before using; bring to room temperature before serving. (Leftovers can be refrigerated in an airtight container for up to 3 days; the sauce will thicken slightly.)

No. 62

Use Steam Power for More Tender Meat

Adding water to the pan doesn't directly add moisture to the meat, but it does create a moist environment that transfers heat to the meat more efficiently than dry air, cooking it fast and keeping it tender.

Fennel–Brown Sugar Pork Ribs
(Rosticciana)

Kosher salt and ground black pepper

2 tablespoons packed
light brown sugar

1 tablespoon fennel seeds, ground

1 teaspoon red pepper flakes

1 teaspoon granulated garlic

6 teaspoons minced fresh
rosemary, divided

Two 2½- to 3-pound racks St. Louis–
style pork spareribs

In Tuscany, rosticciana is cooked on a grill and served with other meats, such as steak and sausage. We chose to focus on the ribs and brought the recipe indoors so we could use the oven to create just the right cooking environment for yielding super-tender and perfectly browned ribs. For the fullest, richest flavor, it's best to pulverize your own fennel seeds in a spice grinder. If convenience is key and you can find ground fennel seed at the grocery store, use the same amount of ground fennel (1 tablespoon). The start-to-finish time for this recipe may be long, but the hands-on cooking is minimal.

Don't substitute baby back ribs for the St. Louis spareribs. Baby backs are smaller and leaner and will end up overdone. St. Louis–style ribs are spareribs that are trimmed of excess meat and cartilage, so the racks have a neat rectangular shape. Try to choose racks that are similar in size so they cook at the same rate.

Heat the oven to 325°F with a rack in the middle position. Set a wire rack in a rimmed baking sheet. In a small bowl, combine 2 tablespoons salt, 1 tablespoon black pepper, the sugar, ground fennel, pepper flakes, granulated garlic and 4 teaspoons of rosemary. Rub the mixture between your fingertips until well combined and the rosemary is fragrant. Sprinkle the mixture evenly over both sides of the racks of ribs, then rub it in.

Place the ribs, meaty side up, on the wire rack on the baking sheet. Transfer to the oven, then pour 3 cups water into the baking sheet. Bake until a skewer inserted into the meat between the bones meets no resistance, 2½ to 3 hours.

Transfer the rib racks to a cutting board and let rest for 20 minutes. Cut the ribs between the bones and transfer to a platter.

No. 63

Don't Marinate Without Also Saucing

Marinades are slow to penetrate meat, so they add limited flavor. To get around this, use them twice—first to season the meat before cooking, then later as a sauce for the finished dish.

MAKING PORK CUTLETS

1. Cut the tenderloin in half crosswise, making the tail end slightly larger.

2. Cut each piece in half lengthwise so that you have a total of 4 pieces.

3. Place 2 pieces between sheets of plastic wrap and gently pound with a meat pounder to an even ¼-inch thickness.

4. Repeat with the remaining 2 pieces of pork, reusing the plastic wrap.

Japanese Ginger Pork
(Shogayaki)

¼ cup soy sauce

3 tablespoons mirin

2 tablespoons sake

1 tablespoon white miso

1½ tablespoons finely grated fresh ginger

1¼-pound pork tenderloin, trimmed of silver skin

2 tablespoons grapeseed or other neutral oil

2 teaspoons white sugar

1 bunch scallions, cut into 1-inch pieces

½ small head green cabbage, cored and finely shredded (about 3 cups)

Cooked Japanese-style short-grain rice, to serve

Shoga means "ginger" in Japanese, and yaki translates as "grilled," though the term sometimes is applied to foods that are fried or griddled. In the popular dish known as shogayaki, thinly sliced pork is cooked with a lightly sweetened, very gingery soy-based sauce. We use pork tenderloin cut into quarters and pounded into thin cutlets. A quick soak in a marinade that later becomes the sauce ensures the cutlets are thoroughly flavored. Shredded green cabbage and steamed rice are the classic accompaniments.

Don't crowd the skillet when cooking the cutlets. It's usually best to cook them in two batches so they brown rather than steam. But how they fit in the skillet depends on their shape after pounding. If you can fit all four in the pan without them touching, cook all at once using the 2 tablespoons of oil.

In a wide, shallow bowl, whisk together the soy sauce, mirin, sake, miso and ginger. Cut the pork tenderloin in half crosswise, making the tail-end half slightly larger, then cut each piece in half lengthwise. Place 2 pieces of pork between 2 large sheets of plastic wrap. Using a meat pounder, gently pound each piece to an even ¼-inch thickness. Repeat with the 2 remaining pieces. Add the cutlets to the soy mixture and turn to coat, then let marinate at room temperature for 15 minutes.

Remove the cutlets from the marinade, letting the excess drain back into the bowl; reserve the marinade. Pat the cutlets dry with paper towels. In a 12-inch skillet over medium-high, heat 1 tablespoon of oil until shimmering. Add the cutlets in a single layer and cook undisturbed until well browned, 2 to 3 minutes. Using tongs, flip each piece and continue to cook until the second sides are well browned, about another 2 minutes. Transfer to a large plate, then wipe out the skillet with paper towels. Repeat with the remaining oil and cutlets.

Return the skillet to medium-high and add the reserved marinade, the sugar and ¼ cup water. Bring to a simmer and cook, scraping up any browned bits, until the mixture thickens and a spoon drawn through it leaves a 1- to 2-second trail, about 3 minutes. Stir in the scallions, then add the pork and any accumulated juices. Cook, stirring gently, until the scallions are wilted and the pork is heated through, about 1 minute. Serve with the shredded cabbage and rice.

CHANGE THE WAY YOU COOK

No. 64

Give Meats an
Acidic Finish

Adding acidic ingredients
at the end lightens and
brightens otherwise rich
and heavy meats.

Spicy Curry-Cumin Pork

½ cup tamarind pulp (4 ounces)

1 tablespoon grapeseed or other neutral oil

2 medium yellow onions, halved and sliced

6 medium garlic cloves, smashed and peeled

3 tablespoons finely grated fresh ginger

1 jalapeño chili, stemmed, seeded and thinly sliced

2 tablespoons ground coriander

2 tablespoons curry powder

1 tablespoon ground cumin

1 tablespoon fennel seeds

Kosher salt and ground black pepper

5 pounds boneless pork shoulder, trimmed and cut into 2-inch chunks

1 cup low-sodium chicken broth or water

1 tablespoon white vinegar

Portuguese influence in southern India explains the preponderance of pork in many of the region's stews. Mangalorean dukra maas was the inspiration for this spicy pork curry with tangy, fruity notes from tamarind pulp and the brightness of vinegar stirred in at the end. If you like chili heat, leave the seeds in the jalapeño and add an extra one or two. Serve with basmati rice.

Don't use tamarind concentrate *sold in a small plastic container. Though it is ready to use (no need to rehydrate and strain), its flavor is dull. Instead, look for blocks of tamarind pulp; it's available in some well-stocked supermarkets, in Asian grocery stores and online.*

Heat the oven to 350°F with a rack in the lower-middle position. In a 2-cup liquid measuring cup or a small microwave-safe bowl, combine the tamarind pulp and 1 cup water. Microwave on high until warm, about 1 minute, then whisk to combine. Let stand for at least 10 minutes.

Pour the tamarind mixture through a fine mesh strainer set over a medium bowl, pressing to extract as much liquid as possible and scraping the underside to collect as much pulp as possible; set aside. Discard the solids in the strainer.

In a Dutch oven over medium, heat the oil until shimmering. Add the onions, garlic, ginger and jalapeño, then cook, stirring occasionally, until the vegetables are softened, about 5 minutes. Add the coriander, curry powder, cumin, fennel seeds, 1 teaspoon salt and ½ teaspoon pepper, then cook, stirring, until fragrant, 1 to 2 minutes. Add the pork, broth and the strained tamarind. Stir to combine, then bring to a simmer over medium-high. Cover, place the pot in the oven and cook for 2 hours.

Uncover the pot and stir. Return, uncovered, to the oven and cook until a skewer inserted into the pork meets no resistance, about another 1 hour. Remove the pot from the oven. Tilt the pot to pool the liquid to one side and use a wide spoon to skim off and discard as much fat as possible from the surface. Stir in the vinegar, then taste and season with salt and pepper.

No. 65

Sear on the Stovetop, Cook in the Oven

Searing a spice-crusted pork tenderloin on the stovetop not only browns the meat, it also toasts the seasonings, heightening their flavors. But it's easy to overcook, so we finish it in the gentler and more even heat of the oven.

Suya-Spiced Pan-Roasted
Pork Tenderloins

2 teaspoons sweet paprika

2 teaspoons ground ginger

2 teaspoons granulated garlic

2 teaspoons onion powder

½ teaspoon cayenne pepper

Kosher salt and ground black pepper

Two 1¼-pound pork tenderloins, trimmed of silver skin and halved crosswise

2 tablespoons grapeseed or other neutral oil

2 teaspoons packed light or dark brown sugar

¾ cup low-sodium chicken broth

4 tablespoons (½ stick) salted butter, cut into 8 pieces and chilled

2 tablespoons lime juice

⅓ cup roasted, unsalted peanuts, finely chopped

This recipe was inspired by Nigerian beef suya, or beef skewers seasoned with chili and peanuts. The pan sauce has a simple base, but gets lots of character from the lime juice and chopped peanuts that are stirred in at the end. Warmed flatbread or steamed rice would be a great accompaniment.

Don't add the butter *all at once when making the pan sauce. Whisking it in a piece at a time creates an emulsified sauce that's glossy and velvety. If the sauce breaks and the butter separates, drizzle in a few drops of water while swirling the pan until the sauce is once again shiny and emulsified.*

Heat the oven to 450°F with a rack in the middle position. In a large bowl, stir together the paprika, ginger, granulated garlic, onion powder, cayenne and 1 teaspoon each salt and black pepper. Add the pork, turn to coat and massage the spice mixture into the meat. Let stand at room temperature for 15 minutes.

In an oven-safe 12-inch skillet over medium-high, heat the oil until shimmering. Add the pork and cook, turning occasionally with tongs, until browned on all sides, about 4 minutes total. Transfer the skillet to the oven and roast until the center of the thickest tenderloin reaches 140°F, 10 to 15 minutes.

Transfer the skillet to the stovetop (the handle will be hot). Using tongs, transfer the pork to a large plate and let rest for 10 minutes. Meanwhile, add the sugar and broth to the skillet. Bring to a simmer over medium-high, scraping up any browned bits, and cook until reduced to ½ cup and slightly thickened, about 2 minutes.

While whisking constantly, add the butter 1 piece at a time; add the next piece only after the previous one is almost fully incorporated. After all the butter is incorporated, stir in the lime juice and cook until a spatula drawn through the sauce leaves a trail, about 20 seconds.

Off heat, stir in the peanuts, then taste the sauce and season with salt and black pepper. Thinly slice the tenderloins and arrange on a platter. Stir any accumulated pork juices into the sauce, then spoon the sauce over the pork.

Fennel-Rosemary Pan-Roasted
Pork Tenderloins

4 teaspoons fresh rosemary, minced, divided

4 teaspoons fennel seeds, ground

2 teaspoons dried oregano

2 teaspoons garlic powder

¾ teaspoon red pepper flakes

Kosher salt and ground black pepper

Two 1¼-pound pork tenderloins, trimmed of silver skin and halved crosswise

2 tablespoons grapeseed or other neutral oil

2 teaspoons packed light or dark brown sugar

¾ cup low-sodium chicken broth

4 tablespoons (½ stick) salted butter, cut into 8 pieces and chilled

2 tablespoons lemon juice

Think of this dish as a weeknight version of Italian slow-roasted porchetta. Fennel seeds and herbs are ideal seasonings for the mild, subtly sweet flavor of pork tenderloin. Serve crusty bread or mashed potatoes alongside for soaking up the sauce.

Don't add the butter *all at once when making the pan sauce. Whisking it in a piece at a time creates an emulsified sauce that's glossy and velvety. If the sauce breaks and the butter separates, drizzle in a few drops of water while swirling the pan until the sauce is once again shiny and emulsified.*

Heat the oven to 450°F with a rack in the middle position. In a large bowl, stir together 3 teaspoons of rosemary, the fennel seed, oregano, garlic powder, pepper flakes and 1 teaspoon each salt and black pepper. Add the pork, turn to coat and massage the seasonings into the meat. Let stand at room temperature for 15 minutes.

In an oven-safe 12-inch skillet over medium-high, heat the oil until shimmering. Add the pork and cook, turning occasionally with tongs, until browned on all sides, about 4 minutes total. Transfer the skillet to the oven and roast until the center of the thickest tenderloin reaches 140°F, 10 to 15 minutes.

Transfer the skillet to the stovetop (the handle will be hot). Using tongs, transfer the pork to a large plate and let rest for 10 minutes. Meanwhile, add the sugar and broth to the skillet. Bring to a simmer over medium-high, scraping up any browned bits, and cook until reduced to ½ cup and slightly thickened, about 2 minutes.

While whisking constantly, add the butter 1 piece at a time; add the next piece only after the previous one is almost fully incorporated. After all the butter is incorporated, stir in the lemon juice and cook until a spatula drawn through the sauce leaves a trail, about 20 seconds.

Off heat, stir in the remaining 1 teaspoon rosemary, then taste the sauce and season with salt and black pepper. Thinly slice the tenderloins and arrange on a platter. Stir any accumulated pork juices into the sauce, then spoon the sauce over the pork.

Caraway-Dill Pan-Roasted
Pork Tenderloins

Start to finish: **50 minutes**
Servings: **6**

1 tablespoon caraway seeds, crushed

2½ teaspoons ground coriander

2½ teaspoons dry mustard

Kosher salt and ground black pepper

Two 1¼-pound pork tenderloins, trimmed of silver skin and halved crosswise

2 tablespoons grapeseed or other neutral oil

2 teaspoons packed light or dark brown sugar

¾ cup low-sodium chicken broth

4 tablespoons (½ stick) salted butter, cut into 8 pieces and chilled

2 tablespoons cider vinegar

2 tablespoons chopped fresh dill

For these pork tenderloins, we looked to the flavors of Eastern Europe. Crushing the caraway seeds releases their essential oils for bigger, bolder flavor. Use a mortar and pestle or the back of a heavy pan to break them up, or pulse them a few times in a spice grinder. Serve the tenderloins with roasted potatoes or winter squash.

Don't add the butter all at once when making the pan sauce. Whisking it in a piece at a time creates an emulsified sauce that's glossy and velvety. If the sauce breaks and the butter separates, drizzle in a few drops of water while swirling the pan until the sauce is once again shiny and emulsified.

Heat the oven to 450°F with a rack in the middle position. In a large bowl combine the caraway, coriander, mustard, 1 teaspoon salt and 2 teaspoons pepper. Add the pork, turn to coat and massage the spices into the meat. Let stand at room temperature for 15 minutes.

In an oven-safe 12-inch skillet over medium-high, heat the oil until shimmering. Add the pork and cook, turning occasionally with tongs, until browned on all sides, about 4 minutes total. Transfer the skillet to the oven and roast until the center of the thickest tenderloin reaches 140°F, 10 to 15 minutes.

Transfer the skillet to the stovetop (the handle will be hot). Using tongs, transfer the pork to a large plate and let rest for 10 minutes. Meanwhile, add the sugar and broth to the skillet. Bring to a simmer over medium-high, scraping up any browned bits, and cook until reduced to ½ cup and slightly thickened, about 2 minutes.

While whisking constantly, add the butter 1 piece at a time; add the next piece only after the previous one is almost fully incorporated. After all the butter is incorporated, stir in the vinegar and cook until a spatula drawn through the sauce leaves a trail, about 20 seconds.

Remove the pan from the heat, then taste the sauce and season with salt and pepper. Thinly slice the tenderloins and arrange on a platter. Stir any accumulated pork juices into the sauce, then spoon the sauce over the pork and sprinkle with the dill.

Mexican Wedding Stew
with Pork (Asado de Bodas)

3 ounces (5 medium) ancho chilies, stemmed, seeded and torn into pieces

3 ounces (10 medium) guajillo chilies, stemmed, seeded and torn into pieces

4 cups boiling water

3 corn tortillas

1 quart low-sodium chicken broth

¾ cup raisins

2 tablespoons extra-virgin olive oil

1 large white onion, chopped

10 medium garlic cloves, chopped

2 teaspoons dried oregano, preferably Mexican oregano

2 teaspoons ground cumin

1 teaspoon ground cinnamon

28-ounce can diced fire-roasted tomatoes, drained

1 tablespoon cocoa powder

Kosher salt and ground black pepper

5 pounds boneless pork butt, trimmed and cut into 2-inch cubes

This is our version of the traditional chili-rich Mexican stew prepared for special occasions. The ingredients vary by region, but to keep things simple, we opted to use widely available ancho and guajillo chilies and cocoa powder instead of Mexican chocolate. With warm spices and a touch of fruitiness from raisins, the flavor profile is reminiscent of mole negro. The corn tortillas that are toasted and pureed with the softened chilies give the sauce a velvety consistency that clings to the fork-tender chunks of pork. Serve with rice or warmed tortillas.

Don't forget to drain the tomatoes *before use. The liquid will add too much moisture and acidity to the stew, throwing off the consistency and flavor balance.*

Heat the oven to 325°F with a rack in the lower-middle position. In a 12-inch skillet over medium-high, toast the chilies, pressing with a wide metal spatula and flipping halfway through, until fragrant, about 30 seconds. Transfer to a medium bowl and add the boiling water; reserve the skillet. Let stand until the chilies are softened, about 20 minutes, then drain.

While the chilies soak, in the same skillet over medium-high, toast the tortillas, turning frequently, until lightly charred, 2 to 4 minutes. Transfer to a plate and let cool slightly, then tear into pieces.

In a blender, combine half the broth, half the chilies, half the tortillas and half the raisins. Puree until smooth, about 1 minute, scraping down the blender as needed. Transfer to a bowl, then repeat with the remaining broth, chilies, tortillas and raisins; stir into the first batch. Measure ½ cup of the puree into a small bowl, cover and refrigerate until needed.

In a large Dutch oven over medium-high, combine the oil and onion. Cook, stirring occasionally, until the onion is lightly browned, about 5 minutes. Stir in the garlic, oregano, cumin and cinnamon, then cook, stirring, until fragrant, about 30 seconds. Add the tomatoes and cook, stirring occasionally, until most of the moisture has evaporated, about 5 minutes. Stir in the chili puree, the cocoa

and pork, then bring to a simmer. Cover, transfer to the oven and cook for 2 hours.

Remove the pot from the oven. Uncover and stir, then return to the oven uncovered. Cook until a skewer inserted into the pork meets no resistance, about 1 hour.

Remove the pot from the oven. Tilt to pool the liquid to one side, then use a wide spoon to skim off and discard as much fat as possible. Stir the reserved chili puree into the stew, then cook on the stovetop over medium until heated through, about 5 minutes. Taste and season with salt and pepper.

No. 66

Lose the Lid to Concentrate Flavors

We often start long-cooked stews covered so the ingredients' natural moisture is trapped in the pot and cooking begins gently and slowly. But we like to remove the cover toward the end to allow the liquid to reduce and the flavors it contains to concentrate.

TAME YOUR GARLIC!

5 Ways to Bring Out Garlic's Sweet, Nutty, Savory and Mellow Sides

In Italy, it seems no matter how much garlic ends up in a dish, the flavor always is subtler than expected. That's because Italians understand that garlic's pungency is easily controlled by how you prep it. Raw, unbruised garlic has only mild flavor, but damaging garlic's cells—by slicing, chopping, smashing, mincing, chewing, or, to a lesser extent, heating—triggers a chemical reaction that produces its telltale flavor and aroma. The more garlic is bruised, the greater the pungency. Heating garlic above 140°F mellows that flavor.

ROAST

Roasting a whole unpeeled head of garlic produces a mellow, sweet flavor because few cells are damaged. Remove the outermost papery skins and lob off the top third of the head. Drizzle with oil, season with kosher salt and black pepper, wrap in foil, then roast in a 375°F oven until the cloves are pale golden brown and creamy-soft, about 45 minutes. Squeeze the roasted cloves out of their skins and into soups, stews and dressings.

Uses: Blend roasted garlic cloves with equal parts miso and softened butter, then toss the mixture with blanched asparagus or sautéed spinach, or dollop on roasted salmon or cod and garnish with crumbled toasted seaweed. Smear roasted garlic cloves on toast and top with a fried egg and melted sharp cheddar cheese, or add whole cloves and a few bay leaves to a pot of simmering rice or bulgur. Blend cloves into mayonnaise with lemon juice for roasted garlic aioli.

STEW

For garlic flavor without the pungent bite, slice off the top third of a whole head of garlic, but keep the rest intact. No need to peel it. Simmer the head in soups and stews until tender. Squeeze the head until the softened cloves pop out, then stir them into the liquid, where they will dissolve with just a little stirring.

Uses: Add mellow garlic richness to chicken, beef and other soups and stews by adding a head to the broth. Enhance and thicken store-bought broth with the same treatment, adding a head and stewing for about 30 minutes until tender, then squeeze out the cloves and stir in. Add a head or two when cooking any type of dried beans, squeezing and stirring the cloves in at the end of cooking.

FRY

Sliced garlic is mild (fewer cells are ruptured than in mincing). Frying those slices in hot oil in a skillet for just a couple of minutes until crisped and browned brings out a sweet, slightly nutty flavor. Save the oil—which will be infused with garlic flavor—to drizzle on soups and stews or blend into vinaigrettes.

Uses: Toss fried garlic slices with a simple bowl of buttered noodles tossed with Parmesan cheese or poppy seeds. Sprinkle them over avocado toast dressed with olive oil and coarse salt or a roasted sweet potato drizzled with soy sauce and sesame oil. Or mix with buttery breadcrumbs and paprika to garnish roasted or steamed broccoli, cauliflower and green beans.

OIL-POACH

Gently poaching whole, peeled garlic cloves in oil produces a soft, spreadable texture and mellow garlic flavor that permeates the oil. Reserve the oil for use in vinaigrettes or to sauté, stir-fry or roast vegetables, meats or seafood. Or drizzle it onto pasta dishes and grain salads.

Uses: Smash poached garlic cloves into softened butter with chopped fresh herbs, then smear on toasted crusty bread for bruschetta, toss with egg noodles or rice, or melt over sliced steak or sautéed chicken breasts. Toss whole poached cloves with roasted potatoes or broccoli, or add them to soups.

SAUTÉ

When sautéing or stir-frying, which involves medium-high to high heat, be careful not to let garlic overbrown, which causes it to taste bitter. To prevent garlic from cooking too quickly, combine it with the oil in a cold pan and heat it gradually.

Uses: Sautéed minced or sliced garlic is a flavor foundation for many dishes, such as tomato sauces and stir-fries. Cooked on its own, sautéed garlic can be spooned with its oil as a finishing touch to bean purees, soups and stews.

RECIPES & RULES

BEEF

BEEF

At Milk Street we **look for thin, well-marbled cuts,** such as skirt steaks or sirloin tips; they deliver good flavor and value. **For soups and stews we skip the sear** and instead **load up on herbs and spices,** repeating flavors across the dish for maximum impact. And we **don't spend a lot of time on marinades,** especially on weeknights, **instead dressing the meat after it's cooked** to keep the flavors brighter.

We eat a lot of beef in the U.S.; the average person consumes an estimated 55 pounds per year. We like it plain or posh, from burgers to barbecued ribs to a plateful of prime rib.

But the relationship can be complicated. We end up spending more than we want to for top-of-the-line cuts such as tenderloin, only to be underwhelmed by the taste. We try our luck with cheaper cuts that turn out tough. Or we waste time (and make a lot of mess) patiently browning chunks of stew meat in hopes of "sealing in" flavor. Spoiler: It won't.

Turns out there are easier ways to infuse stews with flavor than standing at the stove—think layers of herbs, spices and flavorful condiments. And less-expensive cuts of beef cook up just fine in a covered pot if we keep the temperature—and liquid level—low. We can get the rich, beefy dishes we crave with a lot less effort.

At Milk Street, **we add plenty of seasoning to pot roasts, but not much liquid.** It sounds counterintuitive, but adding liquid to the pot doesn't guarantee moist meat. This less-is-more approach to liquid also is key to the French stew known as boeuf à la gardiane, a hearty braise that includes classic Provençal ingredients such as olives, anchovies, garlic and red wine. And we **repeat flavors within a dish,** as in our curry-coconut pot roast, where we use coconut in three forms—oil, milk and flaked—for maximum impact.

A simple way to signal-boost the signature flavors of a dish is to **layer seasonings to keep them bright and distinct.** We do this in our Thai stir-fried beef, which is cooked with basil, then has additional fresh, torn leaves stirred in at the end. Bookending flavor isn't limited to herbs. Our spice rub for Chinese beef skewers goes on before and after cooking.

For our pan-seared steaks with sherry we **let seasonings soak in after cooking.** Flavors stay fresh and vibrant and since the meat fibers relax as they cool, the seasonings are absorbed better. The minced beef in larb, a Thai salad, also is dressed at the end of cooking.

In many parts of the world, cooks **use meat as a garnish for light, but still savory, dishes,** a technique we follow in our hashweh, in which a small amount of beef is added to rice seasoned by Middle Eastern flavors. And our Thai beef stir-fry gets a perspective switch when we **treat garnishes (ginger) as a vegetable, for fragant and robust flavor.**

There's a place for stovetop browning, but when making stews, **we skip the sear;** it's messy and doesn't do a lot for flavor. Instead, we follow the lead of cooks elsewhere and **build flavor by layering herbs, spices and potent seasonings.** We apply this technique to our Chinese-style beef stew, which gets bold flavor from star anise, Sichuan peppercorns and plenty of herbs.

Ground beef is a quick and economical way to get dinner on the table. But it can easily turn out greasy and bland. We fix that with two variations on meatballs, a spicy, Mexican-inspired version, and a Balkan paprika-and-garlic flavored patty. For ease, **we roast, not fry, meatballs.** We also briefly chill them so they hold their shape better. And we follow the lead of Balkan cooks and **add baking soda to patties to improve texture.**

Curry-Coconut Pot Roast

Start to finish: **5 hours**
(1 hour active)

Servings: **4 to 6**

2 tablespoons coconut oil, preferably unrefined

2 large yellow onions, halved and thinly sliced

3 tablespoons ground coriander

2 tablespoons ground cumin

2 tablespoons curry powder

3 lemon grass stalks, trimmed to the lower 6 inches, dry outer leaves discarded, roughly chopped

6 ounces fresh ginger, peeled and sliced into coins

½ teaspoon red pepper flakes

28-ounce can diced tomatoes

5- to 6-pound boneless beef chuck roast, trimmed and tied at 1-inch intervals (see note)

1 cup unsweetened wide-flake coconut

1½ tablespoons cornstarch

½ cup coconut milk

3 tablespoons lime juice

½ cup finely chopped fresh cilantro

Sri Lankan cooks blend South Asian flavorings with several different culinary styles, including that of 17th- and 18th-century Dutch colonizers. In the dish known as smore, Northern European-style braised beef meets aromatic lemon grass and ginger along with curry spices. If your chuck roast is already tied, remove the twine so you can trim off excess fat, then re-tie it with fresh twine. Wide flake coconut adds nuttiness while coconut milk brings richness, and we reinforce these flavors by using coconut oil to sauté the aromatics. If you have unrefined coconut oil, use it for its fuller flavor. Otherwise, regular refined coconut oil works well, too. Serve with steamed rice or warmed bread or flatbread. And for a little heat and even bolder coconut flavor, offer a homemade coconut relish (see following recipe) on the side. If you have leftover pot roast, reheat the slices by layering them in a baking dish, spooning on some of the sauce, covering with foil and warming in a 400°F oven for 15 to 20 minutes.

Don't use sweetened coconut, *as the added sugar will cause it to scorch; unsweetened coconut will brown lightly without burning. We preferred wide-flake coconut, as it toasts nicely and infuses the sauce with nutty flavor. If you can only find finely shredded unsweetened coconut, it will work, too, but it won't brown as well.*

Heat the oven to 325°F with a rack in the lower-middle position. In a large Dutch oven, heat the oil over medium until shimmering. Add the onions and cook, stirring occasionally, until light golden brown, 5 to 7 minutes. Stir in the coriander, cumin and curry powder, then cook until fragrant, about 30 seconds. Stir in the lemon grass, ginger, pepper flakes and tomatoes, then cook, scraping up any browned bits, until the liquid has evaporated, 5 to 7 minutes.

Set the roast in the pot and turn to coat. Spoon about 1 cup of the solids onto the roast, then sprinkle the coconut over it and into the pot. Cover and cook for 3 hours. Uncover the pot, scrape the coconut (which will be toasted) and solids into the cooking liquid, then return uncovered to the oven. Continue to cook until a skewer inserted into the thickest part of the meat meets no resistance, about another 1 hour.

Using tongs, transfer the roast to a shallow baking dish and tent with foil. Set a fine mesh strainer over a medium bowl. Pour the contents of the pot into the strainer and press on the solids with a silicone spatula to extract as much liquid and pulp as possible; scrape the underside of the strainer to collect the pulp. Discard the solids. You should have about 2 cups strained liquid and pulp; let settle for about 5 minutes, then use a spoon to skim off and discard the fat from the surface. Return the liquid and pulp to the Dutch oven, then stir in the coconut milk and bring to a simmer over medium.

In a small bowl, stir together 3 tablespoons water and the cornstarch. Whisk the mixture into the liquid and return to a simmer, stirring constantly, until lightly thickened, about 2 minutes. Stir in the lime juice. Taste and season with salt and pepper. Off heat, stir in the cilantro.

Transfer the roast to a cutting board. Remove and discard the twine. Cut the meat against the grain into ½-inch slices and place on a platter. Pour about ¾ cup of the sauce over the meat; serve with the remaining sauce on the side.

SPICY COCONUT RELISH

Start to finish: **10 minutes, plus chilling**
Makes about **2 cups**

This condiment, a riff on the Sri Lankan coconut relish called pol sambol, is a great accompaniment to curries of almost any kind. Wide-flake coconut works best; shredded coconut does not break down properly.

2 cups unsweetened
wide-flake coconut

½ cup warm water

Kosher salt

2 tablespoons packed
light brown sugar

1 tablespoon red pepper flakes

1 teaspoon sweet paprika

2 tablespoons red pepper flakes

1 Fresno chili, stemmed, seeded
and roughly chopped

½ cup lime juice

3 tablespoons fish sauce

3 tablespoons coconut milk

¼ cup chopped fresh mint

In a medium bowl, stir together the coconut, water and 1 teaspoon salt. Let stand until the coconut has softened, about 15 minutes. Transfer the mixture to a food processor; reserve the bowl. Add the sugar, pepper flakes, paprika and chili, then process until the coconut is roughly chopped, about 1 minute. Add the lime juice, fish sauce and coconut milk and process until finely chopped, about 1 minute.

Return the mixture to the bowl, cover and refrigerate for at least 1 hour or up to 3 days. Bring to room temperature before serving, then stir in the mint.

CHANGE THE WAY YOU COOK

No. 67
Use Less Liquid for More Flavor

Braising meats with minimal liquid in a covered pot allows the meat to cook gently in its own juices. The method concentrates juices that can later make richly flavored sauces.

HOW TO CUT APART A CHUCK ROAST

1. Remove and discard any twine around the roast. Begin pulling the roast apart at its natural fat seams.

2. Use a sharp knife to fully separate the pieces and trim off excess fat and silver skin.

3. Cut the trimmed pieces into strips about 2 inches thick.

4. Cut the strips crosswise into 2-inch cubes.

Beef, Orange and Olive Stew
(Boeuf à la Gardiane)

Start to finish: **4½ hours**
(1 hour active)
Servings: **6 to 8**

6 to 7 pounds boneless beef chuck roast, trimmed and cut into 2-inch cubes

Kosher salt and ground black pepper

4 medium carrots, peeled and cut crosswise into ½-inch rounds, divided

3 anchovy fillets, patted dry

2 tablespoons extra-virgin olive oil

2 medium garlic cloves, thinly sliced

1 medium yellow onion, chopped

1 cup pitted Kalamata olives, rinsed, patted dry and chopped, divided

2½ cups dry red wine

1 medium red bell pepper, stemmed, seeded and cut into 1-inch pieces

1 tablespoon grated orange zest, plus ⅓ cup orange juice

2 teaspoons red wine vinegar

1 cup lightly packed fresh flat-leaf parsley, roughly chopped

Our version of this hearty stew from Camargue, in the south of France, uses chuck roast, a well-marbled cut. It gets robust flavor from Provençal ingredients—red wine, olives, anchovies and garlic. Orange is traditional, too; it lends the braise a balancing touch of brightness. Wine is key to this dish, and we wait until the beef is cooked before we add it, retaining more of the flavors. A bold, full-bodied dry red wine such as Côtes du Rhône or syrah is ideal, as it holds its own among the other big flavors. Serve with rice, egg noodles or potatoes.

Don't forget to zest the orange *before juicing it—it's much easier to grate the zest from a whole orange than from one that's been halved and squeezed. Don't add all of the carrots at once to the pot with the beef. Adding some at the beginning gives the stew a subtle sweetness, but after hours of braising, these carrots are spent. We add more carrots near the end of cooking so that they are tender but still flavorful.*

Heat the oven to 325°F with a rack in the lower-middle position. In a large Dutch oven, toss the beef with 2 tablespoons salt and 2 teaspoons pepper. Add ½ the carrots, the anchovies, oil, garlic and onion, then toss. Cover, transfer to the oven and cook for 2 hours.

Remove the pot from the oven and stir in ½ cup of the olives. Return to the oven uncovered and cook until a knife inserted into a piece of beef meets no resistance, 1 to 1½ hours.

Using a slotted spoon, transfer the meat to a large bowl, leaving the vegetables in the pot. Set a fine mesh strainer over a medium bowl. Pour the meat juices into the strainer, pressing on the solids to extract as much liquid as possible; discard the solids. You should have about 2½ cups liquid; if needed, add water.

Pour the wine into the now-empty pot and bring to a boil over medium-high, scraping up any browned bits. Reduce to medium and simmer, stirring occasionally, until the wine is reduced by half, about 8 minutes. Meanwhile, use a spoon to skim off and discard the fat from the surface of the strained cooking liquid.

Pour the defatted cooking liquid into the pot and add the remaining carrots and the bell pepper. Return to a simmer and cook, uncovered and stirring occasionally, until the vegetables are tender and the sauce is slightly thickened, 10 to 15 minutes. Stir in the orange juice and beef. Continue to cook, stirring occasionally, until the sauce begins to cling to the meat, 3 to 6 minutes.

Off heat, stir in the remaining ½ cup olives, the orange zest, vinegar and half of the parsley. Taste and season with salt and pepper. Sprinkle with the remaining parsley.

No. 68

Finish the Dish the Way You Start

Finishing a dish with a repeat hit of seasoning used during cooking creates layers of interest and helps reinforce flavor.

Thai Stir-Fried Beef
with Basil (Pad Krapow Neua)

1 pound flank steak, halved lengthwise with the grain, then cut against the grain into ¼-inch-thick slices

1 tablespoon soy sauce

3 tablespoons fish sauce, divided

Ground white pepper

4 tablespoons peanut oil, divided

¼ cup chopped fresh basil, plus 3 cups lightly packed, torn

2 tablespoons white vinegar

4 ounces sugar snap peas, strings removed, halved on the diagonal

1 red bell pepper, stemmed, seeded and sliced ½ inch thick

1 or 2 serrano chilies, stemmed and sliced into thin rounds

4 medium garlic cloves, thinly sliced

1 bunch scallions, white and light green parts finely chopped, dark green tops cut into 1-inch pieces, reserved separately

1 tablespoon white sugar

1 teaspoon oyster sauce

The Thai name for this dish includes the word for holy basil. It's not an easy herb to source in the U.S., so we tried the dish with more widely available Italian basil. We found that sweeter, slightly more subdued Italian basil yields a perfectly delicious stir-fry. For the fullest herbal flavor and fragrance, we use both chopped basil (mixed with the cooked steak) and torn basil leaves (stirred in at the end). The snap peas and red bell pepper add pleasing crunch, as well as vibrant colors. Use one or two serranos, depending on your heat preference. Or, if you like, leave out the chilies entirely. Serve with steamed white or brown jasmine rice.

Don't cook the meat *without first draining off the excess liquid and patting the slices dry with paper towels. This ensures the meat browns. Also, don't stir the meat after adding it to the pan. Let it cook undisturbed so the slices get a good, flavor-building sear.*

In a medium bowl, stir together the steak, soy sauce, 1 tablespoon fish sauce and ½ teaspoon white pepper. Let stand for 5 minutes, then drain and pat dry with paper towels.

In a 12-inch skillet over high, heat 1 tablespoon of oil until barely smoking. Add half the meat in a single layer and cook without stirring until well browned, 1 to 1½ minutes. Turn the slices, then continue to cook until the second sides are well browned, another 1 to 1½

minutes. Transfer to a clean medium bowl. Repeat with 1 tablespoon of the remaining oil and the remaining meat. Transfer to the bowl, then stir in the chopped basil and vinegar.

Add the remaining 2 tablespoons oil to the skillet and heat over medium-high until barely smoking. Add the snap peas, bell pepper and chilies. Cook, stirring occasionally, until the peas are lightly browned, about 3 minutes. Add the garlic and finely chopped scallion parts,

then cook, stirring, until fragrant, about 30 seconds, then stir in the sugar. Add the scallion tops and the beef with any accumulated juices and cook, stirring, until most of the juices have evaporated, about 1 minute.

Off heat, add the remaining 2 tablespoons fish sauce, the oyster sauce and torn basil, then stir until the basil is wilted, about 30 seconds. Taste and season with white pepper.

Spicy Chinese Beef Skewers
(Niu Rou Chuan)

1½ pounds beef flat iron steak, sliced against the grain into ¼-inch-thick strips

1 tablespoon dry sherry or Shaoxing wine

1 tablespoon soy sauce

2 tablespoons grapeseed or other neutral oil, plus more for grill grate

2½ tablespoons cumin seeds

2½ teaspoons fennel seeds

1½ teaspoons Sichuan peppercorns

2 teaspoons red pepper flakes

Kosher salt

Chili oil, to serve (optional)

Street vendors in China sell sizzling skewers of meat hot off the grill, rich with cumin and chilies. Some of the heady spice mixture goes onto the beef just before cooking; the rest is sprinkled on at the end. To make lamb skewers instead of beef, called yang rou chuan, substitute boneless lamb shoulder or leg; make sure to slice the meat against the grain. Though these are typically enjoyed as a snack, if served with steamed rice and stir-fried vegetables, the skewers make a satisfying dinner.

Don't trim the fat from the beef before cooking. The fat adds flavor and helps keep the meat succulent. If you're using a gas grill, make sure to give it at least 10 to 15 minutes to heat before cooking the skewers. This ensures the meat gets a nice surface char without overcooking the interior.

In a medium bowl, combine the beef, sherry, soy sauce and oil. Let stand at room temperature while preparing the spice mix and the grill.

In a small skillet over medium-low, toast the cumin, fennel and Sichuan peppercorns until fragrant, about 2 minutes. Transfer to a spice grinder and add the pepper flakes. Process until coarsely ground, about 10 seconds. Transfer to a small bowl and stir in 1¾ teaspoons salt. Measure out 1 tablespoon of the mix and set aside to use as garnish.

Prepare a charcoal or gas grill for high-heat cooking. For a charcoal grill, ignite a large chimney of coals and let burn until lightly ashed over, then distribute the coals evenly over one side of the grill bed; open the bottom grill vents and the lid vent. For a gas grill, turn all burners to high. Heat the grill,

covered, for 10 to 15 minutes, then clean and oil the cooking grate.

While the grill heats, thread the beef onto ten 8- to 10-inch metal skewers, evenly dividing the meat and pushing the pieces together. Sprinkle the remaining spice mixture evenly over both sides of the meat, patting gently to adhere.

Grill until lightly charred, 2 to 3 minutes, then flip and grill until the second sides are lightly charred, another 2 minutes. Transfer to a serving platter, sprinkling both sides of the skewers with the reserved spice mix, then drizzle with chili oil (if using).

OVEN-COOKING METHOD

Follow the recipe through making and portioning the spice mix. Heat the broiler with a rack about 4 inches from the element. Line a rimmed baking sheet with foil, then set a wire rack in the baking sheet. While the broiler heats, thread the beef onto ten 8- to 10-inch metal skewers, evenly dividing the meat. Sprinkle the remaining spice mix evenly over both sides of the meat, patting gently to adhere. Evenly space the skewers on the rack and broil until well browned, 2 to 3 minutes, then flip each skewer and grill until the second sides are well browned, another 2 to 3 minutes. Transfer to a serving platter, sprinkling both sides of the skewers with the reserved spice mix, then drizzle with chili oil, if using.

BOOST FLAVOR FAST

Three Asian-Pantry Shortcuts to Deep, Rich, Savory Success

Miso, soy sauce and spicy gochujang paste are simple solutions for adding instant umami—that savory, simmered-all-day richness. Used widely in Asian cooking, they're good in soups, sauces, noodles, stir-fries, dressings and more. These are Milk Street's go-to choices and how we use them.

MISO

Miso is a Japanese staple typically prepared from fermented soy beans and grains, such as rice and barley. Two varieties are common in the U.S.—white (shiro), which has a mild, salty-sweet flavor; and red (aka), with a rusty hue and big, bold taste. Other types include yellow (shinshu), which falls somewhere between white and red; barley (mugi); brown rice (genmai); and miso made with 100 percent soybeans (hatcho). Miso often is used in soup, but also can boost the flavor of many dishes.

In broth: Miso broth can be cooled and stored in an airtight container in the refrigerator for up to five days. The miso will settle upon standing, so stir to recombine before using. Our recipes take 10 minutes and make about 1 quart each.

In sauces and compound butter: Whisk a spoonful into pan sauces for meat or poultry or even into roux-thickened gravies, or mash an equal amount with softened butter and, if you like, some grated fresh ginger. The butter is great tossed with hot noodles or pasta or melted onto roasted or grilled vegetables.

In vinaigrette: To make a miso-ginger dressing, in a blender, combine **⅓ cup walnuts, ⅓ cup white miso, 1 teaspoon grated lemon zest, ¼ cup lemon juice,** ¼ cup water, **1-ounce piece fresh ginger** (peeled and thinly sliced), **1 teaspoon Dijon mustard, 1 teaspoon honey** and ½ teaspoon ground white pepper. Blend until smooth, about 1 minute. Add **½ cup grapeseed or other neutral oil** and blend until emulsified, about 30 seconds.

MISO BROTH RECIPES

Red Miso Broth

In a large saucepan over medium, combine **4 medium garlic cloves** (smashed and peeled) and **2 tablespoons tomato paste.** Cook, stirring occasionally, until the tomato paste has browned, 2 to 3 minutes. Add 4 cups water, then whisk in **½ cup red miso.** Bring to a gentle simmer, then reduce to medium-low and cook, stirring occasionally, for 5 minutes. Strain through a fine mesh strainer set over a medium bowl. The broth can be used in recipes in place of chicken or beef broth and is appropriate in hearty stews and braises.

White Miso Broth

In a large saucepan over medium, cook **4 medium garlic cloves** (smashed and peeled), **1 ounce fresh ginger** (peeled and smashed) and **1 medium shallot** (roughly chopped), stirring occasionally, until beginning to brown, about 2 minutes. Add 4 cups water, then whisk in **½ cup white miso.** Bring to a gentle simmer, then reduce to medium-low and cook, stirring occasionally, for 5 minutes. Strain through a fine mesh strainer set over a medium bowl. This broth can be used in place of chicken broth or stock and as a poaching liquid for chicken or seafood.

SOY SAUCE

Soy sauce traditionally has been made with a combination of soy beans and roasted wheat that has been cultured, then mixed with a hefty saltwater solution and fermented. Though the condiment is produced in many Asian countries, the dominant varieties are from Japan and China. Japanese soy sauce (shoyu) typically is made with more wheat and tends to be lighter in viscosity and less salty than Chinese soy sauce (jiangyou). When we call for soy sauce, it's usually standard Japanese dark soy sauce (koikuchi shoyu), which is widely available. Whatever variety or brand you buy, check the label. Look for the phrase "naturally brewed" or "fermented." Soybeans, wheat, salt and water should take the lead in the ingredient list. Here is a guide to common soy sauces.

Japanese dark soy sauce (koikuchi shoyu) is the type most widely available in supermarkets. This is the default in Japanese cooking and what we use, too; if a Japanese brand doesn't specify which type of soy sauce it is, it's koikuchi. It is darker in color but is neither saltier nor stronger than Japanese light soy sauce (usukuchi shoyu), so don't be fooled. Soy sauce is used as a seasoning in marinades, sauces, glazes, soups and stews. It's also the base for many dipping sauces and is a standard condiment on the Asian table. In applications where regular soy sauce is too salty, we sometimes call for low- or reduced-sodium soy sauce.

Tamari is made with little to no wheat and, as a result, has a strong soy flavor. The Japanese product—some would argue it's not a soy sauce at all—is more viscous and darker than koikuchi. It's often used as a gluten-free alternative to soy sauce. If you are avoiding gluten, make sure the tamari's label reads "gluten-free" or check the ingredient list to see if it contains wheat.

Sweet soy sauce (kecap manis) is dark, syrupy, sweet and Indonesian in origin. Its flavor contains notes of bittersweet molasses and smoky spices. (Chinese sweet soy sauce is somewhat milder in flavor and less viscous.) Kecap manis is used liberally in Indonesian cooking for marinating, in noodle dishes and stir-fries, as well as in dipping sauces. We include a recipe for making your own.

Soy Dipping Sauce

In a medium bowl, whisk together **½ cup soy sauce, ½ cup unseasoned rice vinegar, 1 tablespoon finely grated fresh ginger, 1 tablespoon white sugar** and **2 teaspoons chili-garlic sauce.** Cover and refrigerate up to 3 days.

Indonesian-Style Sweet Soy Sauce (Kecap Manis)

In a small saucepan over medium-high, combine **1 cup firmly packed dark brown sugar** and **½ cup water.** Bring to a simmer, stirring to dissolve the sugar, then reduce to medium and cook until syrupy and reduced to about ¾ cup, 10 to 12 minutes. Transfer to a small bowl or jar and let cool slightly. Stir in **¼ cup soy sauce,** then cool to room temperature.

GOCHUJANG

Many of the core flavors of Korean cuisine are built on a family of fermented soy-based condiments, each of which is considered a jang. The simplest—made from soy beans, salt and water—is ganjang, or soy sauce. One of the most complex—and the most popular in the U.S.—is gochujang, a spicy red paste with a consistency and savoriness similar to Japanese miso. Traditional methods for making it call for hand mixing a slurry of soy sauce, sticky rice, salt, malt and chili powder, then fermenting it in large clay pots left outside in the sun. The pots—called onggi—are porous, which helps foster fermentation. Though six months is acceptable, the best gochujangs are aged as long as five years. It works as flavoring in marinades, soups, stews, sauces and stir-fries, as well as a table condiment.

No. 69

Sauce Meat as It Rests

As meat rests, the muscle fibers relax, allowing flavors to be better absorbed.

Pan-Seared Steaks
with Sherry and Caper Vinaigrette

Kosher salt and ground black pepper

3 teaspoons sweet paprika, divided

1 teaspoon granulated garlic

1½ pounds flat iron steak (½ to ¾ inch thick), trimmed, cut into 3 or 4 evenly sized pieces, patted dry

4 tablespoons extra-virgin olive oil, divided

2 tablespoons drained capers

3 anchovy fillets

1 medium garlic clove, finely grated

¼ cup sherry vinegar

3 tablespoons Worcestershire sauce

3 tablespoons finely chopped fresh flat-leaf parsley

Flaky sea salt, to serve (optional)

This pan-seared steak gets deep flavor from a basic spice rub and a high-impact, no-cook sauce that uses the juices the meat releases while resting. If you can't find flat iron steak, use two 12-ounce strip steaks (no need to cut them in half before cooking). A cast-iron skillet is best for getting a deep, even sear on steaks and a digital thermometer is the most reliable way to test for doneness. Just make sure you're taking the temperature at the thickest part of the meat. Serve with a green salad and crusty bread to soak up the vinaigrette.

Don't score the steaks too deeply. *Cut only about ⅛ inch into the surface. And score only one side.*

In a small bowl, stir together 2 teaspoons each salt and pepper, 1 teaspoon of paprika and the granulated garlic. Using a sharp knife, score one side of each steak in a crosshatch pattern, cutting only about ⅛ inch into the meat and spacing the cuts about ½ inch apart. Sprinkle the steaks all over with the seasoning mixture, rubbing it into the scored side. Let the steaks stand, scored side up, for 15 minutes at room temperature.

Set a wire rack in a rimmed baking sheet. In a 12-inch cast-iron skillet, heat 1 tablespoon of oil over medium-high until barely smoking. Add the steaks scored side down and cook without disturbing until well browned, about 3 minutes. Flip the steaks and cook until the centers register 125°F to 130°F for medium-rare, about another 3 to 6 minutes. Transfer the steaks scored side up to the rack and let rest for 15 minutes.

Meanwhile, in a small bowl, combine the capers, anchovies, grated garlic and remaining 2 teaspoons paprika, then use a fork to mash to a smooth paste. Whisk in the vinegar, remaining 3 tablespoons oil, the Worcestershire and the accumulated juices from the steaks. Stir in the parsley. Taste and season with salt and pepper.

Transfer the steaks to a cutting board and thinly slice on a diagonal. Place the slices on a platter and pour the vinaigrette over the steak, letting it rest for several minutes. Sprinkle with flaky salt, if using, and additional pepper.

Spicy Beef Salad with Mint
and Cilantro (Larb Neua)

2 tablespoons jasmine rice

3 tablespoons lime juice

2 tablespoons fish sauce

2 teaspoons white sugar, divided

Kosher salt and ground black pepper

2 medium shallots, sliced into thin rings

2 Fresno chilies, stemmed and sliced into thin rings

2 teaspoons grapeseed or other neutral oil

1 pound 85 percent lean ground beef

1 cup lightly packed fresh mint, torn

1 cup lightly packed fresh cilantro leaves

Larb is a minced-meat salad from northern Thailand. Versions abound, but this beef version was inspired by the spicy, tangy Isaan style that's also popular in neighboring Laos. Easy-to-make toasted rice powder, called khao kua, is an essential ingredient here—it imparts a unique flavor, absorbs a small amount of the liquid and adds a subtle crunch. Cabbage leaves and sticky rice are the traditional accompaniments, but lettuce leaves and steamed jasmine rice are equally good. If you like, for more spiciness, add another chili or two.

Don't use extra-lean ground beef. *A little fat keeps the meat moist, adds flavor and balances the acidity of the dressing.*

In a 12-inch skillet over medium-low, toast the rice, stirring often, until golden brown, about 5 minutes. Transfer to a small bowl and let cool, about 10 minutes; set the skillet aside.

Meanwhile, in a medium bowl, whisk together the lime juice, fish sauce, 1 teaspoon of sugar, 1 teaspoon salt and ½ teaspoon pepper. Stir in the shallots and chilies. Let stand for at least 10 minutes or up to 20 minutes while you prepare the rest of the dish.

Using a spice grinder pulse the toasted rice to a coarse powder, 8 to 10 pulses. Return the powder to the bowl and set aside.

In the same skillet over medium-high, heat the oil until shimmering. Add the beef, the remaining 1 teaspoon sugar and ½ teaspoon salt and cook, breaking the meat into very small bits, until no longer pink, 4 to 5 minutes. Immediately add the beef and any juices to the shallot-chili mixture, along with the mint, cilantro and half of the rice powder, then toss to combine. Let stand for 5 minutes. Taste and season with salt and pepper, then transfer to a serving platter and sprinkle with the remaining rice powder.

No. 70

Treat Meat as a Flavoring

Meat doesn't have to be the main event. Much of the world treats it more as a garnish, adding deep savory flavor without weighing down the dish.

Cumin Beef with Rice
and Pine Nuts (Hashweh)

4 tablespoons (½ stick) salted butter

1 medium yellow onion, finely chopped

8 ounces 85 percent lean ground beef

2½ teaspoons ground cumin

1 teaspoon ground coriander

½ teaspoon ground cloves

¼ teaspoon cinnamon

Kosher salt and ground black pepper

2 cups long-grain white rice, rinsed and drained

½ cup dried currants

3 tablespoons lemon juice

¼ cup pine nuts, toasted

1 cup lightly packed fresh flat-leaf parsley, chopped

In the cooking of the Levant, hashweh is a spiced meat and rice dish that's often used as a stuffing. But the richly fragrant mixture, suffused with butter and studded with toasted nuts, also makes a delicious side dish and is hearty enough to serve as a main course. In our version, we include dried currants plumped in lemon juice to add bursts of sweet-tart flavor. Toast the pine nuts in a small skillet over medium-low, shaking the pan frequently, until the nuts are light golden brown and fragrant, about 4 minutes.

Don't add the water *to the Dutch oven until the rice has toasted and is no longer translucent. This gives the ingredients in the pot a chance to build a flavorful foundation for the dish.*

In a large Dutch oven over medium, melt the butter. Add the onion and cook, stirring occasionally, until golden brown, 10 to 14 minutes. Add the beef, cumin, coriander, cloves, cinnamon, 2½ teaspoons salt and 1 teaspoon pepper, then cook, stirring occasionally and breaking up the meat into small bits, until the beef is lightly browned, 4 to 5 minutes. Add the rice and cook, stirring often, until the grains are no longer translucent, 5 to 7 minutes.

Add 2⅔ cups water, scrape the bottom of the pan, then bring to a boil over medium-high. Cover, reduce to low and cook until the rice has absorbed the liquid, about 20 minutes. Meanwhile, in a small microwave-safe bowl, combine the currants and lemon juice. Cover and microwave on high until plumped, 30 to 45 seconds. Set aside.

When the rice is done, stir in the currants and any juice in the bowl.

Taste and season with salt and pepper. Sprinkle with pine nuts and parsley.

Stir-Fried Beef with Ginger

1½ pounds beef sirloin tips or flank steak, cut into 3-inch pieces with the grain, then sliced ½ inch thick against the grain

Kosher salt and ground black pepper

3 tablespoons grapeseed or other neutral oil, divided

6 ounces fresh ginger, peeled and sliced into very thin coins (generous 1 cup)

4 medium garlic cloves, chopped

1 bunch scallions, cut into 2-inch lengths

3 tablespoons fish sauce

2 teaspoons white sugar

This is our take on saiko cha k'nye, a simple but bold stir-fry from Cambodia. The ginger is not just a flavoring here—it's treated almost as a vegetable. A full cup of thinly sliced fresh ginger gives the dish substance; its spiciness and pungency is tamed by cooking. A mandoline makes quick work of slicing the ginger, but a chef's knife works, too. We liked the flavor and texture of beef sirloin tips here, but flank steak also worked. Serve the stir-fry with steamed jasmine rice to soak up the sauce.

Don't crowd the skillet *when browning the beef. Cooking it in two batches ensures the pieces don't steam in the pan.*

In a medium bowl, toss the steak with ½ teaspoon each salt and pepper. In a 12-inch skillet over high, heat 1 tablespoon of oil until barely smoking. Add half the meat in a single layer and cook until well browned on both sides, 2 to 3 minutes total, turning the slices only once. Transfer to a plate. Repeat with 1 tablespoon of the remaining oil and the remaining meat.

In the same skillet over medium, heat the remaining 1 tablespoon oil until shimmering. Add the ginger and cook, stirring frequently, until lightly browned, about 2 minutes. Add the garlic and cook, stirring, until fragrant, about 30 seconds. Stir in the scallions, fish sauce and sugar, then return the meat and accumulated juices to the pan. Cook, stirring occasionally, until the liquid is slightly thickened and the ginger is tender, 2 to 4 minutes. Taste and season with salt and pepper.

CHANGE THE WAY YOU COOK

No. 71

Treat Fresh Ginger
as a Vegetable

Don't consign ginger to a mere
flavoring. Up the volume and treat
it like a vegetable. And don't worry
about the spiciness. Ginger's bite
mellows with cooking.

SMOKE POINT PRIMER

The Best High-Heat Oil Isn't What You Think

Techniques such as searing and stir-frying produce well-browned steaks and crisp-tender vegetables, but they require oil that can hold up to the heat. That means using one with a high smoke point, the temperature at which the chemical compounds that make up the oil break apart, releasing smoke and imparting acrid flavors and smells.

TYPE OF OIL	AVERAGE SMOKE POINT
Grapeseed Oil	494°F
Safflower Oil	470°F
Peanut Oil	467°F
Canola Oil	453°F
Olive Oil	449°F
Refined Coconut Oil	423°F
Avocado Oil	412°F

But we've found that many published smoke points—often listed on the bottles—varied greatly from those we measured at Milk Street. So we gathered eight of the most common home cooking oils and tested how high we could heat them before they became unfit for cooking.

We limited our testing to oils that are highly refined. Less refined oils—meaning they contain impurities that react to heat at lower temperatures—have dramatically lower smoke points than oils with few or no impurities. That ruled out extra-virgin olive oil and unrefined coconut oil, among others

We heated 2 tablespoons of each oil in a stainless-steel skillet over medium-high. When each was barely smoking, we took its temperature using two different infrared thermometers. We repeated this process three times with each oil.

Our favorite oil for high-heat cooking—and the one that consistently had the highest smoke point—was grapeseed oil, which is made from grape seeds, a byproduct of wine-making. Safflower oil—made by extracting oil from the seeds of the safflower, a cousin of the

sunflower—was the second most durable oil for high-heat cooking.

But the biggest surprise was the olive oil. Though the impurities in extra-virgin olive oil make it ill-suited for high-heat cooking, we were impressed by how hot we were able to get refined olive oil. We like to use it for sautéeing vegetables, hearty greens, chicken cutlets and strip steaks because of its light flavor and clean mouthfeel.

Though we often use the faint wisps of smoke that rise off hot neutral oils as a cue for when a pan is hot enough to brown food, when an oil smokes too much or gives off a burnt smell, it's an indicator that the triglycerides—the compounds that make up oil—have broken down into fatty acids and glycerol. If that happens, it's best to remove the pan from heat, discard the oil and start fresh.

MORE ABOUT THE FATS WE USE AT MILK STREET

Coconut Oil

Coconut oil is a fat we use sparingly, generally pairing it with other coconut ingredients. Its flavor is particularly good in Indian and Southeast Asian dishes. Be mindful of its low smoke point.

Cooking Spray

We use nonstick cooking spray judiciously. It's convenient and works well (the lecithin in it ensures that even the stickiest foods release). Baking spray, which contains flour, is ideal for coating pans, especially a Bundt pan's deep grooves.

Grapeseed Oil

We like the neutral flavor, light mouth-feel and high smoke point of grapeseed oil. It's our go-to choice for a neutral cooking oil.

Lard

Though it's a four-letter word for many, we think lard has a place in modern cooking. It tastes good stirred into a pot of beans and adds flakiness to savory baked goods. Most supermarkets sell Armour brand lard, which is hydrogenated (in some stores it will be easier to find Armour labeled in Spanish as "manteca"). Lately, high-quality lard has become more widely available; look for it in jars. If you can find it, "leaf" lard has the lightest flavor. Lard keeps indefinitely in the refrigerator or freezer but will absorb other flavors; wrap it well.

Olive Oil

We probably use olive oil more than any other oil. In most cases, we favor full-flavored extra-virgin olive oil. Buying extra-virgin oil is a gamble; expense doesn't always guarantee quality, and there are few safeguards against adulterated oils. While there are wonder-

ful imported oils, we think California oils are generally fresher and a better bet. California Olive Ranch extra-virgin olive oil, for example, is an excellent product and widely available. Regular olive oil—not extra-virgin—is made from subsequent pressings and thus lacks the more robust flavor of extra-virgin. Its mild flavor and higher smoke point make it better for sautéing.

Peanut Oil

The light, nutty flavor and high smoke point of refined peanut oil make it good for deep-frying. Roasted peanut oil has a more pronounced nutty flavor. Unrefined varieties are not good for high-heat cooking.

Sesame Oil

Sesame oil is pressed from either raw or toasted seeds; we prefer the richer flavor of the latter. Like most nut and seed oils, sesame oil goes rancid more quickly than refined oils. We recommend buying small bottles and storing them in the refrigerator. Let stand at room temperature for 20 minutes to allow the oil to liquify before use. Sesame oil has a low smoke point and is not suitable for sautéing.

No. 72

Stop Searing
Your Meat

Skip the searing. It's easier to
build flavor into a stew by
adding handfuls of herbs and
plenty of robust spices. You'll
save the time and hassle.

Chinese Beef Stew
with Chickpeas and Star Anise

Start to finish: **2¼ hours**
(15 minutes active)

Servings: **4**

2 pounds bone-in beef shanks
(about 1 inch thick), trimmed

Kosher salt and ground black pepper

2 tablespoons grapeseed or
other neutral oil

6 medium garlic cloves, smashed
and peeled

2 bunches scallions, white and light
green parts thinly sliced, dark green
tops cut into 1-inch lengths, reserved
separately

1 bunch fresh cilantro, stems minced,
leaves roughly chopped, reserved
separately

4 star anise pods

2 teaspoons Sichuan peppercorns,
ground

2 teaspoons Chinese five-spice powder

¼ cup soy sauce

Two 15½-ounce can chickpeas,
rinsed and drained

Sichuan chili oil, to serve (optional)

This hearty, aromatic stew, called niu rou fang zang, is a dish from the Hui people of China. Star anise, five-spice powder and Sichuan peppercorns combine to yield warm, subtly sweet and gently tingling spice notes, while a generous dose of herbs adds freshness. We use beef shanks, as the bones contribute richness to the simple braise. Serve with steamed or stir-fried greens and rice or warmed flatbread.

Don't add all of the chickpeas *to the pot with the beef. We add only half with the meat. With long cooking, these chickpeas soften, adding body to the braising liquid. We add the remaining chickpeas at the end so they retain their texture and contrast the tender beef.*

Heat the oven to 325°F with a rack in the lower-middle position. Season the shanks on both sides with 1 teaspoon salt and 2 teaspoons black pepper; set aside.

In a large Dutch oven over medium, heat the oil until shimmering. Add the garlic, scallion whites, cilantro stems, star anise, Sichuan peppercorns and five-spice powder. Cook, stirring frequently, until the scallions begin to brown, 2 to 4 minutes. Stir in the soy sauce and 3 cups water, then add the beef shanks and half the chickpeas. Cover and transfer to the oven. Cook until a skewer inserted into the meat meets no resistance, 1½ to 2 hours, stirring once half-way through.

Remove the pot from the oven and transfer the beef to a medium bowl. Remove and discard the star anise pods. When the shanks are cool enough to

handle, shred the meat into bite-size pieces and return to the pot; discard the bones. Stir in the remaining chickpeas and cook over medium until the meat is heated through, about 5 minutes. Taste and season with salt and pepper. Off heat, stir in the reserved scallion greens and cilantro leaves.

SICHUAN CHILI OIL

Start to finish: **5 minutes, plus cooling**
Makes about **1 cup**

This fiery chili oil is delicious on our Chinese beef stew, but has many other uses, as well. Drizzle it on plain rice and scrambled eggs, or add it to steamed or stir-fried vegetables. If Sichuan chili flakes aren't available, red pepper flakes can be used as a substitute, but the oil won't have the same color.

Don't use hot water *when washing the saucepan after making the Sichuan oil. Rinse the pot with cold water; hot water can cause pepper fumes that irritate your eyes.*

1 cup peanut oil

1 ounce whole dried red Sichuan
chilies (1 cup)

3 tablespoons Sichuan chili flakes
or red pepper flakes

2 tablespoons Sichuan peppercorns

In a small saucepan over medium-low, combine all ingredients. Heat until the oil reaches 275°F, 3 to 4 minutes.

Remove from the heat and cool to room temperature. Strain out and discard the solids. Store in a tightly sealed jar in a cool, dark place for up to 1 month.

Roman Braised Beef
with Tomato and Cloves

Start to finish: **4 hours**
(30 minutes active)
Servings: **6**

6 to 7 pounds boneless beef chuck roast, trimmed and cut into 2-inch chunks

¾ teaspoon ground cloves

Kosher salt and ground black pepper

4 ounces pancetta, roughly chopped

6 medium garlic cloves, smashed and peeled

1 medium yellow onion, halved and thinly sliced

1 medium fennel bulb, trimmed, halved, cored and thinly sliced

28-ounce can whole peeled tomatoes, crushed

2 teaspoons fresh thyme, minced

In Rome, cloves are used to flavor the pot roast-like dish known as garofolato di manzo alla Romana. Cloves, known as chiodi di garofano, give the dish its name. The earthy, subtly smoky and slightly bitter flavor of cloves complements the natural sweetness of the onion, fennel and tomatoes used to flavor this dish. The beef typically is cooked as a large roast, similar to a pot roast. We prefer cutting a chuck roast into chunks and simmering the meat as a stew. This ensures the pieces are succulent and flavorful throughout, while also slightly reducing the cooking time. For cool contrast, we make a salad of fresh fennel, tomatoes and parsley (see following recipe) to serve with the stew. Polenta or crusty bread is an excellent accompaniment for absorbing the flavorful sauce.

Don't use ground cloves that have gone stale, *as they won't add much flavor or fragrance to the braise. If your cloves have been in the pantry for more than a few months, uncap and take a whiff. The aroma should be sharp and strong. If not, it's time to get a new jar.*

Heat the oven to 325°F with a rack in the lower-middle position. Place the beef in a large bowl and season with the cloves, 1 tablespoon salt and 2 teaspoons pepper.

In a large Dutch oven over low, cook the pancetta, stirring occasionally, until sizzling and the fat has begun to render, about 5 minutes. Increase the heat to medium-low and continue to cook, stirring occasionally, until the pieces begin to brown, another 7 minutes. Add the garlic, onion and fennel, then increase to medium. Cook, stirring occasionally, until the vegetables are softened and translucent, about 6 minutes. Stir in the tomatoes and bring to a simmer. Stir in the beef, then cover, transfer to the oven and cook for 2 hours.

Remove the pot from the oven. Stir, then return to the oven uncovered. Cook until a skewer inserted into a piece of beef meets no resistance, another 1 to 1½ hours. Using a slotted spoon, transfer the meat to a medium bowl. With a wide spoon, skim off and discard the fat from the surface of the cooking liquid, then bring to a boil over medium-high, scraping up any browned bits. Cook until the liquid has thickened to the consistency of heavy cream, 10 to 12 minutes.

Stir in the thyme, then return the beef to the pot. Reduce to medium and cook, stirring occasionally, until the meat is heated through, about 5 minutes. Taste and season with salt and pepper.

FENNEL, TOMATO AND PARSLEY SALAD

Start to finish: **15 minutes**

Servings: **6**

1 medium fennel bulb, trimmed, halved and thinly sliced

1 pint cherry or grape tomatoes, halved or quartered if large

½ cup lightly packed fresh flat-leaf parsley, chopped

1 tablespoon red wine vinegar

Kosher salt and ground black pepper

In a medium bowl, toss together the fennel, tomatoes, parsley, vinegar, 1 teaspoon salt and ¼ teaspoon pepper.

No. 73

Chill Your Meatballs

Chilling meatballs firms them up
so they hold their shape better and
won't fall apart as they cook

Meatballs in Chipotle Sauce
(Albondigas Enchipotladas)

Start to finish: **50 minutes**
(15 minutes active)
Servings: **4**

2 tablespoons grapeseed or other neutral oil

1 medium white onion, finely chopped

Kosher salt and ground black pepper

4 medium garlic cloves, minced

1½ teaspoons dried oregano

1½ teaspoons ground cumin

⅓ cup panko breadcrumbs

1 pound 90 percent lean ground beef

¾ cup chopped fresh cilantro, divided

14½-ounce can diced fire-roasted tomatoes

1 or 2 chipotle chilies in adobo and the sauce clinging to them, chopped

Crumbled queso fresco, to serve (optional)

These Mexican meatballs are served in a tomato sauce laced with spicy, smoky chipotle chilies. Canned fire-roasted tomatoes are an easy way to give the sauce flavor that accentuates the smokiness of the chipotles. Instead of browning the meatballs on the stovetop, we roast them in the oven, minimizing splatter and freeing up the skillet for the sauce. Crumbled queso fresco offers a nice color and flavor contrast. Serve with crusty bread, Mexican rice or warmed tortillas.

Don't use ground beef that's fattier than 90 percent lean. *Not only will the meatballs be too greasy, they may end up too soft and delicate because of the additional fat.*

In a 12-inch skillet over medium-high, heat the oil until shimmering. Add the onion, 1 teaspoon salt and ¼ teaspoon pepper, then cook, stirring occasionally, until browned, about 5 minutes. Add the garlic, oregano and cumin, then cook, stirring, until fragrant, about 30 seconds. Remove from the heat, then transfer ½ cup of the mixture to a large bowl; set aside the skillet with the remaining mixture. Line a rimmed baking sheet with kitchen parchment.

Into the bowl with the onion mixture, stir in the panko and ½ cup water. Let stand until the panko softens, about

5 minutes. Using a silicone spatula or your hands, mash the mixture to a paste, then add the beef, ½ cup of cilantro and 1 teaspoon each salt and pepper. Mix well, then divide into sixteen 2-table-spoon portions, rolling each into a ball and placing on the prepared baking sheet. Cover and refrigerate for 15 to 30 minutes. Meanwhile, heat the oven to 450°F with a rack in the middle position.

Uncover the meatballs and roast until browned and the centers reach 160°F, 12 to 16 minutes, stirring once about halfway through. Remove from the oven and set aside.

To the skillet with the remaining onion mixture, stir in the tomatoes and ½ cup water. Bring to a simmer over medium-high, then add the chipotle chilies and cook, stirring occasionally, until a spatula drawn through the sauce leaves a trail, about 3 minutes. Taste and season with salt and pepper. Add the meatballs and stir gently to coat with the sauce, then stir in the remaining ¼ cup cilantro and sprinkle with queso fresco (if using).

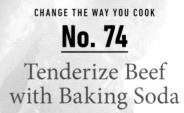

No. 74

Tenderize Beef with Baking Soda

Lowering the acidity of beef makes it more tender. Balkan and Chinese cooks do this by adding an alkali, such as baking soda. This forces the muscle proteins apart, which makes them easier to bite through and better able to retain moisture.

Paprika-Garlic Beef
and Pork Patties

¾ teaspoon baking soda

12 ounces 90 percent lean ground beef

12 ounces ground pork

1 small red onion, grated on the large holes of a box grater (about ½ cup)

2 medium garlic cloves, finely grated

1 tablespoon sweet paprika

1 teaspoon cayenne pepper

Kosher salt and ground black pepper

Traditionally, these hand-formed sausages, called ćevapi, are grilled, but roasting in a 500°F oven is a great year-round cooking method. We use a combination of ground beef and pork, as well as baking soda, as is customary in ćevapi recipes. The baking soda creates a lighter texture and tender springiness in the cooked meat. The most foolproof way to test for doneness is with a digital thermometer; the centers should reach 160°F. Serve with warmed flatbread, shaved red onion, thinly sliced cucumber, roasted red peppers and sour cream.

Don't add the baking soda *directly to the meat mixture. Dissolving it in 1 tablespoon of water ensures the soda is evenly distributed.*

Heat the oven to 500°F with a rack in the middle position. Line a rimmed baking sheet with foil and mist with cooking spray.

In a large bowl, stir together 1 table-spoon water and the baking soda. Add the beef, pork, onion, garlic, paprika, cayenne, 1½ teaspoons salt and ½ teaspoon black pepper. Knead the mixture by hand until well combined and paste-like.

Moisten your hands with water then, using a scant ¼ cup of the mixture for each, form into 12 oval patties, rolling each between your hands until smooth. Place on the prepared baking sheet. Re-moisten your hands as needed to prevent sticking.

Roast until the centers of the sausages reach 160°F, 10 to 15 minutes. Transfer to a platter and serve.

BUILD BETTER COCKTAILS

At Milk Street, we like our cocktails the way we like our food—built from ingredients that add layers of flavor, yet remain light and bright. And we're always looking for simple ways to get better tasting drinks without a lot of effort. So we use reposado tequila to **add gentle smokiness to a classic negroni. We shake from side to side**—not up and down—and **use saltwater to sharpen flavors. We warm a white wine sangria for winter with bay leaf and cardamom** and sometimes **make our own easy grenadine** as well as other syrups to add brightness to drinks. And **we bring the bar showstopper of smoked cocktails home by simply lighting up a cinnamon stick.** Here are some of our favorite recipes and techniques. Unless otherwise noted, recipes serve one.

Cranberry-Gin Smash

Muddling—using a thick baton-like tool or spoon to lightly crush ingredients—helps extract flavorful essential oils and juices. In this recipe, we muddle fresh rosemary and cranberries with a bit of sugar, then add cranberry juice for color and sweetness to balance the gin. Also try this with vodka. In a cocktail shaker, combine **1 sprig rosemary, 6 fresh cranberries** and **1 teaspoon white sugar.** Muddle until the cranberries are broken down. Add **2 ounces gin** and **1½ ounces cranberry juice,** then fill the shaker with ice. Shake vigorously for 15 seconds, then strain into a chilled coupe glass. Garnish with **another rosemary sprig.**

WARMING COCKTAILS FOR COOL EVENINGS

Reposado Negroni

Sid Datta, formerly of Cunard Tavern in East Boston, turned us on to this subtly smoky, slightly fruity version of the classic negroni, which replaces the gin with tequila. Reposado tequila has been aged up to a year, which gives it more nuance and less bite than a blanco. Anejo tequilas—aged for more than a year—would be too robust. In a cocktail mixing glass, combine **1½ ounces reposado tequila, ¾ ounce campari** and **1 ounce sweet vermouth.** Stir with 1 cup ice for 20 seconds, then strain into a rocks glass filled with ice. Garnish with a strip of **orange zest.**

Citrus and Bay Sangria

We often associate white wine sangria with warmer months, but cutting back the sugar and flavoring it with warming spices—cardamom and bay leaf—make it a perfect winter punch. We liked Grüner Veltliner, a grassy white wine with a pleasant minerality. Unoaked chardonnays are a good substitute. Remove the zest in wide strips from **2 oranges.** In a large bowl, combine **¼ cup white sugar, the zest, 5 cardamom pods** (lightly smashed) and **4 bay leaves** (crumbled). Stir, then add a **750-milliliter bottle dry white wine** and **2 ounces dry vermouth.** Stir until the sugar dissolves. Refrigerate at least 4 hours and up to overnight. Strain into a pitcher or punch bowl. Halve and thinly slice **another orange;** add to the wine. Serves 6.

Hot Brown Buttered Cider

This alcohol-free drink combines the flavors of two winter favorites—mulled cider and hot buttered rum. Lemon juice keeps the cider tasting light and bright. We top it with browned butter in which we bloomed cinnamon, nutmeg and vanilla bean. The butter can be made up to a week ahead and refrigerated; melt and stir before using. The cider can be made up to three days ahead, then rewarmed. In a small saucepan over medium, melt **4 tablespoons salted butter.** Cook, swirling, until the milk

solids at the bottom are browned and the butter has a nutty aroma, 1 to 3 minutes. Transfer to a small bowl, stir in **1 teaspoon ground cinnamon, ¼ teaspoon ground nutmeg** and **the seeds of 1 vanilla bean.** Set aside to cool slightly. In a large pot over medium-high, combine the **pod of the vanilla bean, ½ gallon apple cider, ¼ cup lemon juice, 2 tablespoons maple syrup, 3 star anise pods** and **3 cinnamon sticks.** Bring to a simmer, then reduce to low. Steep for 5 minutes. Ladle into mugs, then top each with **1 teaspoon of browned butter** and **1 cinnamon stick.** If you'd prefer a cocktail rather than a mocktail, stir **1 ounce bourbon** into each serving. Serves 10.

Coquito

Coquito is a traditional holiday cocktail from Puerto Rico that often is compared to eggnog. Though creamy and rich, it contains no eggs. It's traditionally made from a blend of evaporated milk, sweetened condensed milk and coconut milk, but we preferred a lighter version that replaced the evaporated milk with whole

milk. We liked this with 8 ounces white rum, but use more or less to your taste. The blender ensures the ground spices are evenly dispersed, but it also can be whisked. Refrigerate for up to two days. In a blender, combine a **14-ounce can coconut milk, 14-ounce can sweetened condensed milk, 1¼ cups whole milk, 8 ounces white rum, ½ teaspoon ground cinnamon, ¼ teaspoon ground nutmeg** and **⅛ teaspoon ground cloves.** Blend until slightly frothy. Transfer to a pitcher, cover and chill until very cold, at least 1 hour. Stir to recombine, then serve dusted with additional cinnamon. Serves 8.

Orgeat Old Fashioned

We tend to be dogmatic about old fashioneds. Bourbon, bitters, a hint of sugar, a suggestion of ice. No soda water. No juice. No fruit. Never fruit. But after we encoun-

tered the rich, almond-orange infused syrup orgeat, (pronounced OR-zsa) we had to admit there was room for improving our favorite cocktail. Classic old fashioneds are made with Angostura bitters, but we liked the way orange bitters accent the orgeat. We like Woodford Reserve Orange Bitters best, but the more common Fee Brothers West Indian Orange Bitters also are good. The intensity of the orgeat flavor varies by brand. Taste yours; if it's particularly strong, reduce it to ¼ ounce and add ¼ ounce simple syrup. Mid-range bourbons, such as Bulleit or Jefferson's Very Small Batch, work best for an old fashioned. Save top shelf bottles for enjoying neat. In a rocks glass or other tumbler, combine **2½ ounces bourbon, ½ ounce orgeat** and **3 dashes orange bitters.** Stir well, then add 1 to 2 ice cubes and **a strip of orange zest,** if using. Stir briefly.

DRINKS FOR SUMMER SOIRÉES

Pomegranate Mimosa

Inspired by the classic Champagne cocktail, we wanted to dress up a glass of sparkling wine without masking the flavor. We kept the bitters, but rather than sprinkle them on a sugar cube, we combine them with tart pomegranate

juice, creating a beautiful layered cocktail with a gentle fruitiness. Fill a flute glass **⅔ full with sparkling wine,** about 4 ounces. Allow the bubbles to settle, then gently tilt the glass to the side and slowly pour in **¾ ounce pomegranate juice.** Top with **4 dashes Angostura bitters,** then garnish with **several pomegranate seeds.**

Grenadine

At London's retro-modern Dandelyan bar on the banks of the River Thames, we discovered a refreshing update of grenadine, a cocktail mixer traditionally made of pomegranate juice and sugar. Most commercial grenadines today are toothachingly sweet, fluorescent red syrups made from high-fructose corn syrup and artificial colors and flavors. But at Dandelyan, they simmer elderberry, sour cherry and pomegranate juices into a syrup spiked with cumin

for a sophisticated sweetener used in their version of a Manhattan made with scotch. We created a simpler, but equally delicious grenadine by simmering **1 cup each pomegranate juice** and **sour cherry juice** with **6 tablespoons white sugar, 1½ tablespoons coriander seeds, 1 tea-** spoon fennel seeds and ¼ teaspoon kosher salt. Cook, stirring occasionally, until reduced to about 1 cup, about 20 minutes. Strain and cool, then refrigerate for up to a month. We like it in a gin daisy (**2 ounces gin, 1 ounce each lemon juice** and **grenadine,** shaken with ice and strained, then topped with **4 ounces seltzer**), or mixed with soda water for a grown-up Shirley Temple.

Rose-Lemon Syrup and Cherry-Rose Sparkling Lemonade Mocktail

We love the way the delicate sweetness of rose water mingles with the bright zip of lemon in this flavored simple syrup. It adds wonderful dimension brushed on a simple cake or drizzled over fresh fruit, and also makes an elegant addition to cocktails and mocktails. A splash of tart cherry juice harmonizes perfectly with the gentle sweetness of the syrup for a refreshing spritzer. It's the perfect companion to a hot summer day. For the syrup, add ½ cup water to a small saucepan. Slowly pour **½ cup white sugar** into the center of the pan, being careful not to get any on the sides of the pan. Add **eight 2-inch strips lemon zest** and cook over medium-low heat, swirling occasionally, until all the sugar has dissolved and the syrup just begins to bubble, 3 to 4 minutes. Let cool slightly. Pour into a heatproof bowl or storage container and stir in **¾ teaspoons rosewater.** Cover and refrigerate. To make the lemonade, in a 16-ounce glass, stir together **5 tablespoons rose-lemon syrup, 1 tablespoon lemon juice** and **2 tablespoons tart cherry juice.** Top with **¾ cup sparkling water** and adjust tartness to taste with additional lemon juice. Serve over ice. This makes enough for one glass but can easily be scaled up to make two or even a pitcher.

No. 75

Salt Your Drinks, Not Your Glassware

Unlike salting the rim of a glass—which overwhelms the flavors inside—a tiny amount of salt added to the drink itself enhances and brightens the other ingredients.

GET SALTY

Just as salt improves the taste of food, it can sharpen cocktails, too. We tried various saline tinctures and found a 4 percent solution made all manner of cocktails—negroni, Moscow mule, daiquiri—taste more complete and smoother. To make, mix **4 grams (a generous ½ tablespoon) Diamond Crystal kosher salt** and 96 grams (6 tablespoons plus 1 teaspoon) water until the salt dissolves. The saline can be stored indefinitely at room temperature.

French 75

A half-teaspoon of saltwater solution—and Angostura bitters—give exceptional balance to this slight tweak on the classic French 75. In a cocktail shaker, combine **¾ ounce lemon juice, ¾ ounce simple syrup, ½ teaspoon 4-percent saltwater** solution, **1½ ounces gin** and **2 dashes Angostura bitters.** Fill the shaker with ice, then shake vigorously for 15 seconds. Pour into a coupe or flute glass and top with **2 ounces sparkling wine.**

BE A BETTER SHAKER

There are three styles of cocktail shaker: the **cobbler,** the **Boston** and the **Parisian.** Nearly all are made of metal, which chills and contracts when loaded with ice, creating a vacuum seal. Breaking that seal to pour the drink can be difficult. Most people shaking cocktails at home use the cobbler, which has three parts: a cup, a lid and a cap that includes a built-in strainer. Trouble is, most of them are made of thin metal that's prone to freezing shut. If you opt for this style, look for one with thick walls, such as those made from heavy-gauge steel. The two-piece Boston shaker consists of two cups, one smaller and one larger. To shake, the smaller cup—which can be made from steel or glass—is inverted into the larger. Thickness is less important in this design. Focus instead on how deeply the smaller cup fits into the larger. A deeper fit makes a better seal and is easier to open. A small mesh strainer or cocktail strainer is used to pour the drink. The third type of shaker—the Parisian—is less common. It resembles a cobbler shaker in shape, but functions more like a Boston shaker in that it has two cups and no strainer. Whichever style you pick, **proper shaking is a two-handed operation.** Grasp the bottom

of the shaker with one hand and the top with the other. **Hold the shaker parallel to the floor and shake it side-to-side, not up and down.** The latter doesn't circulate the ingredients as thoroughly. If you don't have a cocktail shaker, use a lidded jar large enough to accommodate about 6 ounces of liquid plus 2 cups of ice.

SHAKE IT

Gin Alexander

In a cocktail shaker, combine **3 ounces gin, 1½ ounces crème de cacao** and **1½ ounces heavy cream.** Fill the shaker with ice, then shake vigorously for 15 seconds. Strain (twice, if desired) into chilled glasses and sprinkle with **freshly grated nutmeg.** Makes 2 drinks.

Tequila at High Noon

We substitute the mildly bittersweet Italian spirit Aperol for the typical (and often too sweet) grenadine. A dose of chocolate bitters—½ teaspoon's worth—complements the orange juice. In a cocktail shaker combine **4 ounces tequila blanco, 4 ounces orange juice, 1 ounce lemon juice, 1 ounce Aperol** and **½ teaspoon chocolate bitters.** Fill the

shaker with ice, then shake vigorously for 15 seconds. Strain into **chilled rocks glasses.** Makes 2 drinks.

Pisco Sour

This Peruvian staple traditionally is made with lime juice, but we preferred a brighter blend of lemon and lime. "Dry shaking" the cocktail with one ice cube helps create the sour's signature foam. In a cocktail shaker, combine **3½ ounces pisco, 1 egg white, ½ ounce lemon juice, ½ ounce lime juice** and **½ ounce simple syrup.** Add 1 ice cube and shake vigorously for 15 seconds. Fill the shaker with ice, then shake vigorously for 15 seconds. Strain into chilled glasses and sprinkle **3 to 4 dashes of Angostura bitters** over each. Makes 2 drinks.

SMOKED COCKTAILS

A flaming orange peel, a smoke gun, torched woodchips, smoldering coals— these are just a handful of methods bartenders use for smoking cocktails. But you don't need special equipment to smoke a cocktail at home. A cinnamon stick is perhaps the easiest thing to smoke—and is reusable. To make a **cinnamon-smoked whiskey sour,** which we learned from bartender Zachary Blair in Lake Placid, New York, using a brulee torch, gas stove burner or a match, set fire to one end of a **3-inch cinnamon stick.** It will burn briefly, then extinguish. Once it does, set it on a plate or other heatproof surface and cover with a wine glass. In a cocktail shaker filled with ice, combine **2 ounces bourbon, ½ ounce maple syrup, ½ ounce lime juice, 1½ ounces grapefruit juice** and **a splash of orange juice.** Shake for 15 seconds, then turn the glass upright and double-strain the drink into it. Slap **2 sage leaves** to release their oils. Garnish the drink with the sage leaves and **2-inch strip orange zest.**

INDEX

ACKNOWLEDGMENTS

Milk Street is a real place with, oddly enough, real people. It's a small crew, but I want to thank everyone who has made this book a reality.

In particular, I want to acknowledge J.M. Hirsch, our tireless editorial director, Matthew Card, food editor, Michelle Locke, books editor, and Dawn Yanagihara, recipe editor, for leading the charge on conceiving, developing and editing all of this. Jennifer Baldino Cox, our art director, and the entire design team who deftly captured the look and feel of Milk Street, including our associate art director, Brianna Coleman, who directed all photo shoots in addition to being our prop stylist; Connie Miller, our photographer; Christine Tobin, our food stylist; Gary Tooth, book designer; and special thanks to Catherine Smart and Brian Samuels for additional food styling and photography. Our team of production cooks and recipe developers kept the bar high, throwing out recipes that did not make the cut and improving those that did. Our team includes Diane Unger, Erin Register, Courtney Hill, Julia Rackow, Phoebe Maglathlin, Rose Hattabaugh, and Angie Marvin. Also, Elizabeth Germain, Bianca Borges, Erika Bruce, Laura Russell and Jeanne Maguire. Deborah Broide, Milk Street director of media relations, has done a spectacular job of introducing Milk Street to the world.

We also have a couple of folks to thank who work outside of 177 Milk Street. Michael Szczerban, editor, and everyone at Little, Brown and Company have been superb and inspired partners in this project. Yes, top-notch book editors still exist! And my long-standing book agent, David Black, has been instrumental in bringing this project to life both with his knowledge of publishing and bourbon. Thank you, David!

Finally, a sincere thank you to my business partner and wife, Melissa, who manages our media department, from television to radio. Melissa has nurtured the Milk Street brand from the beginning so that we ended up where we thought we were going in the first place! Thanks.

And, last but not least, to all of you who have supported the Milk Street project. Everyone has a seat at the Milk Street table, so pull up a chair and dig in!

Christopher Kimball

ABOUT THE AUTHOR

Christopher Kimball is founder of *Christopher Kimball's Milk Street*, a food media company dedicated to learning and sharing bold, easy cooking from around the world. It produces the bimonthly *Christopher Kimball's Milk Street Magazine*, as well as *Christopher Kimball's Milk Street Radio*, a weekly public radio show and podcast heard on more than 220 stations nationwide. Kimball is host of *Christopher Kimball's Milk Street Television*, which airs on public television. He founded *Cook's Magazine* in 1980 and served as publisher and editorial director through 1989. He re-launched it as *Cook's Illustrated* in 1993 and founded *Cook's Country* magazine in 2004. Through 2016, Kimball was host and executive producer of *America's Test Kitchen* and *Cook's Country*, the two highest-rated cooking shows on television. He also hosted *America's Test Kitchen* radio on public radio. Kimball is the author of several books including, most recently, *Fannie's Last Supper*.

Christopher Kimball's Milk Street is located at 177 Milk Street in downtown Boston and is home to our editorial offices and cooking school. It also is where we record *Christopher Kimball's Milk Street television* and radio shows. *Christopher Kimball's Milk Street* is changing how we cook by searching the world for bold, simple recipes and techniques. Adapted and tested for home cooks everywhere, these lessons are the backbone of what we call the new home cooking. For more information, go to 177milkstreet.com